Intellectuals and the People

Intellectuals and the People

Angie Sandhu
Sheffield Hallam University

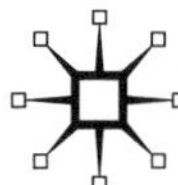

First published 2007 by
PALGRAVE MACMILLAN
Houndmills, Basingstoke, Hampshire RG21 6XS and
175 Fifth Avenue, New York, N.Y. 10010
Companies and representatives throughout the world

PALGRAVE MACMILLAN is the global academic imprint of the Palgrave Macmillan division of St. Martin's Press, LLC and of Palgrave Macmillan Ltd. Macmillan® is a registered trademark in the United States, United Kingdom and other countries. Palgrave is a registered trademark in the European Union and other countries.

ISBN-13: 978–0–230–54923–4   hardback
ISBN-10: 0–230–54923–3   hardback

This book is printed on paper suitable for recycling and made from fully managed and sustained forest sources. Logging, pulping and manufacturing processes are expected to conform to the environmental regulations of the country of origin.

A catalogue record for this book is available from the British Library.

Library of Congress Cataloging-in-Publication Data

Sandhu, Angie, 1966–
   Intellectuals and the people/Angie Sandhu.
       p. cm.
   Includes index.
   ISBN 0–230–54923–3 (alk. paper)
   1. Intellectuals. 2. Social role. I. Title.

HM728.S275 2007
305.5'52—dc22   2007021652

10   9   8   7   6   5   4   3   2   1
16   15   14   13   12   11   10   09   08   07

Printed and bound in Great Britain by
Antony Rowe Ltd, Chippenham and Eastbourne

For my parents

Contents

Acknowledgements

I would like to thank the Social Sciences team at Palgrave Macmillan and Jill Lake in particular for their interest in this project. I would also like to thank the English department at Sheffield Hallam for giving me a research post. This book has been long in the making and would not have been possible without the support of my friends and family. I would particularly like to thank Soledad Alvarado, Claudine Domoney, Paula Fitzgerald, Rachel Gundry, Kate Jones, Becky Lyall, Julia Swindells, Dal Sandhu, Roy Smiles and Katy Watson. Huge thanks to my partner Malcolm Artley and to Hana Sandhu, Carla Sandhu and Paul Sandhu for their love and support. Sara Mills' careful readings of the manuscript and her suggestions have been invaluable and I am delighted to finally have the opportunity to thank her for her generosity, intellectual camaraderie and support over the years.

Note

The term 'people of color' is a useful generic term for identifying those who do not benefit from racial privilege as encompassing more than simply 'black people'. The term refers to Chicana, Latino, Asian, Arab and many other indigenous groups as well as to those of strictly African descent.

1
Introduction: The Role of the Intellectual

This book is an intervention into contemporary debates concerning the social and political role of the intellectual. As Stefan Collini[1] points out, this issue continues to preoccupy theorists across the political spectrum and reflects long-standing anxieties about the status of both the intellectual and intellectual labour. Collini documents how this anxiety has resulted in two specific and interrelated ideas being repeatedly circulated in debates about the intellectual. First, there is, he argues, the notion that intellectuals are currently in a state of acute decline which can be verified by the second idea which is that intellectuals did perform a vital role in some past era or are fulfilling it in a society different from the one under review.[2] Collini contends that the fact that this argument is advanced across national boundaries suggests that we should pay attention to this search for intellectual purity rather than be seduced into accepting the validity of the proposal that intellectuals are either absent or in decline. He argues that the perception of the intellectual as either extinct or as existing in other societies is often accompanied by accounts that are either hopelessly idealistic or vehemently antagonistic to intellectuals. This distancing of the intellectual in space and time, or through idealisation or mockery, prompts Collini to emphasise the need for us all to acknowledge, 'the sheer ordinariness of the role of the intellectual'.[3]

Collini's attempt to insert intellectuals into a more mundane social location parallels the arguments advanced by theorists writing under the broad influences of postmodern theory. For theorists such as Michael Walzer,[4] Richard Rorty[5] and Zygmunt Bauman,[6] the passionate truthteller of Edward Said's[7] and Julien Benda's[8] imagination needs to be replaced by a more realistic assessment of the intellectual and intellectual labour. Thus, Walzer rejects Benda's definition of the intellectual as

a fierce prophet in favour of the 'connected critic', who is like everyone else except that 'he' devotes himself with 'passion' to truths that 'we all know'.[9] For his part, Rorty argues that the pursuit of truth is pointless since everything is contingent and there are no absolute truths to which we could or should insist upon realising. Meanwhile, Bauman perceives the intellectual as primarily a translator and interpreter of contemporary discourses.[10]

The sense that this contemporary reassessment of intellectuals constitutes an emphatic break from earlier, more exaggerated models of intellectual labour is very much in evidence in the recent anthology, *Intellectuals In Politics: From the Dreyfus Affair to Salman Rushdie*.[11] Significantly, the editors, Jeremy Jennings and Anthony Kemp-Welch, and the contributors to the anthology dutifully accept that contemporary dismissals of high ideals for intellectual work really do signify a cataclysmic shift on the part of intellectuals. Accordingly, Walzer's 'connected critic' and Rorty's assertion that the point of intellectual work is to 'keep the conversation going',[12] amount to a dramatic rupture with older models of intellectual labour. But, given that scholars such as Rorty and Walzer are occupying the *same* intellectual prominence that their supposedly radically different predecessors enjoyed, the question arises as to in what way intellectuals' modifying, and even abandoning, previous definitions of intellectual labour constitutes a shift in the relation between intellectuals and society.

Indeed, it is arguable that in Europe and North America, where information is particularly abundant since the spread of the Internet and the multiplication of media channels, the intellectual as one who is particularly able to sift through information and extract what is pertinent for the public as commentators such as Walzer and Bauman suggest they should, is performing a decidedly eminent function. In other words, the intellectual as an 'interpreter' and provider of 'moral clarity' could be said to be reflective of precisely what is prestigious today.

The constant juxtaposition that the editors and contributors to the anthology draw between old-style intellectual concerns – 'freedom', 'justice', 'truth' and so forth – and more modest contemporary ones ensures that there is a noticeable lack of attention to what is being evoked through the use of such terms as 'community' and 'participatory democracy' and such intellectual skills as 'clarification' and 'demystification'. For, while terms such as participatory democracy, diversity and decentralisation undoubtedly lack the dramatic resonance of 'revolution' and 'the proletariat', they are yet to emerge as somehow more straightforward. In particular, the question of how localised communities and

participatory democracy relate to the national state and international free-market capitalism is not addressed in the anthology. Neither is there any reference to the problems of defining what is meant by 'the community', despite the fact that 'communities' can be both united and divided by the dominant political culture's enforcement of race, class and gender 'difference'. And given that there is no attempt in the anthology to engage with the work of those who have attempted to enact and theorise alternative democratic models, notably in Latin America,[13] it remains unclear to me in what way 'the concreteness of community' functions as an obvious reference point.

Edward Said's definition of the intellectual as a courageous and isolated individual who is compelled to, 'speak the truth to power'[14] functions as an almost obligatory context in contemporary discussions about the intellectual and intellectual labour. The hubris of Said's romantic depiction of the intellectual as a 'voice of the voiceless' proved too tempting a target to ignore.[15] In particular, commentators noted the discrepancy between Said's progressive political views and his highly individualistic reading of the intellectual as a gifted and unique champion of the oppressed. The contradiction that was detected between Said's model of intellectual labour and his political affiliations proceeded upon the assumption that a more modest estimation of intellectual labour would enable intellectuals to continue their work without any accompanying claims to genius and omnipotence.

Unfortunately, the unwillingness of commentators to subject their own assumptions about what it is that does distinguish intellectuals from other people to any scrutiny ensures that it is not just Said who articulates seemingly contradictory arguments. Indeed, the frequency with which modest definitions of intellectuals and their labour rapidly develop into far-reaching claims for that labour is striking. Thus, Bauman's intellectual may have been relegated to the role of an 'interpreter' but 'his' role remains crucial, for as Bauman reminds us, '[i]t still remains the function of the intellectuals to bring the project of modernity towards its fulfilment'.[16]

Similarly, Charles F. Gattone[17] concludes his recent survey of social scientists by noting that in the contemporary world the growing power and influence of government and business over social life have drastically undermined the potential for enlightened democratic participation. Consequently, he argues it is increasingly difficult for social scientists to maintain their independence and work as 'public intellectuals'. Moreover, social scientists can no longer assume themselves to be equipped to 'guide' humanity to new levels of consciousness but should

rather view themselves as 'uniquely able to frame information in ways that help others to make sense of the world'.[18] The contrast between the new, more unassuming model for intellectual labour, and the significance of that labour for society as a whole is reflected in references to such grand entities as 'modernity' and 'civilisation'. Thus Gattone notes that social scientists can yet 'provide a valuable contribution to the ongoing reformation of traditional knowledge and to the future directions of modern civilization'.[19]

The ongoing struggle within intellectual debate about what model best describes the role and identity of intellectuals is, of course, marked by attempts to overcome previous or dominant stipulations made by prominent intellectuals. Thus, Michel Foucault[20] pitted his notion of the 'specific intellectual' against a 'faded Marxist story' in which the barely conscious proletariat embodies universal humanity and the intellectual humanity's consciousness and conscience.[21] Foucault identified Jean Paul Sartre's evocation of the grand universal intellectual as the epitome of this delusion. Pierre Bourdieu,[22] for his part, placed his notion of the 'critical intellectual' against the versions of intellectuals advanced by theorists such as Walzer, Bauman and Rorty. Rather than viewing such notions of intellectuals as 'interpreters' and 'translators' as constituting a progression from more elitist models of intellectual labour, Bourdieu instead criticised them as denoting the emergence of a 'new' individualistic intellectual'.[23] However, the problem is that while Foucault and Bourdieu both redefine the intellectual, their accompanying prescriptions for intellectual labour maintain the very elitist principles that they condemn in their intellectual opponents.

Thus, Bourdieu argues for a managerial role for social scientists because they are particularly equipped to understand and prevent the imbalances of power that occur within organisations.[24] But the problem here is surely that the roles that Bourdieu has outlined for social scientists are ones that could be enacted by non-intellectuals and may well confound intellectuals, including critical ones. Ironically, it is precisely because Bourdieu is willing to take seriously the determination of the dominant social, economic and political elites to impede the political consciousness of the public that he ends up overestimating the extent to which they can or do achieve this.

More importantly, his focus upon the effects of social inequality confirms that the political consciousness of the public mirrors the existing hierarchies that divide the public. In other words, women and the less educated lack an equivalent degree of political consciousness,

not because they are intrinsically unpolitical, but because they are further away from sites of political engagement and influence. Thus, he argues that

> the media are, overall, a factor of depoliticisation, which naturally acts more strongly on the most depoliticized section of the public, on women more than men, on the less educated more than the more educated, on the poor more than the rich. It may be a scandalous thing to say this, but it is clearly established from statistical analysis of the probability of formulating an explicit response to a political question.[25]

But what Bourdieu's conclusion overlooks is that the fact that women and the less educated may be less forthcoming when confronted by 'a political question', not because they do not have a political opinion, but because they do not have the confidence or desire to respond to political questions when they are posed by social scientists or other professionals.

Moreover, given that women in particular are also frequently placed in subordinate positions in left-wing organisations, notably trade unions and radical political parties, it is little wonder that 'expressing' as opposed to 'possessing' a political opinion is fraught with difficulties. Bourdieu's assumption that political consciousness can be assessed through academic research overlooks entirely the extent to which public speaking and the expression of political opinion are themselves bound up with power. And if political consciousness really does conform to existing hierarchies then what are we to make of the wealth of evidence that documents the refusal of women and the less educated to accept their political illiteracy and accompanying marginality?

Furthermore, by confining his interest to Europe, Bourdieu not only accords the European worker a uniquely privileged location in international struggle but also misses the opportunity to learn from those social movements and revolutionary governments that have attempted to rethink knowledge, power and education. David Archer and Patrick Costello's[26] exploration of literacy in Latin America in the late 1980s demonstrates that viewing education only in terms of its privilege is of little use for societies that are attempting to rethink their social and political relations. In other words, the emphasis upon education as a privilege can, as it does in Bourdieu's work, lead to the assumption that a progressive society will simply extend education to more people. And in the process the productive challenge that lies in rethinking the role

of both education and the educators is ruled out. This is unfortunate; for, as Paulo Freire[27] points out:

> One of the tragic mistakes of some Socialist societies is their failure to transcend in a profound sense the domesticating character of bourgeois education, an inheritance that amounts to Stalinism.[28]

By identifying the role of critical intellectuals as one that equips non-intellectuals with the means to understand and overcome the manipulations of the dominant medias, Bourdieu rules out any chance of critical intellectuals learning from non-intellectuals. And in the process he misses the opportunity for intellectuals to reconsider and overcome the pedagogical nature of bourgeois education.

Significantly, Bourdieu's identification of critical intellectuals as offering social movements the weapons with which to resist the destructive effects of the dominant medias does not extend to the capacity of these intellectuals to investigate their own claims to knowledge. Foucault, for his part, contended that the 'specific intellectual' was not assuming a universal significance but was addressing those questions that 'he' was qualified to explore. But this substitution of access to the truth for an ongoing search for the truth was one that failed to notice that in both cases *knowledge* of what it is that constitutes truth is an underlying assumption. Foucault's work for the Prison Information Group[29] and Bourdieu's attempt to connect his 'critical intellectual' to a model of collective intellectual engagement through a 'Parliament of Writers'[30] attests to both theorists' commitment to collective work and to political activism. Therefore, it is difficult not to conclude that elitist assumptions underpinning ideas concerning the intellectual and intellectual labour are not so easy to discard.

As Collini observes, the debate about the role of the intellectual has always been marked by a striking absence of any attention by intellectuals to their own status as intellectuals.[31] Certainly, for Jeremy Jennings the irony of Francois Lyotard declaring the death of the intellectual is able to pass entirely unnoticed.[32] Collini draws particular attention to the growing literature devoted to distinguishing between supposedly 'free' and 'independent' intellectuals and those supposedly domesticated individuals working within academic institutions. But, as Collini points out, the assertion that being accountable to editors and publishers, as opposed to academic institutions, is somehow more conducive to independence is at the very least open to question. Moreover, as he notes the irony of this claim lies in the fact

that it is one frequently advanced by those who themselves work in academia.[33]

The tenacious appeal of notions of intellectual distinction and accompanying assertions that emphasise the need to maintain and extend intellectual autonomy is evident across the political spectrum and explains why opposing models of intellectual labour can be advanced by utilising common assumptions about both intellectuals and their labour. Thus, for Steve Fuller the 'true' intellectual, functioning as a 'superhero of the mind', is accountable to ideals that are beyond the scope of ordinary people and can best demonstrate her credibility by demonstrating her intellectual autonomy.[34] Whereas, for Bourdieu, the value of intellectual autonomy lies in its potential to reduce the powerful effects of dominant institutions and encourage instead collective political activism. As Collini points out, arguments that extol the benefits of intellectual autonomy are based upon the dubious premise that any of us are 'unattached' to the world that we live in.[35]

Collini concludes his discussion of intellectuals by arguing that the inability of intellectuals to reflect upon their own status, the widespread allusion to intellectuals as existing in a different time and place to our own, and the defence of intellectual autonomy all suggest that the intellectual is operating primarily as an object of fantasy and desire. Consequently, he suggests that the appropriate corrective to this is to insist upon the 'ordinariness' of intellectuals:

> Perhaps its time that someone wrote an essay entitled 'Intellectuals are ordinary'. 'Ordinary' in the sense that they are indeed part of the cultural landscape of all complex societies; ordinary in the sense that it is neither unthinkable nor shocking to recognize that the noun 'intellectual' might be applied to some of the contemporaries one reads, or occasionally to some of one's colleagues or friends, or even, in some circumstances, to oneself; and above all, ordinary in the sense that carrying on the activities of intellectuals should not be seen as exceptionally heroic or exceptionally difficult or exceptionally glamorous or ... even exceptionally important. Important yes, but not exceptionally important.[36]

The modesty and caution of Collini's project is clear. Thus, he attributes the existence of intellectuals to a combination of 'education, occupation, circumstance, talent and luck'[37] and notes that intellectuals are merely the recipients of an unusual amount of time and access to the 'best' thinking and writing.[38] By pitting his study against the contexts

of elitism and condescension that underlie discussions of intellectuals, Collini is able to provide a valuable corrective to contemporary discussions about intellectuals. In particular, his suggestion that we resist 'fashionable' readings of 'the public' as 'duped' or 'dumbed down' points towards more egalitarian readings of the relation between intellectuals and society.

However, Collini's plea for the 'ordinariness' of intellectuals and their work avoids addressing the fact that what he defines as intellectual labour – 'disciplined intellectual enquiry' and 'aesthetic creativity'[39] – are actually qualities and practices that are utilised to *explain* the intellectual's difference from 'ordinary people'. Arguably 'the public' deserve something more than a recognition stating that they are not wholly ignorant of or indifferent towards the value of intellectual labour. In other words, proposing more mundane contexts for intellectual labour and encouraging us to extend our perceptions of who intellectuals are, stops short of challenging the material and theoretical conditions that maintain the authority and power of the intellectual.

The disinclination to address the power and authority of the intellectual is evident in debates about intellectuals. The almost permanent anxiety about the survival of the intellectual and her ability to exercise a useful social role ensures that little attention is paid to what it is that intellectuals do authorise; namely, a supposedly accidental or natural division of intelligence perception, and responsibility within society that in turn justifies the division of cultural resources and access to those resources within society. And while conservative theorists can ignore their own privileges, precisely because they accept their own advanced intellectual abilities as merely another example of 'natural' inequalities, radical theorists who contest social and political inequalities have no equivalent excuse. Therefore, identifying the hierarchical underpinnings of liberal democracy should extend to a consideration of how existing models of intellectual distinction intersect with wider social and political inequalities.

For me this is politically crucial, because I would argue that the failure of large sections of the radical left to seriously consider the basis and conditions for intellectual work has obstructed their attempts to realise a radically different and egalitarian society. Of course, to argue for the erosion of notions of intellectual distinction is also to argue for a different role for intellectuals in the present time. Thus rather than directing our energies towards curter clarification of our difference from other people, we could use our power to criticise those theories, institutions and practices that imprison us in unproductive and unequal relations with non-intellectuals. This is not, in short, a gleeful embrace of intellectual nihilism but an

attempt to place intellectuals in a constructive relation to the extension of thought within society. For, the dismantling of intellectual privilege is surely essential if we are to have any hope of living in an 'intellectual society'.

A central concern of this book is to challenge the alleged benefits of notions of intellectual autonomy. The persistent efforts of the dominant culture to obliterate, marginalise or suppress the thoughts of radical intellectuals has not, surprisingly, led to a passionate defence of 'freedom of thought' on the part of radical intellectuals.[40] Unfortunately however, defending the freedom of Western intellectuals, whatever their particular political objectives are, involves a simultaneous defence of principles that are strikingly hierarchical and elitist. Thus the right of intellectuals to speak freely is often attributed to their possession of an original and extraordinary perception. Arguably, advocating notions of intellectual autonomy only serves to ensure that radical intellectuals will continue to be perceived as self-interested elites committed in the first instance to the stable reproduction of their privileges. Moreover, critical intellectuals need to take note of the fact that intellectual autonomy functions equally well as a weapon for the dominant political and economic elites in their struggle against both radical intellectuals *and* the wider publics.[41]

How else can we account for the determination of the political and economic elites to insist upon the differences between intellectuals and 'the people', so that intellectuals who refuse to express their difference from 'the people' are routinely upbraided for their failure to demonstrate the point of intellectual labour? Consequently, a failed intellectual is one who has failed to distinguish herself from the 'ordinary' people with whom she should be contrasted. Unsurprisingly, those intellectuals who produce work that 'anyone could do' are guilty of 'pretension'; namely, the pretension of believing that their interests and talents are not necessarily so different to those of 'ordinary people'.[42]

Here the hierarchies of cultural production return with a vengeance, since those who are told/taught that critical discernment and artistic production are out of their reach expect – reasonably enough – intellectual production to *do* something that they themselves cannot. This, far from signalling the need for intellectuals to prove their excellence, seems to me to suggest that radical intellectuals need to direct their energies towards building connections with 'the people'. For, the current lack of attention to our own implications as theorists creates an absence that is politically disenabling for us as radical intellectuals. Consequently, until

radical intellectuals themselves demonstrate their commitment to dismantling their own elite locations, it should come as no surprise to find that their fervent support for 'freedom of thought' continues to be considerably less inspirational for the population as a whole.

My examination of the ways in which the Liberal, Marxist and anti-colonialist traditions have articulated their visions of intellectuals and 'the people', 'public' or 'publics' is offered as a challenge to those who look to these traditions for evidence of an inevitable difference between intellectuals and 'other people'.

Part 1   Literature and Civility: Liberal Solutions to Political Conflict

2
Matthew Arnold, Culture and the Intellectual

Given that this book is primarily an intervention into current radical theory, it seems appropriate to begin with another intellectual intervention into the role of the intellectual that took place in the late nineteenth century. I begin, then, with Matthew Arnold, not least because he continues to be cited across the political spectrum as a 'major influence' on critical theory today.[1] Arguably, it is precisely because Arnold succeeded in obscuring the connections between intellectual authority and other sites of social, economic and political power that he continues to be embraced by theorists across the political spectrum. For, it is the very magnitude of the role that Arnold accorded to 'culture', and 'cultural' critics, which has succeeded in obscuring the connections between cultural authority and other sites of power. By contrasting 'culture' with other sites of authority, Arnold was able to detach cultural authority from state authority even as he declared the 'proper' study of culture to be the most crucial task confronting nineteenth-century Britain. His elevation of bourgeois 'culture' to the very top of the national political agenda effectively expelled other cultures from possessing any equivalent national legitimacy.

And if Arnold's attempt to connect the bourgeoisie with 'culture' remains effective today, then so too does the pedagogical relation that he recommended exist between the cultural elites and 'the people'. None more so, in fact, than in the literary arena, which Arnold singled out for its 'civilising' potential both at home and abroad.[2] For, the pedagogical authority of the literary arena ensures that the entire subject of reading, writing, speech and comprehension continues to function as a site of considerable anxiety for most people. Deborah Cameron points out that the arbitrary roots of our contemporary grammar system continue to

arm those with a privileged education with the opportunity to 'correct' those who fail to know or to obey the rules:

> Linguistic conventions are quite possibly the last repository of unquestioned authority for educated people in secular society. Tell such people that they must dress in a certain way to be admitted to a public building, and some at least will demand to know why; they may even reject the purported explanations as absurd and campaign for a change in the rules. Tell them, on the other hand, that the comma goes outside the quotation marks rather than inside (or for that matter vice versa as is conventional in North America) and they will meekly obey, though the rule is patently as arbitrary as any dress code ... Moreover, the social function of the rule is not arbitrary. Like other superficially innocuous 'customs', 'conventions' and 'traditions' ... rules of language use often contribute to a circle of exclusion and intimidation, as those who have mastered a particular discourse use it in turn to intimidate others ... linguistic bigotry is among the last publicly expressible prejudices left to members of the Western intelligentsia. Intellectuals who would find it unthinkable to sneer at a beggar or someone in a wheelchair will sneer without compunction at linguistic 'solecisms'.[3]

In Britain it is significant that the supposed need to enforce literacy targets and so-called standards of English is increasingly voiced by governmental officials, while linguists and other literary professionals are increasingly at odds with such educational programmes.[4]

Perhaps inevitably, the tensions that accompanied Arnold and his supporters' mission to install the 'correct' study of literature[5] continue to mark contemporary debates concerning the teaching of English and literature and its relation to the wider political arena.[6] Therefore, when Stefan Collini celebrates Arnold for contributing more than 'any other single figure' to equipping 'the critic with the cultural centrality it has come to enjoy in the English-speaking world',[7] then this 'achievement' surely needs to be placed into the volatile historical contexts that Arnold sought to pacify with bourgeois education and leadership.

Matthew Arnold's 1869 polemic, *Culture and Anarchy: An essay in social and political criticism*,[8] was a passionate appeal to the English bourgeoisie to prepare themselves for the vital task of uniting the nation and ending the violent discord that for Arnold so characterised and mired English society. In the wake of the expansion of literary production in mid-eighteenth-century England,[9] the literary commentator and

companion was replaced by those who demanded a far more serious role for what was to become the 'study' of literature. No longer was reading to be accompanied by the irreverent generalisations of Samuel Johnson's *The Rambler* or *The Idler*.[10] Rambling and idling your way through books was, for people like Arnold, altogether too relaxed and complacent a posture for the emerging middle classes to adopt. Arnold saw little hope of stamping bourgeois authority over the public sphere without a radical reform of traditional reading habits. For, unlike the aristocracy before them, the bourgeoisie were confronting the increased literacy and confidence of the working classes, thus making literature and reading a fundamental political issue.

As Terry Eagleton argues, modern literary criticism 'was born of a struggle against the absolutist state.'[11] But, for the men struggling to assert their moral and political leadership over England, this struggle was conducted with one eye firmly trained on the alarming nascent threat posed by the working classes. The working classes had found, in literature, a useful way to communicate their interpretations of the proper relations between the public and the state. E.P. Thompson[12] notes the emergence, in the late eighteenth century, of intensive class struggle. This was visible in the 'counter-public sphere' in which a radical press, Owenism, William Cobbett's *Political Register,* Thomas Paine's *Rights of Man,* feminism and dissenting churches communicated through an extensive network of dissenting journals, clubs, pamphlets, debates and institutions. All this led one commentator to observe in 1793 that the

> lowest of the people can read; and books adapted to the capacity of the lowest of the people, on political and all other subjects, are industriously obtruded on their notice ... The newspapers ... communicate the debates of opposing parties in the senate; and public measures ... are now canvassed in the cottage, the manufactory, and the lowest resorts of *plebeian* carousal. Great changes in the public mind are produced by this diffusion; and such changes must produce public innovation.[13]

As the bourgeoisie dispensed with the elite gentlemanly public sphere of the old order, they confronted for the first time the possibility of losing it. Not surprisingly, anxiety rather than elation accompanied the steady bourgeois acquisition of social and political power. As Chris Baldick notes, Arnold's original idea of establishing France as an exemplary intellectual centre was shattered by the shock of the Paris Commune and the Prussian win over France. Arnold looked at Europe, and far from seeing the unfolding of a victorious bourgeois hegemony,

saw instead the possible, if not probable, *loss* of the public sphere in vivid and depressing detail:

> It is of itself a serious calamity for a nation that its tone of feeling and grandeur of spirit should be lowered or dulled. But the calamity appears far more serious still when we consider that the middle classes, remaining as they are now, with their narrow, harsh, unintelligent, and unattractive spirit and culture, will almost certainly fail to mould or assimilate the masses below them, whose sympathies are at the present moment actually wider and more liberal than theirs. They arrive, these masses eager to enter into possession of the world, to gain a more vivid sense of their own life and activity. In this their irrepressible development, their natural educators and initiators are those immediately above them, the middle classes. If these classes cannot win their sympathy or give them direction, society is in danger of falling into anarchy.[14]

Arnold's prescriptions for his society were informed by his evident consternation at the volatile character of Victorian England. His urgent call to the middle classes to assert their moral leadership over the nation was prompted by his sense that England was perilously close to disintegration as an unguided and unrestrained working class adopted ideas of freedom. It was fear that led Arnold to distinguish between freedom and the anarchy that working-class confidence and discontent threatened. For Arnold, the increased literacy of the working classes far from civilising them had provoked instead an alarming thirst for emancipation. Thus, he observed that they were beginning to

> put in practice an Englishman's right to do what he likes; his right to march where he likes, meet where he likes, enter where he likes, hoot as he likes, threaten as he likes, smash as he likes. All this I say tends to anarchy … he comes in immense numbers, and is rather raw and rough … And thus that profound sense of settled order and security, without which a society like ours cannot live and grow at all, sometimes seems to be beginning to threaten us with taking its departure.[15]

Arnold's solution to this apparent crisis lay in persuading the middle classes to abandon what he characterised as their trivial and self-interested concerns and safeguard the interests of the nation. Thus he insisted that the bourgeoisie cease claiming power on the basis of their class and present it instead as serving the interests of *all* classes. In short,

Arnold was urging the bourgeoisie to adopt the universalising pretensions of the old ruling elite.

Arnold searched for a way in which to establish a harmonious public sphere where class differences would no longer engender class hostility. Religion had proved unable to secure concord and so Arnold looked to literature to secure a strong, 'natural', social and political hierarchy. Thus, in his address as Professor of poetry at Oxford in 1857, Arnold announced that the present age demanded nothing less than an 'intellectual deliverance'.[16] The deliverance he had in mind was one that would replace the squabbles and conflicts of the public sphere with the luminous presence of great literature.

Arnold was by no means alone in his desire to find, in literature, the means to subdue dissatisfaction and secure, in its place, social coherence and order. Baldick notes that nearly every theorist of popular literary education in this period attempts to show that great literature is capable of breaking down class differences.[17] Lord Avebury was effusive in his praise for the social benefits of literary education in F.D. Maurice's Working Men's College and cited the study of literature as providing 'one of the good influences which in our country so happily link different classes together'.[18] The naturalisation of class inequalities that underscored this 'linking' of the classes was more honestly formulated by H.G. Robinson, who detected in literary education the means for revealing class inferiority.[19]

Certainly, dismayed though commentators such as Arnold and Robinson were by the apparent hostility between the English working classes and the bourgeoisie, for them the solution did not lie in advocating the dismemberment of privileges that differentiated the classes. Harmony needed to be produced in order to secure a viable social order, but commonality was to be established as far away as possible from the material sites of class differences. The notion that the study of literature could perhaps solve the political crisis swiftly gained currency in bourgeois circles. Literature, they conjectured, could perhaps transport the working classes away from attending to their social and political inequality and direct them instead to consider their own aesthetic limitations.

Accordingly, the aesthetic realm of great art emerges at once as the site of commonality and rare genius. As Robinson explained,

> Large views help to develop large sympathies; and by converse with the thoughts and utterances of those who are intellectual leaders of the race, our heart comes to beat in accord with the feeling of universal humanity. We discover that no difference of class, or party,

or creed, can destroy the power of the genius to charm and to instruct, and that above the smoke and stir, the din and turmoil of man's lower life of care and business and debate, there is a serene and luminous region of truth where all may meet and expatiate in common.[20]

Perhaps inevitably, given the enormity of its task, literature proved to be disappointingly incapable of providing the basis for the harmonious public sphere that Arnold insisted was needed to avert the impending crisis. He searched for a kind of literature that could circumvent any engagement on the part of the reader and encourage instead feelings of awe and wonder. However for Arnold, contemporary literature, with a few welcome exceptions, was singularly lacking in the kind of universal pretensions necessary to fulfil such a role. He concluded that great art, understood as that which communicated universal and timeless truths, could not be produced under such vulgar conditions; it was the task of criticism (the only contemporary sign of literary life) to demonstrate the grandeur of past art and in so doing 'beckon' in a time when once more art could be produced. Dismissing the present time as largely empty of any literature capable of fulfilling the vital role that he had in mind, Arnold turned instead to the Greeks. Greek poetry emerged as the most obvious literary candidate for the task of redeeming the public sphere and inoculating it from any future disturbances.

Given Arnold's assessment of his contemporary situation, it is not altogether surprising that he invested so heavily in the past and future. Of course ancient poetry was recruited for Arnold's entirely contemporary purposes, but it had the advantage of offering a more amenable flight from any unnecessary contaminating political disturbances that marked literature in the present. Naturally, Greek poetry was not going to be addressed in any historical or political contexts but purely in terms of its supposed ability to transcend such concerns. What would have proved near impossible in assessments of contemporary literature was altogether easier in the selection of past literature, which had the supreme advantage of a deceased audience with which to read it in.

However, for all Arnold's investment in the past and future the problem remained that such investments would come to nothing unless they could be installed at a general level in his contemporary society. Mediation and direction of some kind was clearly essential if the golden age of poetry was to be appreciated by sufficient people to mobilise a future 'deliverance' from the present age. Thus, commentaries upon Greek poetry were necessary but it was imperative that those who were selected to disseminate such literature be aware of their own relative

insignificance. Commentators needed to be mindful of the paucity of their own contribution to the cultural life of the nation and adopt instead an attitude of dutiful and humble servitude.

For this essentially mundane but politically crucial task the modern literary critic was born. The modern literary critic appeared on the literary stage not with a flourish but with a murmur; rather than staging a dramatic entrance, the literary critic appeared in the guise of a discreet servant. All that was required of the literary critic was that 'he' possess the ability to recognise great poetry and experience the necessary awe to compel 'him' to silence. Arnold as both a poet and a critic described his own approach to 'criticism' by way of example: 'I wish to decide nothing as of my own authority; the great act of criticism is to get oneself out of the way and let humanity decide.'[21]

But Arnold's intention was to confine 'humanity's' decision-making capacity to an absolute minimum; noticeably no such invitation to 'decide' was extended to which texts best constituted a proper literary education. The texts that Arnold singled out as providing transcendental relief from the struggles and concerns of everyday life were selected in order to ensure that humanity decided not to engage with the literary arena but to learn from it. Consequently, for all the humility assigned to the modern literary critic in his relation to great literature, his relation to the public at large was anything but modest. As Baldick comments, literary criticism as the 'appointed guardian' of general culture was invested with the authority to 'deny [a] book the right to existing'.[22]

However, by focusing upon the cultural 'improvement' of the nation, Arnold and his fellow 'reformers' were able to simultaneously assert the social and political dominance of the bourgeoisie and avert any charges of self-interest. By linking his prescriptions to the overall health of the nation, Arnold was able to dismiss his opponents as mere ideologues pursuing their own narrow self-interests. His insistence that the literary arena should transcend class interest successfully extracted the literary arena from any direct investment in contemporary politics even as he proposed that it be viewed as the only safeguard against violent social and political conflict. Arnold's 'disinterested' critic could thus be marshalled against his opponents as free from too direct an involvement in the vulgar political realities of the day. William Cobbet served as a pointed example of the shallow 'unliterary' critic, 'blackened as he is with the smoke of a lifelong conflict in the field of political practice'.[23] The effect of this reading of Cobbet is, of course, to mask the obvious fact that Arnold too was busily conducting a wholesale intervention into nineteenth-century political life.

By insisting upon a distinction between culture and politics, whereby culture enables us to transcend our individual interests, Arnold was able to obscure the power and authority that his prescriptions granted to the English middle classes. Instead, the bourgeoisie, as guardians of the national culture, were fruitfully connected to the disinterested pursuit of harmony and perfection:

> Culture being a pursuit of our total perfection by means of getting to know, on all matters which most concern us, the best which has been thought and said in the world; and through this knowledge, turning a stream of fresh and free thought upon our stock notions and habits ... Culture, which is the study of perfection, leads us ... to conceive of true human perfection as a *harmonious* perfection, developing all sides of our humanity; and a *general* perfection, developing all parts of our society.[24]

Significantly, the projection of these values onto the literary arena has proved to be a powerful and seductive point of origin for modern literary studies. As Robert Young notes,

> After Arnold literature became the privileged embodiment of a culture assigned the role of truth within the university and in school at large. In England it replaced philosophy. Arnold's arguments for literature form the basis for its teaching to this day. Dismayed by the roots of English Literature leads some to advocate a transformation to cultural or communication studies.[25]

Moreover, Arnold's elevation of the study and pursuit of 'culture' into a vital and humanitarian social mission has proved impressive enough to ensure his survival in new disciplines such as 'cultural studies'.

Thus, Kwame Anthony Appiah and Henry Louis Gates Jr include Arnold in their *Dictionary of Global Culture*, which is presented as 'the global citizen's guide to culture emphasizing the achievement of the non-Western world'.[26] Appiah and Gates present Arnold as an educational reformer who also took up 'the issue of societal reform'.[27] Arnold's prescriptions for a specific pedagogical canon that privileged poetry over the narrow concerns of contemporary literature becomes, in 'the global dictionary', a call 'for a revision of literary canons and for a shift in the class-specific participation that characterised Victorian England.'[28] By linking Arnold's 'revision' of the proper hierarchy of literature with the explanation that Arnold wanted to move beyond the

Victorian class system, the editors manage to imbue Arnold's vision with democratic credentials. The study of literature then becomes seamlessly connected with an explicitly egalitarian agenda, as Appiah and Gates make clear: 'Arnold believed literature to be a powerful cultural force, the centrepiece of a democratic education'.[29]

What is interesting in more contemporary celebrations of Arnold is the extent to which the elitism that underlies Arnold's conception of culture are suppressed by an appreciative reading of him as someone who strived to think beyond his own interests. In such readings, the argument goes, he may not entirely have succeeded but that is to be expected given that no one can entirely escape their own social and political locations. Thus the crucial insight that Arnold and his literary heirs have bestowed upon us is that the correct study and practice of 'culture' is one that strives to transcend individual interest and attach itself instead to general, universal 'human' interest. Of course, the fact that this noble mission is reliant upon an acceptance of rare individual brilliance is not a theoretical assumption but merely an irrefutable observation. In this sense, Arnold's attempt to render the pursuit of culture as uniquely free from specific class interests and concerned only to cultivate 'human' perfection has achieved considerable success. Subsequent critics have dutifully attempted to rid themselves of any narrow parochialism and looked to Arnold as one who exemplified the struggle to transcend mere self-centred individual concerns.

Raymond Williams, for whom Arnold was an unambivalent champion of educational reform, draws attention to Arnold's 'intense and sustained' efforts to establish 'a system of general and humane education'.[30] Significantly, Williams shared Arnold's sense of the urgent need to create the harmonious class relations necessary for social unity. Writing about his contemporary society in the mid-twentieth century, Williams argued that

> we lack a genuinely common experience, save in certain rare and dangerous moments of crises. What we are paying for in this lack, in every kind of currency, is now sufficiently evident. We need a common culture, not for the sake of an abstraction, but because we will not survive without it.[31]

Williams' dissatisfaction with the habitually fractured character of society mirrors Arnold's gloomy appraisal of his contemporary society, even as his recommendations point in an entirely different direction. However, it is Williams' commitment to overall social unity that leads

him to congratulate Arnold for demonstrating the social costs of unfettered individual freedom:

> Arnold was an excellent analyst of the deficiencies of the gospel of 'doing as one likes': partly because of his reliance on the traditional idea of man's business as the 'pursuit of perfection'; and partly, in social terms, because he lived through a period in which the freedom of one group of people to do as they liked was being challenged by that much larger group who were being 'done as others liked'. He saw the consequences in both spheres: the danger of the spiritual anarchy when individual assertion was the only standard; the danger of social anarchy as the rising class exerted its power.[32]

Here Arnold's identification of both 'social' and 'spiritual' anarchy serves to demonstrate his ability to see beyond his own class interests. Interestingly, Williams preserves intact the assumption that the middle classes are not only representing 'individual freedom' but also are themselves best viewed as a collection of individuals rather than as a group with a relatively coherent set of interests. By contrast, the working classes are assumed to somehow exist only as a collective mass and can accordingly be represented as opposing 'the individual'. The consequences of this reading are that while the working classes by sheer weight of homogeneity and numbers threaten to provoke social collapse, the middle classes threaten the more internal condition of 'spiritual anarchy'.

Williams' identification of Arnold as someone who was capable of thinking beyond his class was not, however, entirely without qualification, and he documents a selection of Arnold's more nervous and recriminating assessments of the 'rough' and 'raw' masses. Williams' disappointment is palpable: 'It is here, at so vital a point, that we see Arnoldt surrendering to a "stock notion or habit" of his class'.[33] However, rather than exploring the implications of Arnold's 'stock notions', Williams instead corrects Arnold's vilification of the British working classes with a romantic invocation of their inherently 'civilised' nature:

> Calm, Arnold rightly argued, was necessary. But now the Hyde Park railings were down, and it was not Arnold's best self which rose at the sight of them. Certainly he feared a general breakdown, into violence and anarchy, but the most remarkable facts about the British working class, ever since its origin in the Industrial revolution, are its conscious and deliberate abstention from general violence, and its firm faith in other methods of advance. These characteristics of

the British working class have not always been welcome to its more romantic advocates, but they are a real human strength and a precious inheritance. For, it has been, always, a positive attitude: the product not of cowardice and not of apathy, but of moral conviction.[34]

Williams, in other words, reinserts the working classes into a dignified and crucial part of the cultural revolution that Arnold was attempting to install. Moreover, in Williams' reading, Arnold's negative portrayal of the working classes is read as one that damages Arnold's own otherwise-admirable efforts to transcend his own class interests. Sympathy is directed at Arnold, who – having extolled the need to transcend class interest in favour of a 'better' self – here reveals his own inability to do so. Arnold's distrust and antipathy is removed from its connection with the working classes and returned to Arnold as an unfortunate theoretical mistake. Fortunately, Williams as a working-class intellectual is able to correct Arnold's version of the working classes with an account that Arnold himself would usually recognise. Thus Williams notes that 'the case is one in which Arnold detached from his particular position would readily understand'.[35]

The irony of this supplementary role that Williams adopts is that he employs his own particular position to correct Arnold's particular position and then concludes that both of them adhere to the same philosophical precepts. In other words, Williams does not correct Arnold by demonstrating his own ability to transcend class but by demonstrating his more intimate knowledge of the working classes. The implication of this is that a universally beneficial culture needs the equal participation of all classes in order to avoid incorrect stereotypes, which is precisely the scenario that Williams elsewhere explicitly advocates and that Arnold himself wishes to avoid. However, Williams in his haste to connect his vision of cultural practice and activity to that of Arnold, ends up juxtaposing Arnold's degradation of the working classes with his own idealisation of them.

The tensions that arise in Williams' reading of Arnold are derived from their qualitatively different assessments of the capacity of the working classes for unsupervised participation in cultural practices and debates. As Eagleton points out, Arnold's refusal to support Bishop John William Colenso's attempts to demythologise the Bible stemmed from his distrust of the masses and his conviction that they should only be exposed to poetic works that could refine their raw and uncultivated understanding of the world. Educational reform was based explicitly on

the assumption that it was the primitive and volatile character of the masses that were in need of urgent attention. Thus Arnold argued that

> the great mass of the human race have to be softened and human-ised through their heart and imagination, before any soil can be found in them where knowledge may strike living roots ... only when [ideas] reach them in this manner do they adjust themselves to their practice without convulsing it.[36]

Arguably, the championing of the individual that characterises bourgeois rhetoric and is so evident in Arnold's writings is a necessary linguistic and philosophical emphasis that serves to both define the middle classes and protect them from the repercussions of their dependency upon a widen-ing public sphere. For, in order to pursue their profits the bourgeoisie needed a consuming public; in order to establish their cultural authority they needed a literate population; and, finally, in order to represent them-selves as democrats committed to the preservation of each and every indi-vidual, they needed to obtain electoral support.

In short, the expansion and education of the public that the bour-geois needed in order to expand the consumer market produced the very developments that threatened to escape from their direct control. It was the potential weakness of minority governance that the ideology of 'the individual' sought to resolve. By linking bourgeois governance with the category of 'the individual' – a category that reveals as much about the middle classes as a group as it does about any 'individual' – the bourgeoisie were able to define themselves as a class uniquely dedi-cated to 'the individual'. For, as long as 'the individual' is assumed to be the very foundation of bourgeois rule then any other claim to power can be dismissed as merely the claims of a self-serving particular group which would by definition be unable to enact a universally beneficial social order. It is the remarkable ability of the middle classes to obscure their considerable hegemony – notably educational, legal, economic and social advantages – through their professed attachment to the val-ues of 'the' individual that enables them to be figured as exceeding the confinement of class interest. The notion that if we challenge the power of the bourgeoisie we simultaneously issue a challenge to the very exis-tence of the individual follows quite logically from this.

The representation of the 'individual' as a precious and fragile human entity still dominates contemporary Western criticism and cultural pro-duction. Such representations of the individual continue to normalise a representation of human relations as best understood to be a perpetual battle between 'the' individual and society at large. The narrative of

individual freedom flourishes in a plethora of routine characterisations of human collectivities as a threatening and 'faceless' mass. Underpinning this conception of human collectivities is the nascent threat of all those people not assigned value in celebrations of 'the individual'. The poor, the unemployed and the refugees – those supposedly marking society's borders – are recruited as evidence of and justification for fear and loathing on the part of 'civilised' society. Fear and distrust is thus encouraged and normalised as an inevitable human reaction to specific human groups in particular and, at a more subdued level, to human groups in general.

Arnold's fear of the working classes continues to preoccupy the dominant culture. The bourgeoisie are confronting an even greater instability than Arnold ever did, and the scale of this insecurity can be measured in the harshness of the arguments advanced by today's educational 'reformers'. While education becomes ever more authoritarian for the domestic British population, education for the refugees and asylum seekers is one of the benefits of a Western democratic life that they are depicted as trying to steal. Moreover, the ability to speak and understand English, 'our' culture and 'our' way of life is sufficiently vague to bestow upon the government and their 'cultural' accomplices the requisite power to determine who is and who is not a viable member of the Western nation. Cultural identity in this scenario is simply a possession that you can prove to have or be proved to lack.

In the aftermath of the collapse of the Berlin Wall in 1989, new differences are being assembled, on the basis of old ideologies of racial difference, giving 'Europe' once again a sense of unity. The asylum seekers, the migrant workers and the indigenous Roma are increasingly paying the price of European 'integration' as Europe once again prepares to protect itself from those who do not understand its values and its 'way of life'. As categories of difference, 'us' and 'them' combine to produce the necessary urgency and drama to the establishment of borders and controls between civilised Europe and its old/new Islamic adversary residing 'outside' of Europe.

And central to this difference is the distinction between 'the' Western individual and amorphous non-Western masses. The non-Western subject as one who has not been nurtured in a society that honours the individual above the human group is repaid in Western theory and practice by having any claim to individual sovereignty revoked. As people rather than individuals it follows that any lofty Western ideals equating individual sovereignty with life, liberty and freedom are quite simply not applicable. Similarly, the danger that refugees and asylum seekers pose is never attributable to them as individuals. Thus, like the

few individuals from marginalised groups who enter the public sphere, the rare asylum seeker who wins the right to stay becomes an instant exception. As an instant exception, the rare success stories of the marginalised and excluded become proof merely of the accuracy of the stereotypes about the group which she has proved she transcends.

This persistent multiplication of 'the' non-Western other into a general otherness parallels the equally insistent multiplication of non-white citizens within Europe and North America. Patricia J. Williams' acidic comment on being 'seen' captures precisely the ease with which Afro-American individuality can be refused:

> The partially blind see part, but not all of me. They say, 'I like you. I don't even see you as black.' I just use the following magic words: 'You don't see me as black because I'm not black,' and in a sulphurous flash, they see me as black again … I have trouble getting them to see just one of me … if I spill soup in a restaurant, they tend to see hundreds of me; if I have a baby, I tend to have a population explosion; if I move into a neighbourhood, I come as the forward phalanx of an invading army; if I have an opinion, it is attributed to 'you people'.[37]

Raymond Williams attempted to make both the individual and the working classes equally valuable and performed the necessary modifications to Arnold's writing to do that. But Arnold's 'raw' and 'uncultivated' masses were the necessary backdrop to his evocations of the individual, for, without recognising them, how would we ever recognise those who transcend their classes as rare and brilliant 'aliens'? A degraded working class was essential to the entire mission of pursuing excellence since excellence was, Arnold was sure, eminently lacking in those who expressed a class identity. And since the working classes were the most closely allied to a class identity that promised social disruption, it followed that they were the least excellent of them all.

Arnold's juxtaposition of the valuable and talented individual with the rest of society continues to appeal to the vanities of those who would see in their individual success a sign of their human distinction. Significantly, those who do rise to critical stardom from the dubious particularity of gender, race or class 'difference' are often the most keen to reinforce the fantasies of their bourgeois governors. They, more than most, are likely to be rewarded for demonstrating that an original position of inequality and inferiority is but a detail when compared with the grandeur of liberal democratic thought. Their contribution to the health of Western-styled democracy is invaluable when we consider how much more credible

Western democracy is when its underdogs themselves declare the system to be the best in the world.

Kwame Anthony Appiah and Amy Gutmann, in their recent, award-winning examination of 'the political morality of race',[38] utilise Thomas Jefferson and Matthew Arnold in order to redress what they regard as an increasingly acrimonious public sphere. In particular, they are concerned to demonstrate that the American nation is founded on a surmountable tension between liberal ideals and the realities of racism. For, the contiguity of contemporary American society to its enlightened origins is, they argue, in danger of being forgotten:

> There is a great deal of angry polemic about race in this country today. Accusations of racism, warranted and unwarranted abound. *Rodney King, O. J. Simpson, welfare queens, quota queens, the bell curve –* each of these conjures debates with a distasteful tone. In this respect, discussions of race are perhaps typical, since, as many observers have noticed, public debate on many questions has developed an uncivil reflection ... We in the academy are sometimes angry, also; but even when we are not, we are adversarial, argumentative, disputatious. Our debates, too, can seem divided and divisive.[39]

Appiah and Gutmann hope to demonstrate that such conflicts are at odds with the better elements of American history. Like Arnold before them, Appiah and Gutmann distinguish between a chaotic present and a history that provides the evidence for social and political cohesion. Ironically then, the fact that Arnold lamented the turbulence of his society does not prevent him from being employed, a century later, to provide evidence for the lengthy existence of commonly agreed-upon social and political customs.

Appiah and Gutmann present history as an entity that we can sift for positive and negative traditions of thought. Thus, Arnold's acceptance of hierarchical notions of race should be read alongside his enlightened commitment to the general improvement of humanity. Indeed, Appiah suggests that Arnold's conception of culture can be usefully applied against those who insist upon notions of racial difference. He counters assumptions that black people prefer hip hop and jazz while white people are drawn to the works of Shakespeare and Homer with Arnold's conception of culture:

> For Arnold, true culture is a process 'which consists in becoming something rather than in having something, in an inward condition

of the mind spirit', whose aim is a 'perfection in which characters of beauty and intelligence are both present, which unites, 'the two noblest of things' ... Arnold's aim is not, in the proper sense, an elitist one: he believes that this cultivation is the proper aim of us all.[40]

Arnold's recruitment of culture as a means to transcend the class divisions that he regarded as endangering his society are replicated by Appiah and Gutmann in their attempt to overcome the racial divisions marring contemporary American society. Thus, they emphasise that founding fathers such as Arnold and Thomas Jefferson are the proper point of origin for all Americans. They argue that in Jefferson

> we see something entirely representative of the best thinking of his day: the running together of biology and politics, science and morals, fact and value, ethics and aesthetics. Jefferson is an intelligent, sensitive, educated American shaped by the Western intellectual currents we call the Enlightenment: if we query these conflations, we are querying not so much an individual as the thinking of a whole culture.[41]

Appiah's assumptions that there is such a thing as a 'whole' culture, that elite thought constitutes the 'best' thought, and that an individual can exist as a concentrated form of 'a' culture are accompanied by the advice that unless we dispense with the need for racial identities, we will not produce a non-racist society.

In line with many other contemporary theorists, Appiah places the problem of racism within the context of the problem of continuing to talk about race as though it possessed biological, scientific or cultural meaning:

> There is a danger in making racial identities too central to our conceptions of ourselves; while there is a place for racial identities in a world shaped by racism ... if we are to move beyond racism we shall have, in the end, to move beyond current racial identities ... current ways of talking about race are the residue, the detritus ... of earlier ways of thinking about race; so that it turns out to be easiest to understand contemporary talk about 'race' as the pale reflection of a more full-blooded race discourse that flourished in the last century.[42]

The argument that we have much to lose by remaining attached to racial identities is one that has been addressed by contemporary critical

theory. Not surprisingly, dispensing with 'race' as a meaningful category has appealed to those of us who have direct experience of the force of racist stereotypes. However, as many commentators point out, 'race' may well be a fiction but the realities of racism to the overwhelming majority of black people and people of color are far from fictional.

The ensuing debate as to how far 'race' is demonstrably 'real' and how far it is fictional does not constitute the site of a bitter disagreement. Few commentators who argue for the adoption of a post-racist discourse are doing so with the assumption that 'race' does not exist as a profoundly destructive phenomenon in society. However, the focus upon the degrees of reality or unreality we should attach to race has had the unfortunate result of limiting attention to the question of *who* is in a position to determine the effects of racial assumptions and discourses upon society as a whole. The real tension is not so much between the degrees of weight that specific commentators attach to race-as-fiction or race-as-reality but to the ideological arena in which such debates take place.

As Arnold discovered, practising disinterested observation and critique is far easier if it is done without the irritating disagreements of a contemporary public. Certainly, Appiah's conjectures upon the history of race in the United States and his recommendations for overcoming racism do not point to an emerging academic consensus but to a dispute. In particular, his contention that we are now witnessing the dissolution of an old and powerful racist history is one that many commentators devote their energies to disproving.

Marek Kohn,[43] in his 1995 study of the continuing relevance of racial assumptions in contemporary science, notes the frequently made observation that even if race is no longer fashionable as an academic category, the same cannot be said for ethnicity, which is in many respects taking up the traditional work of race as a meaningful category of human differentiation. Throughout his book, Kohn details the racial assumptions that continue to be held by those in a position to effect educational policies.[44] Furthermore, as Kohn points out, racial classifications are very much in evidence outside of the domain of science, with the widespread governmental practice of using census material to estimate, among other things, the racial numbers of a population. All this leads him to conclude that

race is the great repressed of twentieth-century science. Conventional wisdom holds that, like Marxism in politics, race in science is an idea whose historical moment has passed … the historical moment of race science as a dominant system of belief has passed. But intense passions

are invested in smaller, newer race galleries. A white scientist devotes himself to the hypothesis that American children of East Asian descent do well in school because their distant ancestors evolved to cope with a particularly severe Ice Age. And a European museum curator struggles, largely successfully, to defend his hall of skulls and what they represent.[45]

Verena Stolcke also challenges Appiah's presentation of contemporary society as one that has progressed from the cruder scientific assumptions of earlier centuries. For Stolcke, the move to distinguish incorrect, scientifically inspired racial assumptions from an otherwise laudable Enlightenment heritage is to misread the context for racial stereotyping in the first place. The coexistence of social inequality with the ideals of the Enlightenment is not for Stolcke a problem that can be resolved by returning to Enlightenment principles:

Modern Western society has been characterized from the start by a universalist and individualistic ethos according to which all humans are born equal and free. This doctrine is, however, permanently contradicted by really existing social inequality. Racism is an ideological sleight of hand which serves to neutralize the conflicts that result from this tension by naturalising the socio-political order which produces them. In this sense racism is neither an outgrowth of colonial expansion nor is it simply in our own times an anachronistic residue. Significant socio-economic changes have, indeed, occurred since the colonial period but the basic economic and ideological logic has not changed.[46]

Meanwhile, for Toni Morrison, it is not just an unequal political system that benefited from racist declarations of the alleged innate inferiority of black people and people of color; racism also enabled the new arrivals to secure a distinctive cultural and racial identity for themselves. Thus Morrison argues that the racial presence of the black person as the polar opposite of the white person permeates early American literature as it grappled with the task of fashioning a national American identity:

The rights of man ... an organizing principle upon which the nation was founded, was inevitably yoked to Africanism. Its history, its origin is permanently allied with another seductive concept: the hierarchy of race ... The concept of freedom did not emerge in a vacuum. Nothing highlighted freedom – if it did not in fact create it – like slavery. Black

slavery enriched the country's creative possibilities. For in that construction of blackness and enslavement could be found not only the not-free but also, with the dramatic polarity created by skin color, the projection of the not-me.[47]

Morrison agrees with Appiah that race discourses have undergone historical change but is considerably less sanguine about those changes. Rather than seeking comfort in the demise of older racial discourses, she suggests instead that we pay careful attention to the resilient influence of older racial assumptions that Appiah proposes have all but expiredall but expired:

> Race has become metaphorical ... racism is as healthy today as it was during the Enlightenment. It ... has assumed a metaphorical life so completely embedded in daily discourse that it is perhaps more necessary and more on display than ever before ... there is still quite a lot of juice to be extracted from plummy reminiscences of 'individualism' and 'freedom' if the tree upon which such fruit hangs is a black population forced to serve as freedom's polar opposite.[48]

Appiah's reading of the present time as representing a significant progression away from the limitations of nineteenth-century science can and should be disputed not least because such celebrations of the present as opposed to a faulty past in fact limit the political and imaginative work that is required before any such celebrations can take place. Moreover, Appiah and Gutmann's contention that the extraction of obvious truths about an entire culture either in the past, or in the present, overlooks the extent to which we all function within cultural and political discourses and realities that derive their power from their seemingly natural and inevitable existence. This is not to suggest that we are all determined by the world that we inherit, but rather that we are enmeshed within society in complex ways. In this sense the present is no more obvious than the past which has brought it into being. As Robyn Wiegman argues,

> If rethinking the historical contours of Western racial discourse matters as a political project, it is not as a manifestation of an other truth that has previously been denied, but as a vehicle for shifting the frame of reference in such a way that the present can emerge as somehow less familiar, less natural in its categories, its political delineations, and its epistemological foundations.[49]

Appiah and Gutmann's comfortable depiction of the more noble elements of the American tradition are accompanied by an equally ingenuous depiction of 'traditional' societies with which America can be usefully contrasted. Thus they depict the pluralism through a contrast with an idealised fictional description of 'traditional' societies:

> The very idea of a coherent structure of beliefs and values and practice depends on a model of culture that does not fit *our times* – as we can see if we explore for a moment, the *ideal type* of a culture where it might seem appropriate. There is an *ideal* – and thus to a certain extent *imaginary* – type of small-scale, technologically uncomplicated, face-to-face society where most interactions are with people whom you know, that we call *'traditional'*. In such a society every adult who is not mentally disabled speaks the same language. (my emphasis)[50]

Significantly, while Appiah is willing to extend some degree of fictionality to the non-West, or those societies that are unlike 'ours', he is far from willing to perform the same reading upon 'America'. He distinguishes between a unified non-Western society and a pluralistic American society in order to argue that although America lacks the cohesion that arises from the existence of a single language or faith, it is nevertheless marked by an underlying political consensus that dates back to the Enlightenment. Thus, he depicts the present 'squabbles' of American political debate as precisely that: superficial irregularities that contradict and vaguely threaten the 'real' underlying consensus. However, and unfortunately for Appiah, Jefferson and Arnold also signify the limits of the Enlightenment's supposedly universal principles. Unsurprisingly, Jefferson as an enlightened thinker *and* a slave-owner hardly functions as a unified point of origin for all contemporary Americans.

Ironically, Appiah may have done rather better at arriving at points of commonality if he had dispensed with his tired replication of the supposed differences between 'modern' and 'traditional' societies. For as Toni Morrison points out, 'ancestor worship,' far from distinguishing the pluralistic West from a supposedly primordial non-West, is common to both:

> The practice of honouring or worshipping ancestors is prevalent worldwide. The symbols of European-American cultural icons are both physical and literary ... the ancestral spirits of Confederate soldiers and slaveholders, in iconic statues in Memphis Jackson, or Birmingham parks, inspire devoted visitors. The fervour of canonical

reverence in universities belies the disdain that many European-descended Americans feel for ancestral worship. Popularized ancestors such as George Washington, Thomas Jefferson and Elvis evince complex relationships to and facile representations of white American freedom and civilization that are dependent on enslaved or exploited African-Americans. Increasingly, since the civil rights movement, American culture has jumbled the contradictory values embodied in ancestors who manifest oppositional worldviews: holidays, coins and postage stamps pay tribute to Washington and Jefferson as well as Ida B. Wells and Martin Luther King Jr ... All collectively comprise community.[51]

Indeed, it is tempting to include Appiah and Gutmann's identification of Arnold and Jefferson as America's most illustrious forebears as a striking example of the very ancestor worship that is supposed to be absent in liberal democracies.

Furthermore, as Uma Narayan's discussion of 'Indian' culture makes clear, arguments that posit a definitive point of cultural unity or supposedly universal points of historical consensus are as contentious in the non-West as they are in the West. She observes that, notions of cultural difference, whether they were being advanced by colonialists or anti-colonialists, were idealised constructions that were very different from the values that actually pervaded institutional practices and daily life.[52] Narayan reminds us of what Appiah chooses to ignore, namely, that assertions of the presence of a whole culture are more a reflection of specific cultural power than of the production or existence of a unified culture.

Appiah and Gutmann extract a common American culture only to find, as Arnold did before them, that this culture is one that is concerned above all with the freedom of the bourgeois individual. Appiah's cursory allusion to what it is that creates common cultures reflects his underlying disinterest and antipathy for such an occurrence. For, having established that there are no feasible common cultures in America, he is able to dispense with the value of human collectivities in general. Thus, his bland evocation of a present in which race has largely lost its basis in scientific fact hints at the welcome opportunity for dispensing with the burden of collective identities altogether:

Nowadays there is widespread agreement that the insults to their dignity, the limitations of their autonomy imposed in the name of these collective identities are seriously wrong.[53]

In this sense, collective identities, whether recruited by racists or antiracists, are guilty of assaulting the integrity of the individual, who is depicted as struggling to escape from the confines of any collective identification.

The fictionality of race is not simply a matter of degradation and error but more importantly an obstacle that prevents us from recognising the existence of the individual that both predates and exceeds the human engineering performed by political and cultural theorists. Gutmann agrees, arguing that

> the very act of identifying with people 'of one's own race' simply by virtue of their being one's own race has had the psychological effect of undermining mutual identification among individual human beings.[54]

In a world in which the costs to black people and people of color have been grave – in terms of an assumed racial difference – Appiah and Gutmann urge us instead to return to the individual in order to shed the suffocating skin of imposed categories of human differentiation. The individual emerges as the only essential human category that merits collective identification. Thus Appiah's individual, like Arnold's 'alien', is only ever figured as one who finds in society nothing but obstacles to her freedom and autonomy. This individual is one that is forever held back by the crushing inconvenience of any group identity:

> The main reason why people currently worry about minorities that fail is that group failure may be evidence of injustice to individuals ... The issue can only be kept clear if we look at the matter from the point of view of the individual. Suppose I live in a society with two groups, blacks and whites. Suppose that, for whatever reason, the black group to which I obviously belong scores averagely low on a test that is genuinely predictive of job performance. Suppose the test is expensive. Suppose I would have, in fact, a high score on this test that I would, in fact, perform well. In these circumstances it may well be economically rational for an employer, knowing what group I belong to, simply not to give me the test ... The employer has acted in a rational fashion ... But most people will understand me if I say that this outcome is unfair. One way of putting the unfairness is to say, 'What I can do and be with my talents is being held back because

others, over whose failings I have no control, happen to have the characteristics they do.'[55]

Here we are invited to imagine a scenario in which there are no details about the test or the evaluators of that test. This obscure scenario is then purported to explain why it would be 'rational' for an employer to deny a black person the opportunity to demonstrate their racial equality. Equally obvious is the fact that 'most people' will recognise the rationality of the employer and the rationality of the individual who complains about unfairness. In other words, 'most people', including presumably those from the 'black group', understand that only a few of them possess the individual merit worthy of recognition. Most people, as is customary in such critical narratives, willingly accept their own dull mediocrity.

As Pierre Bourdieu[56] points out, the nineteenth-century bourgeoisie constructed two versions of the poor and found that both portraits served to legitimise their own social, economic and political dominance. Thus there was on the one hand, the 'deserving poor', a captive group that did not threaten bourgeois legitimacy so much as stir its humanitarian will to do good and, on the other, the *un*deserving poor, namely all those who displayed any antagonism towards bourgeois power in its many forms. As Bourdieu demonstrates, the terminologies may change and the criteria for a *theoretically* possible inclusion may change as well but the underlying assumption of natural individual intelligence survives intact:

The State nobility also has its 'poor' (or in the current terminology, the 'excluded'), who, rejected from work ... are condemned, sometimes in their own eyes too, in the name of what is now supposed to determine and justify election and exclusion, namely competence, the raison d'etre and legitimation that the State alone is supposed to guarantee, through rational, universal procedures. The myth of the 'natural gift' and the racism of intelligence are at the centre of a sociodicy, experienced by all dominant groups, beyond the differences in their declared ethical and political commitments, which makes (educationally measured) 'intelligence' the supreme principle of legitimation and which, in a civilization of 'performance' where success is everything – imputes poverty and failure not to idleness, improvidence or vice, but to stupidity.[57]

However, Appiah's contention that natural individual intelligence is a haphazard fact of life is clearly so obvious to him that we do not need to bother ourselves with analysing why it is that such a natural and random fact of life occurs with such dependable frequency in bourgeois individuals.

In keeping with the notion that universal statements and arguments can only be trustworthy if they are made outside of 'political' arenas, it follows that only arguments made on behalf of individuals can attain the necessary levels of disinterested objectivity that can then be applied to society. Focusing on the individual as the best possible means to realising a good society removes the complicated connections of individuals with society and, better still, places the issue of social justice on a subordinate level to individual freedom. Thus the individual is illuminated precisely so that the reasons for deepening social inequality can be reduced, as they are in Appiah's account, to a 'whatever'. Social justice and equality thus emerge as laudable ideals that should be attended to as long as they do not displace individual freedom.

In a familiar and truly surreal account of the pressing issues 'facing a great nation', Appiah and Gutmann invite us to consider very carefully the matter of individual freedom lest we are tempted to dive into a potentially illiberal programme of enforcing collective goals of social improvement. They argue that although the alleviation of inequalities is an implicit ideal in their work, their primary aim is to consider the issues of freedom and justice in the 'real world'. The question of social and economic justice is thus shifted into an ideal political realm, and capitalism is centred as an inevitable 'natural' expression of human relations.

Thus capitalism as a philosophy that honours self-interest and self-motivation cannot be avoided by recourse to naive political idealism. Moreover, capitalism is right to place such faith in individual freedom because it seems that individuals left to themselves are more than willing to alleviate gross poverty and exclusion. While capitalism may not solve social and political inequality *directly*, it does have the advantage of providing us with a model that faithfully reflects life itself, making any desire to overthrow it akin to moral and political suicide:

> Capitalism – like life – is full of such unfairness: luck from lotteries to hurricanes. We can't get rid of all unfairness; for if we had perfect insurance, zero risk, there'd be no role for entrepreneurship, no markets, no capitalism. But we do think it proper to mitigate some risks. We think, for example, that we should do something about bad luck

when it has large negative effects on individual people, or if it forces them below some socio-economic baseline.[58]

By positing insecurity along a spectrum marked by the random effects of hurricanes and lotteries (leaving aside the fact that global warming and increasing poverty may have something to do with their existence), Appiah is able to dismiss any connection between insecurity and the deliberate policies pursued by those who adhere to the doctrines of capitalism. Instead we are presented with a scenario whereby capitalism merely reflects life rather than influences or conditions it. Indeed the only visible sign of influence here is when 'we', that is to say, 'we capitalists', intervene to protect those who fall prey to particularly 'bad luck'. Of course, we cannot remove 'bad luck' altogether since that would be a patently naive denial of 'life' but 'we' can at least provide a degree of protection from its unkinder moments. Unfortunately, this 'we' is one that is either unable or unwilling to notice that capitalism is remarkably predictable in its effects upon the lives of women, black people, people of color and the poor. Ascribing the poverty of 43 percent of all black children in America today to 'bad luck' is an example of liberal theory at its irresponsible worst.

Appiah's concern for those who do not fare well in an unregulated market were in fact voiced by the classical political economists who first outlined what was to become the foundations of our contemporary economic order. Adam Smith's[59] belief that the property-owning individual should be left free to increase his wealth was nevertheless accompanied by a concern for the effects of such freedom for society as a whole. David Ricardo[60] too worried about the economic impact upon the working class, while Thomas Malthus[61] went further and insisted that workers should be paid well for their labour. For the classical political economists it was precisely their real faith in the progressive sensibilities of the bourgeois, property-owning male that prevented them from abandoning their faith in the free market. In this sense, their often-passionate arguments for universal social justice were based upon their conviction that the bourgeoisie should and would take the needs of society as whole seriously.

But while the theorists of the emerging capitalist system can be excused for not knowing how their free-market model would actually work, such an excuse is hard to find for those who continue to equate individual freedom with the common good. The emerging crisis for the majority of the world's population can, according to Appiah and Gutmann, be solved by maintaining our faith in the ability of the individual to administer justice.

Thus, Appiah's answer to the problem of growing inequality is to apply ourselves to the task of being 'fair':

> Responding to racial injustice is a matter of individuals acting in a way that they can reasonably defend as fair and consistent with their self-understandings. Fairness suggests that more advantaged blacks have greater obligations than less advantaged blacks, but not that they must fulfil their obligations in the way in which the majority – black or white – deems appropriate. There are multiple ways in which we all can identify with each other and reciprocate the beneficial acts of others. In fairness, none of us should be tied to the way chosen by others, provided that we too find a way to do our fair share.[62]

Significantly, individuals are here figured as drawn towards fair social conduct through the realisation that their efforts will be reciprocated by others. This exchange of 'benefits' between individuals avoids the obvious fact that many people do not possess the means to offer reciprocal benefit in individual relations because they are structurally excluded from national, social and political resources. By denying the force of social inequality, such individuals can be safely classified as lacking the higher democratic yearnings of their more enlightened social counterparts.

The resulting scenario is of a collection of individuals heroically able to overcome the limitations of society to find within themselves a proper and fair way in which to conduct human relations. The safety and intimacy of individual judgement contrasts starkly with the oppressive censure attached to 'the majority': a reference simply to the point at which the presence of too many individuals somehow makes individuality impossible.

Irritatingly enough, for Appiah and Gutmann though, is the fact that some intellectuals persist in challenging the foundations of liberal ideology. Consequently, like Arnold before them, Appiah and Gutmann see their intellectual role as one that restores civility, order and rationality to civil society. And it is this liberal evocation and celebration of rationality that we will turn to next.

3
The Habermasian Public Sphere

The inherent connection between the human capacity for reason and the human desire for consensus is an argument that Jürgen Habermas has been advancing since the late 1960s. As Alex Callinicos points out, Habermas himself formulated his defence of the Enlightenment principles of rationality, progress and eventual human emancipation in the context of growing political dissatisfaction with liberal democracy in Germany in the late 1960s.[1] It was, Habermas explains, the rise of the extreme left and right and the appearance of new social movements like the Greens who seemed to offer a challenge to modern industrial civilisation itself that drove him out of 'the theoretical ivory tower to take a stand'.[2] Habermas produced a defence of the Enlightenment as an unrealised process that had yet to fulfil its full promise and provided many leftists and left-leaning academics with a useful anchor point against the increasingly dominant post-structuralist direction of academic institutions. Reconstruction, rather than deconstruction, was, Habermas argued, what was needed in order to safeguard the achievements of the Enlightenment.

But while Habermas's explicit appeal to material political goals offered for many a welcome antidote to the perceived self-indulgence, elitism and unnecessary esotericism of post-structuralist theory, the problem remained that Habermas based his theory upon the very historical phenomena that was proving to be a problem not just for post-structuralists but for many leftists, feminists, black people and people of color. For, whilst many political dissenters were uneasy about the post-structuralist privileging of language and discourses above material and social conditions, Habermas's invitation to return to the Enlightenment proved to be no less problematic. The ability of the noble ideals of the Enlightenment to coexist in tandem with slavery and the denigration of the rational

capacities of women and the poor were for many not simply evidence of the unfinished potential of the Enlightenment but rather pointed to a fundamental problem with the privileging of reason itself.

Moreover, the continued ability of liberal narratives to claim a monopoly on a commitment to justice, truth, tolerance and freedom in a world in which most people are struggling to ensure their survival has yet to lose its irony. A historical overview of the friendly relations between Western and non-Western nations does not yield a list of like-minded democratic aspirations. It merely unveils the yoking together of economic interests that provide non-Western nations with despotic tyrants uninterested in promoting any national wealth and Western nations with access to cheap labour and materials to ensure their continued dominance in the world market.[3]

The public sphere, as Habermas rightly observes, is not the same as the governmental sphere and given the blatant hypocrisy of Western governmental foreign policy and rhetoric this is just as well. Habermas tracks the emergence of the public sphere back to the turn of the eighteenth century when the disciplines and activities of science, law, morality and art emerged as distinct cultural practices, each regulated by their own specific principles. As Pauline Johnson observes, this separation of science, morality and art into autonomous spheres with their own specific values, world constructs and institutional frameworks prompted individuals to thematise and question their world and through this reconstruct new ways of perceiving human social existence.[4] The old hegemony of nature and religion gave way and a new disenchantment with the world forced people to see the world not as some intimate and knowable entity but as an alien object with its own causal laws.

For Habermas this historical development constituted a progression that distinguished Western nations and enabled them to evolve a modern consciousness. Implicit in this celebration of Western modernity is a judgement upon non-Western nations where the pre-modern power of myth (in Habermas's account, the result of a confusion between nature and culture) still prevailed. Meanwhile, in modern Western nations, the break-up of science, art and morality removed this option for Western subjects and in doing so propelled them onto the modern stage.

In Habermas's reading, the advantage of the declining authority of religion and nature as universal contexts for human beliefs and knowledge was that people were deprived of any transcendent categories with which to explain both themselves and their world and were forced instead to establish their society and conduct upon clear and pragmatic

grounds. The newly emerging grounds for human knowledge and conduct become, in Habermas's account, those of human communication. Language and debate amongst people become the grounds for knowledge, and the autonomous cultural spheres in which these debates take place become the vital determining force for human society.

The emergence of rational debate and its location in liberal democratic institutions was, according to Habermas, accompanied by the increasing autonomy of the market and state from the fabric of everyday life. For Habermas, the distinction between the market, state and 'life world', while not absolute, constitutes a valuable advance from premodern society. The differentiation of society into governmental, economic and cultural spheres enables cultural activity to exercise a specific role in monitoring the excesses of capitalist expansion. This emphasis upon the difference of cultural activity to economic and governmental activity enables Habermas to stress the *particular* function of cultural activity and diminish its relation to both the economic base and governmental policies.

This stress upon the virtues of the rational differentiation of cultural sites and the corresponding distance of cultural activity from the market and the state underestimates the extent to which these sites overlap. For those people not included in the cultural debates of the eighteenth century, the degrees of coherence and consensus between the interests and concerns of those in charge of government, market, state and culture would no doubt have been more readily apparent. Similarly, in our own times, for the asylum seekers attempting to reside in Western nations it is the powerful consensus between these supposedly differentiated sites that makes their exclusion so profound.

Habermas's emphasis upon the difference between cultural activity and economic and governmental activity gives him a free rein to find altogether more amenable contexts for the evolution of liberal democracy. Thus, the welcome evolution of rational debate and the achievement of a liberal consensus in the eighteenth century reflected humanity's desire to reach a shared understanding. This did not emerge from any encounter with the effects of conflict and confrontation but obeyed instead humanity's desire to reach a shared understanding which in turn constitutes 'the inherent telos of human speech'.[5]

Divorced from any direct connection to the realm of economics, human history becomes instead merely the gradual realisation of pre-existing truths embedded deep inside human consciousness. Thus, humanity is predisposed towards rational consensus because that is the original purpose of language, and modern cultural spheres merely

reflect this disposition and enable this fundamental human instinct to achieve a concrete form. This leads to the collapsing of any difference between individual consciousness and human history, as Habermas makes clear when he speaks about 'the homologous structures of consciousness in the histories of the individual and the species'.[6] As Callinicos comments, Habermas's determination to avoid a materialist account of the mechanisms of social change leads him to 'a strange kind of idealism, in which the stages of the development of the individual person are assimilated to those of humanity'.[7]

In Habermas's historical account both the individual and the species undergo a learning process through which a shared moral consciousness culminates in 'a universal ethics of speech'.[8] This universal ethics is the foundation of rational debate, whereby implicitly shared norms are 'debated'. The limit upon any excessive disagreement in the public sphere in which rational debate supposedly takes place is underlined by the emphasis that Habermas places upon an already existing consensus and unity. As Callinicos points out, such suppositions come dangerously close to reinstating 'a kind of social macro-subject' when he argues that 'even modern largely decentred societies maintain in their everyday communicative action a virtual centre of self-understanding' and 'a diffuse common consciousness'.[9]

Arguably, Habermas's assertion that modern society reflects the evolving moral consciousness of humanity not only, as Callinicos argues, overwrites the means of production and social labour from having any meaningful role in producing historical change, but in doing so risks transporting the entire issue of historical change to the very transcendent sites that he finds so unhelpful in pre-modern societies. Habermas's modern rational subject may have dispensed with God or Nature as its guide but it does so only to follow the course of a mysterious pre-existing imperative rooted in his or her individual consciousness. And this is, very emphatically, a model of universal human *consciousness*; for, the evolutionary path of moral consciousness is not one that is complicated by complex subconscious deviations, contradictions or undue modifications arising out of competing arguments, but one that stays resolutely true to the path of universal moral Enlightenment. The internal history of both the individual and the species is always already bound by a common purpose and mission enabling Habermas to make sweeping allusions to a commonality that precedes and informs entire nations.

Thus the polemical grounds of Habermas's theory are rooted in a temporal order that encompasses the entirety of history. The desire for

consensus and liberal democracy is presented as the context for liberal democracy, which in turn becomes a decidedly *natural* inevitability. The subsequent liberal democratic institutions are as such the embodiment of a moral consciousness that was at last sufficiently evolved to found concrete institutions with which to shape the material world.

The symbiotic relation that Habermas depicts between the individual, the species and liberal democratic institutions marks the triumphant coalescence of liberal democracy, which is constituted as existing deep within human consciousness even before the appropriate democratic institutions were in place. Accordingly, the rule of law, which Habermas places particular emphasis upon, is not only the means through which consensual ideals regarding morality and ethics can be administered but is integral to democracy itself:

> The argument developed in *Between Facts and Norms* essentially aims to demonstrate that there is a conceptual or internal relation, and not simply a historically contingent association, between the rule of law and democracy.[10]

Habermas's allusion to the 'internal' history of the rule of law and democracy is the key to understanding why his accounts of individual development and historical change often prove to be descriptions of a supposedly identical evolutionary process. For it is this recourse to notions of historical inevitability that infuses Habermas's avowedly pragmatic mission to defend the goals of the Enlightenment with mysticism.

The Western subjects that he depicts as inheriting the enabling structures of Western modernity are, as such, both its heirs and its founders since rationality and liberal democratic institutions are, it would seem, predestined outcomes. In this sense, Habermas's account of the beneficial effects of Western modernity is not so much a historical reading, in the sense of aiming to convince readers of the empirical evidence and subsequent reliability of the account, as a historical conclusion. His reference to 'the homologous structures of consciousness in the histories of the individual and the species' reflects his desire to locate the Western subject as someone who both anticipates and carries out the modernist project of creating a good society. Habermas's description of Western modernity and the Western subject are brought so closely together as to make the unfolding of Western modernity as inevitable as birth and death.

Thus, while Habermas defines his mission as one that aims to protect the Enlightenment heritage from destruction at the hands of those who

have no faith in human rationality, his defence ultimately asserts the existence of norms that are entirely unstoppable and inevitable. The evolving rationality of Western individuals becomes not so much an argument set out in order to convince others of its validity but functions instead as both a statement and a conclusion. Habermasian polemic is thus anchored by categorical statements that invite no rational objection. Declarations that reaching a shared understanding constitutes 'the inherent telos of human speech' indicate the limits that are to be placed upon the supposed universal framework of rational 'debate'.

For Habermas the evolutionary moral cognitive processes that make up the lifeworld do not simply stop in the eighteenth century. The lifeworld as the public arena dedicated to the pursuit of rational argument is itself the means by which the excesses of capitalism can and should be challenged. Moreover, the excesses of late capitalism themselves threaten the lifeworld with economic ideologies that attack the moral grounds upon which it was founded. Habermas does not suggest that contemporary liberal democracy is currently producing an enlightened modernity but remains convinced that abiding by Enlightenment values will temper what he terms the 'surrealism' of late capitalism and keep humanity upon the path to moral Enlightenment.

What Habermas identifies as the 'really existing surrealism of life under late capitalism' can, he argues, be countered by a renewed faith in liberal democratic procedures and principles. However, the obstacle that confronts Habermas in this plea is the very universal authority that he has accorded to liberal democratic thought and institutions in the first place. For depicting liberal democracy as the expression of a universal and timeless moral consciousness raises several unanswered questions.

If human moral consciousness was, and is, always tilted towards consensual norms, then what prevented liberal democracy from flourishing in earlier centuries? If humanity is motivated by a desire for consensus, then how do we account for revolutionary struggles aimed at producing a different order? If *universal* norms of consensus operate in the public sphere then why has it been, and why does it remain, so necessary to exercise such caution in determining *who* should occupy it? If what we are dealing with is a universal unfolding of moral consciousness, why did it occur in Western Europe and not the rest of the world? If the cultural spheres that make up the public sphere are so distinct from mere economic factors, then why are those excluded from the 'public' sphere so easily identifiable as lacking economic power? If Marxism is, as

Habermas maintains, guilty of overstating the relevance of the economic base, then what does his model offer by way of explanation for economic exploitation by modern democratic liberal nations? Indeed, how do we account for different nations at all, if what we are committed to are universal processes of moral evolution?

Ultimately, the Habermasian model is unable to account for historical change or to register the long running 'debate' as to the morality of liberal democratic principles and practices. Arguably, because Habermas locates the processes of change *within* the internal histories of bourgeois Western subjects and liberal democratic institutions, he is left at something of a loss when it comes to demands for change in the here and now. Human agency, because it is supposedly committed to deep moral evolutionary processes, becomes markedly suspect when it comes to articulating radically different values, beliefs and aspirations. Habermas, like Appiah and Gutmann, is ultimately unable to account for dissent in the public sphere and criticisms of the democratic credentials of the public sphere, because he pins his argument upon the self-evident existence of an overwhelmingly liberal consensus. Inevitably, their subsequent historicising of this liberal consensus is characterised by a desire to expel any evidence of historical dissent to the margins and to continue this practice into the present.

Indeed, at times, the sense that all we need to do is to support the development of the already existing cultural spheres comes perilously close to making the question of human agency inconsequential. For a theorist who places such optimism in the ability of humanity to produce a rational and progressive society, human beings themselves frequently appear to be little more than conduits for a prior historical mission. Thus, Habermas explains that the evolution of normative structures such as law and morality are not reducible to economic relations because they possess and act upon '"an internal history", which is the pacemaker of social evolution'.[11] Interestingly, the more Habermas attempts to underpin his arguments with empirical evidence the more he drifts towards decidedly more nebulous contexts for his argument. Arguably, Habermas's frequent identification of 'internal' relations legitimates liberal democratic institutions with a progressive capacity that is less discernible in the visible practice and procedures of law as it is practised in modern Western nations.

Habermas's mission to define and protect the Enlightenment heritage has been advanced against two opposing camps. His defence was aimed at subduing those who would like to see a radically different lifeworld and those who would resist the insights offered by the cultural spheres

and pursue instead merely wealth and power. Feminist commentators in particular have battled with the consequences of his early hostility towards new social groups like themselves, who Habermas suspected of being less interested in reforming the public sphere than in demolishing it altogether.

However, Habermas's ambivalence towards the new social movements ran parallel with a recognition that the public sphere, if it were to have any critical force upon the spheres of government and economics, had to incorporate contemporary evidence of rational progress. Moreover, what Habermas described as the 'surrealism' of life under late capitalism prompted him to concede that he had previously failed to 'utilise the whole range of potential contributions to his theory'.[12] Accordingly Habermas has now declared his theory open to those contributions which, far from demolishing the public sphere, will renew its critical energy. As Johnson notes, the early Habermas assumed that an understanding of the common good could only be achieved by the deliberations of private individuals who refrained from burdening the public sphere with their personal needs. However, in his 1996 work *Between Facts and Norms* he breaks with this fundamentally liberal premise to argue that the principle of public discourse is not only compatible with but is built upon the recognition of the plurality of private need interpretations. Habermas's new openness to diverse human needs has mollified some feminist commentators, but others remain unconvinced that Habermas's life world is really capable of any significant transformation.

Whether or not one declares oneself to be willing to enter the Habermasian public sphere, it is worth remembering that 'the' public sphere and the public sphere as envisaged by Habermas are not necessarily the same thing. Indeed, Habermas's delineation of the public sphere has rather conveniently airbrushed out the past influence of marginalised social movements that in their very articulation of exclusion produced change in the public sphere itself. In other words, 'the' public sphere never was a secure entity following its own evolutionary imperative but was, and is, a contested sphere that exists in relation to other social and political sites in the wider public arena.

Moreover, because 'the' public sphere is a contested site it is also a permeable one that responds to demands for change in order to guarantee its survival. As Neera Chandhoke points out:

> It is of course a historical fact that rights have never been as encompassing as they should be. Governments and civil societies have

often maintained a truncated system of rights that have been based upon exclusions rather than inclusions. If rights have become emancipatory mechanisms ... if they have proved to be weapons of enfranchisement, it is because of social struggles. The struggles of subordinate classes have considerably expanded the entire sphere of rights. Any dynamic theory of civil society has to take this into account. Habermas ... does not recognise that his bourgeois public sphere was constantly interrogated and considerably mediated by social groups placed initially outside the discourse of bourgeois society. And if the bourgeois public sphere had succeeded in challenging the absolutist state, it was in turn subjected to challenges by subaltern groups. Thus Habermas' bourgeois public sphere existed in a field of conflictual social relations. And because its discourse was couched in universal terms, it had to respond and modify itself.[13]

Habermas's depiction of the public sphere as an entity that evolved from the developing moral capacities of individuals and their subsequent desire to realise this development in institutional forms produces an account that is cleansed from any contact with bodily matters. The Habermasian public sphere is the result of a universal process of consensus and as such is unmarked by the history of struggle and conflict. The result is a public sphere that derives its clarity and purpose from a suppression of material history. Questions of exclusions are therefore ones that need to be considered very carefully, since they might divert the public sphere from its integral commitment to universal democracy and tilt it towards some particular interest or group. In other words, those who are excluded become suspect by the very fact that they are not inside the public sphere, while the regulatory character of the public sphere becomes merely a necessary device to safeguard the deployment of universal norms.

Habermas's public sphere has little interest in remembering precisely how it came to be expanded since such histories would undermine its claim to permanent universality. Thus, previously excluded groups demonstrate not so much the questionable universality of the public sphere but rather their own relatively recent adoption of 'human' as opposed to 'particular' interests. It is this that allows those already established in the public sphere to decide *when* it is the right time to include others.

Unfortunately Habermas's 'defence' of rationality has proved to be a remarkably effective strategy for convincing his contemporaries that by criticising Habermas somehow one is repudiating rationality itself.

Or, to put it another way, there is nothing unusual in seeing your own version of rationality as being the one that really does transcend mere self-interest and apply to humanity as a whole. Detached agreement whereby 'the force of the better argument' wins by its superior claim to universal validity hints at the presence of power but expunges it with a vision of a universal agreement to abide by the higher logic of reason. Not surprisingly, having detailed precisely why subjective experience is so detrimental to the pursuit of reason the Habermasian public sphere is marked by an overwhelming absence of any 'experience' at all.

The public sphere that Habermas depicts is not one of people but of words, of language. The 'force of the better argument' that will determine the norms and maxims of the public sphere are the force of words imagined here as transcending the bodies of those who speak them. Habermas's insistence that we can and should view our words as answerable only to the logic of 'reason' is one that has already defined reason as something that humanity possesses solely in order to escape from embodied living. As such rationality towers over humanity and can be realised only by a complete surrender to it as a universal and transcendent historical imperative. Interestingly, as Stale R.S. Finke points out, Habermas's refusal to admit to any connection between our reasoning and our experience signals his difference from Kant, who in his *Third Critique* insisted that the fragility or *partiality* of Reason is the condition under which we communicate.[14] In other words, Kant, unlike Habermas, recognised that communication and in particular the need to justify ourselves springs from our awareness of the *limits* of our own rationality not of our universal agreement and surrender to 'it'.

Significantly, those commentators who profess themselves to be optimistic about the capacity of Habermas's theoretical model to encapsulate feminism share Habermas's own unwillingness to consider the questions of access and intelligibility in the Habermasian public sphere. For, Habermas offers no answer to those who wonder at the capacity of his public sphere to engage with the questions of exclusion, inequality and oppression that are reflected in the very public sphere that he insists is necessary for human progress and emancipation. Thus, Maeve Cooke finds in Habermas's model of discursive rationality an implicit commitment to the recognition of the legitimacy of difference. Her positive reading of Habermasian discourse theory, in fact, echoes Habermas's own response to those who charged him with being incapable of giving any concrete or philosophical space to feminism. Accordingly, Cooke's essay notes with approval Habermas's retort, that sensitivity to diverse points of view and to the multifarious claims of

private individuals is built into the 'richness' of the theory's communicative and intersubjective presuppositions.

Consequently, all that is required for a commitment to 'difference' to be realised is that participants in the public sphere be

> willing (in principle) to consider the arguments of *everyone* no matter how poorly they are articulated ... In addition, since argumentative willingness to reach understanding requires a genuine openness not just to new arguments but also to the needs, desires, anxieties, and insecurities – whether expressed or unexpressed – of the other participants: at times this will require a special sensitivity and a willingness to look beyond explicit verbal expressions and deficiencies in argumentative skills.[15]

I am struck by Cooke's assumption that a radically different perspective is likely to be so incompetently articulated that it will require the skills of a detective rather than a listener to unravel her meaning.

This is not to propose that communication between people is always mutually intelligible but to suggest that the answer to incomprehension can be resolved simply by making allowances for another person's linguistic (and implicitly cerebral) shortcomings is to reduce the potential for *shared* communication to a laughable minimum. Clearly, what is not up for 'sharing' is 'meaning' itself, since communicative exchange here is entirely under the control of the Western rational subject. But before we rush to pin our egalitarian principles upon our own 'willingness' to expend our intellectual energy in unravelling the 'other's' discourse, we might want to consider the possibility that what 'the other' says may extend beyond the knowledge and experience of the Western subject. For, this very centring of the Western *rational* subject, as both the producer and the interpreter of meaning, enables her to not just listen but also to dismiss those forms of speech and knowledge that fail to demonstrate evidence of rationality and sense.

The power of the Western subject here is at its most extreme precisely because it is evoked through the representation of her as an unthreatening and empathic 'participating' subject. Indeed, such is the obvious virtue of this model of communication that it goes beyond theory and appeals instead to commonsensical notions of tolerance and benevolence on the part of the rational Western subject. By contrast the non-Western subject (and indeed the many Western subjects who have yet to establish their rational credentials) is here depicted as one who is potentially compatible with the public sphere so long as she is lucky

enough to be talking to a particularly generous member of the rational elite.

Significantly, this recourse to homely notions of common sense occurs at precisely the point where we might want to explore *how* understanding is reached between people, rather than assume that the parameters of what constitutes 'debating difference' have already been successfully laid down. For as Trinh T. Minh-Ha points out, the desire to reduce meaning and comprehension to a simple matter of common sense principles (in this case 'listening'), reveals that the eschewing of complex theory for easily agreed upon norms far from promoting shared communication licenses, instead, linguistic and philosophical authoritarianism:

> The resistance to theory ... constantly runs the risk of reinstituting naively naturalized theoretical concepts as alternatives to theory; as if a pure, self-evident, and pre-theoretical state of meaning can always be returned to, whenever immediate access to language is thwarted. Such concepts are often the result of a nostalgic desire for a return to 'normalcy' – a state of validated 'common sense' in which polarizing opinions and uncomplicated familiar forms of analysis, interpretation, and communication can be made possible once again. Ironically enough, accessibility in such a context takes on a universal character: to be 'accessible,' one can employ neither symbolic and elliptical language, as in Asian, African, or Native American cultures (because Western ears often equate it with obscurantism); nor poetic language (because 'objective' literal thinking is likely to identify it with 'subjective' aestheticism).[16]

However, for Antje Gimmler, Habermas's version of deliberative democracy has the advantage of supplying normativity:

> There is no plausible alternative model to rational and uncoerced discourse as the normative basis for democracy. That discourse is constituted by equality among participants, the complete disclosure of procedures, the temporary suspension of domination and structural power, and the creation of a situation in which themes for discussion can be freely chosen.[17]

Anticipating the objections of those who would point out that such an idealised description of democratic discourse is far from taking place in modern Western nations, Gimmler queries whether that in itself is a

good enough reason to abandon the model. Declaring yourself to be opposed to equality, political transparency and the temporary suspension of the violent effects of power relations is of course to stake out what would be for many an absurd position. However, it is not so absurd to question whether remaining faithful to dominant liberal values and institutions will ever actually usher in such an idyllic scenario.

Gimmler is able to celebrate the normative basis of Habermasian theory because she too accepts Habermas's premise that in modern Western societies the moral, legal and functional spheres are distinct from one another. Thus, differentiation and acceptance of diversity is not so much a premise as an observation that Habermas rightly makes about modern Western societies:

> Habermas's model ... takes account of an important sociological observation, namely, that in pluralistic societies the moral, legal and functional spheres are distinct from one another; and the diversity of values, forms of life and attitudes that compose them is an established fact of modern societies. Indeed, this diversity is seen as valuable in itself ... The public sphere plays an important role in pluralistic societies as an arena for expressing and constituting this diversity.[18]

Unfortunately, for those deemed lacking in the necessary qualifications or linguistic competence for inclusion as citizens in the public sphere, the various sites of law, morality and administration are experienced as anything but diverse. The poor face the hegemonic hurdles of a hierarchical class system, which perpetuates educational, social and material disadvantage with wearying predictability from one generation to the next. Women still have to battle with the powerful degree of hegemony between supposedly unrelated social and political spheres that together ensure the survival of patriarchal privilege. And asylum seekers and refugees prove more visibly still that the authoritative versions of law, culture and 'public' morality are marked by a forbidding coalescence of values and principles that combine to criminalise their plight.

The routine appeal to a notion of 'our' championing of 'diversity' conceals the 'fact' that only some diversions are welcome in modern liberal nations. 'We' are not so keen to welcome the diverse experiences offered by those with a lack of economic independence and 'we' are even less keen when this is accompanied by the wrong skin colour or nationality.[19] Fortunately, the condition of linguistic competence and the required evidence of a benign cultural 'contribution' ensure that

any such embrace of diversity will remain a matter strictly for those already established at the heart of the public sphere.

Gimmler's decision to celebrate rather than analyse the characteristics of modern nations glosses over the central problem of defining who occupies 'the' public sphere. Ignoring this question at the same time as asserting the capacity of 'the' public sphere to 'express' and 'constitute' diversity leaves the urgent question of what precisely this diversity is diverging *from* unaddressed. This celebration of modernity proceeds by masking the continued positioning of those with a classed, raced or gendered identity as external to 'the' public sphere while somehow being faithfully represented by that same public sphere. Such a model of tolerance and inclusion when applied to institutions operates to include 'others' while preserving the self-evident neutrality and universality of the site in which they are 'included'.

Certainly, the benign tolerance of the modern liberal public sphere is apt to evaporate if the other makes the fatal mistake of refusing to express her difference. Multicultural celebrations of the kind that Gimmler proposes depend finally on the acceptance of those deemed to be marginal agreeing that they really are bereft of universal credentials; depend finally on the power to decide who can and who cannot declare themselves able to express universal human principles.

As Jan Blommaert and Jef Verschueren demonstrate in their examination of diversity and tolerance in modern Western nations, underlying the congratulatory rhetoric of toleration and respect lurk older certainties regarding the inalienable 'difference' of some people from 'ourselves'. It is precisely this intolerance that ensures that 'public' debates about diversity are conducted without any necessary involvement on the part of those deemed to be the harbingers of this supposedly welcome diversity:

> Conventional wisdom tells us that *debates* are open discussions of opposing points of view. In that capacity they are associated with democracy, and they are seen as the absolute opposite of authoritatively imposed *dogmas*. This dichotomy hides the fact that public discourse in democratic societies is not as free and open as it might seem at first. In other words, debates are themselves objects (as well as instruments) of control. They are not controlled by just a few individuals … [B]ut they are controlled none the less. Wide societal debates tend to be dominated by the economically and politically powerful segments of society, availing themselves of influential means of communication … The free flow of ideas and arguments is a cherished but dangerous illusion.[20]

As Blommaert and Verschueren's enquiry makes clear, the problem with replacing nature and religion with the supposedly more democratic contexts of language and debate is that any consideration of their hierarchical contexts is pushed to the margins. It is this overwriting of the histories of communication and their connections with other material sites of power, notably private property, that robs Habermasian discourse theory of its assumed basis in universal norms.

As Gayatri Spivak observes in her interview with three Indian colleagues, their assumption that they are attempting to engage in a reciprocal debate which she is blocking by an apparent 'solipsism of meditation' reveals the power concealed in the assumption that your own speaking position and intentions are transparent and neutral and as such can be used to measure the failures of others to attain the same democratic level of debate and subsequent political relevance. As Spivak comments,

> since we have been talking about elite theory, let me suggest that that is the kind of position Jürgen Habermas articulates: a neutral communication situation of free dialogue. Well, it is not a situation that ever comes into being – there is no such thing. The desire for neutrality and dialogue, even as it should not be repressed, must always mark its own failure ... The idea of neutral dialogue is an idea which denies history, denies structure, denies the positioning of subjects. I would try to look, how, in fact, the demand for a dialogue is articulated.[21]

Spivak's invitation to explore how the 'demand for a dialogue is articulated' reintroduces the question of power and history into celebrations of the public sphere and accompanying idealisations of rational debate. The ability of commentators such as Gimmler to concede that the concept of deliberative democracy does entail a 'certain rigidity' that 'might usefully' be amended by 'a widening and differentiation of the model'[22] looks towards the future but refuses to subject the history of the public sphere and liberal concepts of civil society to any serious scrutiny.

As Rey Chow argues, it is only by insisting on the need to question rather than assert culture or cultural 'difference' that cultural studies can perform any valuable work:

> Especially at a time when everything seems equivalent and we could all happily return to our own 'cultures,' 'ethnicities,' and 'origins'. To put it a different way, it is precisely at the time of multiculturalism, when 'culture' seems to have become a matter of 'entitlement' rather than struggle that we need to reemphasize the questions of power

and underscore at every point the institutional forces that account for the continual hierarchization of cultures. Instead of perpetuating what Spivak terms the 'revolutionary tourism' and 'celebration of testimony' that seem to characterise too much of what goes under the name of cultural studies these days, it is the meticulous investigation of such legitimating structures of power that would, in the long run, give cultural studies its sustenance and integrity as a viable and pedagogical practice.[23]

Moreover, now that Soviet Russia no longer functions as the evil that can unite the guardians of Western civilisation and the material and ideological battle shifts to the 'Islamic' threat, 'cultural' identity has become a new and deadly arsenal. Indeed, Habermasian invocations of the individual appear almost as quaint anomalies in the face of the new standoff between 'the West' and 'Islamic terrorism'. And for this reason the need to challenge ideas of cultural absolutism are now more necessary than ever. The extent of the challenge is clear when we remember that it not just the powerful who draw sustenance from an idea of cultural difference.

Thus, Appiah and Gutmann ransack the Enlightenment in order to insist that the raced individual be freed from the constraints of race, which have prevented the Enlightenment from achieving its promise of universal progress and emancipation. Feminist commentators, such as Antje Gimmler, too insist that the Habermasian public sphere is supple enough to open its borders and Habermas himself declares that such progress is already built into his theory. But Lucius T. Outlaw proves that you do not have to stand by a notion of universal individualism to support Habermasian liberalism. For, if Appiah and Gutmann want to shake off the shackles of race and enter a clear rational public space, Outlaw wants to do precisely the opposite. And if Appiah and Gutmann speed over the convergence of ideas of racial superiority and Enlightenment principles in its founding figures, Outlaw stops to draw attention to the 'glaring contradictions of the American democratic revolution'. He identifies the creation of race-based slavery and apartheid as receiving support from 'some of the best "philosophical" minds of the country'. Furthermore, he castigates philosophy for only very recently overcoming its 'virtual silence' and 'complicity' in the 'African holocaust'.[24]

But for all that Outlaw, like Appiah and Gutmann, is able to see a viable future for humankind – one in which the 'contradictions' of the Enlightenment can finally be put to rest. While Appiah and Gutmann

perceive racial identity as a veritable affront to the 'real' underlying individual that racial labelling conceals, Outlaw argues that it is precisely racial identity that is in urgent need of preservation:

> I think we would be wise to take up once again the quest for critical understanding that ushered in modernity and carry it through, but this time conserving raciality and ethnicity in reconceptualizing the ordering of social life as a means of providing understandings more appropriate for ordering social formations with a diversity of racial/ethnic cultural groups.[25]

Turning his back on the white spokesmen and founders of the Enlightenment, Outlaw looks to W.E.B. Du Bois for inspiration and in particular his essay, 'The Conservation of Races', which sought to conserve race in the context of democratic pluralism. As Outlaw relates

> he was concerned that … 'communities of meaning' constituting and constituted by distinct racial (and we might add ethnic) populations, be 'conserved' and nurtured as the most basic unit of social life in and through which each race developed its own cultural 'message' manifested in various forms of achievement … Of particular importance to him were the prospects of cultivating, refining and sharing the 'messages' of what he termed the Negro race.[26]

Interestingly, while Outlaw turns to Du Bois's essay as a source of inspiration for the understanding of race as a flexible but workable reality, Appiah cites it for its inability to adequately define race, concluding that such a failing merely confirms that there is no such thing as race. And yet the argument between Outlaw and Gutmann as to how clear Du Bois's conception of race was combines to misrepresent Du Bois's own thinking on race which he revised substantially throughout his life.

As Outlaw emphasises here, his purpose in drawing upon Du Bois is to recapture the work of black commentators on the subject of race. In other words, rather than simply seeing race as part of a history of subjection, we should retrace its other developments as part of a 'decidedly *political* project'. But ironically, by selecting Du Bois as providing us with an alternative history of race, Outlaw ends up replicating the silences and omissions that he himself levels against traditional philosophy. For as Kate A. Baldwin has demonstrated in her detailed account of Du Bois's engagement with the Soviet Union, the popular academic

practice of focusing on Du Bois's early work and parallel inattention to his later work is one that misrepresents the development of Du Bois's thinking on race which underwent seismic changes arising out of his travels and commitment to the Soviet Union.

Thus, Outlaw's selection of an essay Du Bois wrote in 1897 as providing definitive grounds for thinking about race in contemporary modern liberal nations is problematic because it suppresses the extent to which Du Bois grappled with and ultimately changed his thinking about race. As Baldwin relates, in *Russia and America*[27] written some 30 years after 'the Conservation of Races', Du Bois explains how his encounter with Marxism helped him to rethink his earlier intention of proving the humanity of the Negro. The later Du Bois identifies and condemns the exclusion of Marxism from formal education and the censorship of accounts of the Russian revolution as in part responsible for what he reviewed as his early misplaced energies:

> In my early years then the problems of property, work and poverty were to me but manifestations of the basic problem of color ... Race problems, therefore, to my mind became the main cause of poverty ... Nothing in my college courses at Harvard led me yet to question the essential justice of the industrial system of the nation ... still there came no word of Karl Marx.[28]

It is, as Baldwin's detailed account of Du Bois's engagement with the Soviet Union demonstrates, something of an irony that the exclusion and demonisation of Marxist thought and the Russian revolution in Du Bois's education has been so successfully replicated by subsequent work on Du Bois himself. For, while his early essay advocating the preservation of (some kind of) racial difference may well provide Outlaw with the tools for reconsidering how concepts of race and ethnicity can be preserved in modern liberal nations, this can only be achieved by treating Du Bois's early work as a definitive summary of his literary-political output.

As Baldwin recounts, by the early 1940s Du Bois's interests had moved from a concern for black American liberation to an alignment with the decolonising agenda and anti-imperialism of the Pan-Africanist movement. Allied to this was his investigation of and commitment to the Soviet Union as providing an alternative political model to that of US capitalist expansion. It was this that led Du Bois to refer to the Soviet Union's 'refusal to be white'[29] and his subsequent reworking of race as inextricably connected to the imperialist-capitalist economy.

Du Bois's rethinking of race did not take place within America but was generated more by his many visits to the Soviet Union which led him to open up the issue of race beyond the national parameters of America. The point, as Baldwin emphasises, is not that Du Bois idealised the Russian revolution and its legacy but that as a black American he was welcomed in a way that had been unthinkable for him in the United States. For as she reminds us Du Bois's America was one that was governed by Jim Crow laws, the monopolies of corporate capitalism, the legal suppression of civil liberties and the vilification of all things 'un-American'. What Du Bois saw in the Soviet Union was the *possibility* of a different future and the material existence of a different encoding of race:

> Whether or not Russian Communism is a success is beside the point; the point is, are the ideals of human uplift as conceived by Marx and Lenin ideals which ought to be realized? ... even if Communism as tried in Russia had completely failed, it was a splendid effort, a magnificent vision.[30]

Du Bois's movement towards a vision, which ultimately identified economic exploitation as the fundamental motor for the enslavement and subordination of the poor and dispossessed, makes attempts to recruit him for the buttressing of enlightened liberalism, on the grounds of an alleged racial-cultural essentialism, questionable in the extreme.

While Appiah and Gutmann 'rescue' the individual from the debilitating implications of a racial identity, Outlaw moves in the opposite direction by restating the fundamental importance of race to individual identity. In both accounts the individual (raced or not) emerges as the proper foundation for any prescriptions for contemporary society. The effect of this extraction of the individual from history is an inevitable privileging of the individual over his or her social and political locations both in the past and the present. What we are presented with is a curiously ahistorical individual; one who is profoundly resilient to the succession of historical mistakes that are traced back to the Enlightenment.

Thus Outlaw argues that the mistake was not to privilege reason but to restrict the existence of 'reasons', while Appiah and Gutmann in a countermove insist that the mistake was to think that black people were not capable of the *same* reasoning as white people. But since all agree that reason itself is something that all individuals possess (albeit measurable by different registers and here class 'difference' operates as a subtle and insidious new possibility) the project becomes simply a matter

of bringing Enlightenment discourses up to date. And while they tinker with the correct way in which to view the intersections of race and individuals, the social and political contexts that inform such processes gradually slip away from view.

Thus, Appiah and Gutmann's individual emerges victoriously autonomous as *simply* individual, while Outlaw's individual emerges proudly aware of her racial identity. Such an individual can, of course accept all other individuals because they have been subjected to the same process of extraction from any social and political contexts. Context here is simply a matter of remembering that as individuals we should be concerned to treat all other individuals in a way that we would want to be treated ourselves. Not, of course, that this will always be an easy project, since one cannot advance a project of individualism without the parallel caveat that we are all *different*. Outlaw aligning himself with the new form of 'cosmopolitan liberalism,' as espoused by Michael Novak, explains what such work involves:

> A firm commitment to the laborious but rewarding enterprise of full, mutual, intellectual understanding; and a respect for difference of nuance and subtlety, particularly in the area of those diversifying 'lived values' that have lain until now, in all cultures, so largely unarticulated.[31]

What is strikingly absent in such accounts is any sense that individuals might want to challenge or change their world (and themselves).

This is a model that is profoundly averse to any notion of individuals ever experiencing their individuality as meaningless isolation. Instead we are presented with a representation of humanity as rigidly adhering to their individual boundaries and dutifully undertaking the laborious labour that is necessary for a 'civil' society. In essence it is a profoundly joyless representation of human contact and as such is profoundly resistant to any notion that people not only learn from contact with other people but also, and perhaps more importantly, change.

The capacity of human beings to change and the importance of including the material contexts of poverty and oppression in any account of humanity is something that Du Bois himself did not discount. His curiosity about humanity and the world grew directly out of his experiences of US racism but it was his travels in Europe, Africa and the USSR that inspired him to reach beyond individual experience and struggle with the *international* dimensions of race, class and empire:

I made my first visit to Africa in 1923 ... I became vividly aware of a Negro problem far greater than I had envisaged in America, and my mind leaped further; more or less clearly I found myself asking: is the problem of color and race simply and mainly a matter of difference in appearance and cultural variation, or has it something in common with the industrial organization of the world? With Poverty, Ignorance and Disease? Has Revolution in Russia something fundamental for the Negro Problem in the United States and the Colonial Problem in Africa?[32]

The questions that Du Bois posed in the aftermath of the Second World War continue to preoccupy those of us who want not only to question the existing economic, social and political realities of our world but to change them. Those who argue that individual autonomy must be increased in a world in which ever growing numbers of people are subject to the interests of capital are conveniently silent about the extent to which those in power are more than happy to protect their individual interests through the formation of anonymous and unaccountable organisations such as the World Bank, the IMF and the giant multinationals. And if liberal humanists are reluctant to consider the purposes of collective action then there is notably no such reluctance on the part of those committed to extending their wealth to form alliances with what ought to be the most unlikely partners.[33]

The efforts of liberal theorists to occupy and control the 'public sphere' have been vigorously contested by Marxist theorists who have applied themselves to the task of exposing the liberal discourse of individualism as nothing less than a convoluted attempt to conceal their own class interests. The expulsion of the masses from the dominant cultural and political spheres of influence was, for Marxist intellectuals, precisely what needed to be overturned. And it was this task that prompted Oskar Negt and Alexander Kluge[34] to return to Habermas's 'public sphere' in order to identify and condemn its rigorous exclusions of much of 'the public' from any participation in it. Negt and Kluge's scepticism at the ability of Habermasian delineations of the public sphere to adequately define civil society, let alone secure a democratic future, led them to advocate a wholesale walkout from his proposed public sphere into a new anti-bourgeois counter-public sphere that would, they hoped, bring the project of radical democracy to life.

Part 2 Contesting Civil Order with Proletarian Experience

4
The Counter-Public Sphere

Ten years after the publication of Habermas's influential *The Structural Transformation of the Public Sphere*,[1] Alexander Kluge and Oskar Negt produced a polemical reply to Habermas's thesis with their 1972 collaboration entitled, *Public Sphere and Experience: Analysis of the Bourgeois and Proletarian Public Sphere*.[2] Kluge and Negt subjected Habermas's public sphere to a forensic examination in order to affirm Habermas's notion of a public sphere while disputing his definition of it. The Habermasian public sphere was, they pointed out, one that ignored the existence of other public spheres and reflected and protected the specific interests of the bourgeoisie. In particular, they pointed to the connection that early philosophers of reason had made between economic privilege and reason. Kant[3] asserted that only those who owned property possessed the freedom necessary to exercise disinterested rational judgement. He argued that those who owned property were 'their own masters' as opposed to the propertyless who were still locked into the competitive social relations that prevented them from being able to deliberate upon universal, moral and political concerns.

Thus, as Habermas conceded, although the public sphere was theoretically open to anyone, it was in practice restricted to those who owned property:

> Only *property-owning private people* were admitted to a public engaged in critical political debate, for their autonomy was rooted in the sphere of commodity exchange … While the wage labourers were forced to exchange their labor power as their sole commodity, the property-owning private people related to each other as owners of commodities through an exchange of goods. Only the latter were their own masters; only they could be enfranchised to vote – admitted to

> the public use of reason ... Consequently, the propertyless were excluded from the public of private people engaged in critical political debate ... In this sense they were not citizens at all, but persons who with talent, industry and luck might someday be able to attain that status; until then they merely had the same claim to protection under the law as others, without being allowed to participate in legislation themselves. (emphasis in the original)[4]

As Kluge and Negt demonstrate, Habermas records the history of the public sphere but fails to subject the connection between freedom and property in the classical public sphere to any serious scrutiny. Clearly, Habermas was more interested in tracing the *development* of the classical public sphere than in analysing its foundations, and his evolutionary conception of the public sphere directed him away from questioning its economic foundations.

Kant's founding equation between property owners and the capacity for reason and his immediate dismissal of economic privilege from any discussion of rationality mirrors Habermas's parallel flight from any undue consideration of the material structures of inequality for his liberal democratic project. It is a touch ironic that the existing inequalities of the material world are given such short shrift by both Habermas and Kant considering both philosophers assert their commitment to the development of social democracy. Such a development will be, of course, unlikely to challenge the reproduction of material inequality since it is precisely the privileged status of the property owners that have provided us with the fortuitous birth of modern and rational enlightenment.

Property ownership becomes, in liberal-democratic history, the proper context for intellectual freedom and the ground for transcendental considerations of such conundrums as freedom, justice and ethics. Having utilised the inherited structures of material bourgeois privilege as constituting the grounds for modern rationality we witness nothing short of a full scale race away from any contamination of emergent bourgeois ideologies and values with class privilege. Transcendence of any problematic material contexts becomes not only the preferred flight path for bourgeois commentators but exhibits convincing proof of their democratic credentials. The material world becomes, and remains in liberal democratic commentaries, something best ruminated upon from above. Any niggling problems such as poverty and oppression are best solved by a proper distance from any unhelpful self-interest or partiality. The material world is in short, only to be viewed from a distance; the

possibility for transcendence and with it rational judgement is doomed to disappear if one gets too close.

Unfortunately, this means that when it comes to offering any universal prescriptions and insights into the material world, those who lack material wealth remain as redundant now as they were in Kant's times. By submerging the propertyless into the material world, Kant was able to expel them from any rational insight into that world. For Kant and Habermas, the material world figures as something to be transcended by the human faculty of reason which will, *in time*, direct humanity to democratic enlightenment. It is the temporal logic of this theory that renders both the material world and its disenfranchised members unenlightened.

The expulsion of any consideration as to how some individuals came to own property from liberal democratic discourse has enabled the property-owning hero of liberal democratic theory to be cherished in subsequent accounts as embodying the very essence of democratic freedom. In liberal democratic theory it is this sly entanglement of economic privilege with freedom that enables the economically advantaged to insist that the protection of liberty applies most crucially to themselves. Thus, while state welfare reflects the enlightened benevolence of the economically advantaged, wholesale state protection of the bourgeoisie's property and finances becomes simply the correct protection of 'individual' liberty. The suppression of the ways in which the wealthy amass and maintain their wealth is of course a necessary philosophical procedure.

Significantly, Kant viewed service as incompatible with the aspiration of freedom, which is presumably why he elected to exclude servants from any claims to the political rights of citizenship. Thus, the servant by being a servant demonstrates not his lack of freedom but his irrelevance to any discussion of freedom. In a stroke of historical 'disinterest' Kant presents servants as those who are either unable or unwilling to choose a life befitting that of a free citizen. Accordingly, Kant argues that, a free citizen does not allow, 'others to make use of him; for he must in the true sense of the word *serve* no-one but the commonwealth'.[5] In other words, the economic inequalities that produce servants and masters are less significant than the loss of autonomy which the servants have 'allowed' to take place.

The effects of this removal of any social and political contexts for freedom, and its displacement onto the realm of philosophical conjecture, ensure that the issue of domination and exploitation need not be connected to discussions of freedom. Unsurprisingly, the reluctance of

women and other marginalised groups and individuals to view themselves as embracing a state of servitude has accompanied liberal democratic narratives from their inception. However, liberal discussions of freedom continue to assert that freedom is best represented by those who have the power and the resources to be free. As Susanne Kappeler comments:

> If anything ... we deem service and servitude incompatible with freedom, rather than the power of mastery which commands that service. Thus while Kant emphasises that a free citizen must not allow others to use him, he fails to insist that therefore a free citizen must neither use others in service. Thus the 'freedom' which liberal democracy has aspired to and realized is not universal freedom for all, but the continuation of the 'freedom' of rulers and masters, now extended to a larger number of men. Or to put it differently, the foundation of liberal democracy meant a wider group of men being enfranchised, without disenfranchisement fundamentally being challenged.[6]

The suppression of the histories of opposition to the modernist dream were then, as they are now, marginalised precisely because they undermine the preferred depiction of Europe's organic development into Kant's well-lit beacon guiding all of humanity to an enlightened future. But as Couze Venn comments, there has always been opposition to the dominant culture, surviving now in the recorded histories of the Diggers, the writings of Wollstonecraft and, long before postmodernists discovered the liberation of infinite ambiguity and undecidability, Spinoza had argued that the project to discover the final causes of things was an impossible dream.[7]

Not surprisingly, Europe's growing imperial ambitions and burgeoning overseas acquisitions were regularly punctuated by peasant and slave revolts. And naturally, such expressions of hostility and opposition could be dismissed as ignorant of the ways of reason and as such in need of further subjection, since reason itself was firmly located in the property-owning body of the white male subject. As Venn points out,

> Logocentric discourse displaces the basis of inequality onto something else namely reason itself. For instance, the cunning of Locke (1690) was to argue that the possession of reason determined the possession of other things; property can then appear as the metonym of reason, the natural result of its proper exercise, namely through

the efficient use of one's labour. We know that it is America that offers the stage for Locke's demonstration of the rationality and greater benefit for 'mankind' of the institution of private property and the invention of money. The displacement shifts the gaze from the contingent and socially established reality of inequalities to apparently unchanging and universal features intrinsic to human subjectivity. The discursive stratagem produces narratives in which reason and property came to refer to and relay each other in a specular signifying system. It is difficult to see the join since the differential distribution of power and property appears to correspond neatly to the (assumed to be natural) differential distribution of rationality; each instance performatively validates the 'truth' of the other. The double séance performs two simultaneous substitutions: it naturalizes inequality and difference, either as the consequence of what was intended by divine providence or as the necessary result of 'man's' use of his rational powers, and it secularises them in the form of rational necessity, and thus brings them within the intentionality of subjects and their action. Reason is made to scupper all forms of oppressive relations and exploitation-colonial, 'patriarchal,' class – while the 'Man of Reason' is installed as the centre of a new *logos,* namely as the free, autonomous agent of History, the 'I' who decides the future.[8]

The intrinsic connection that Kant made between property ownership and the capacity for rational thought provides liberal democratic theory with its specific historical point of origin. The bourgeoisie are thus propelled onto the modern stage as a new and innovative ruling class – one that will deliver humanity from the dark superstitions and chaos of pre-modern Europe.

The self-presentation of the emerging bourgeois elite as humanists dedicated to the task of installing progress beyond the localised, and partial interests of all those placed outside the bourgeois public sphere depended upon a peculiar distinction between the bodies of the enlightened few and the unenlightened multitudes. The autonomous figure of the enlightened white male subject attains its indivisible sovereignty and inherent connection to all of humanity precisely through an interpretation of others as fragmented parts of humanity. While the rest of the world could be inspected in the smallest detail and divided into so many species of plant and fauna and categories of class and race, this could only be accomplished by those who had no particular interest – being instead simply 'human'. The autonomy and authority of enlightenment man was realised in practice by his power to define,

order and classify the rest of the world, which, of course, needed ordering and classifying precisely so that he could retain his credentials as a
disinterested humanist.

For the many people that fell under the disinterested scrutiny of the
enlightenment scholar and politician, their failure to embody principles
of freedom, autonomy and rationality was punished by a gaze that dissected them into so many disparate parts. As property ownership was
connected to the male bourgeois subject as an integral part of his
emancipated identity, the workers were subjected to a countermove that
justified their disenfranchisement in terms of their material inequality.
A durable connection was thus established between poverty and self-
interest. For, black people, women, the poor and any one else who
needed a description, this removal of them from any obvious commitment to 'humankind' has meant that the onus falls relentlessly upon
them to prove their ability to articulate human interest. Or put another
way, having being defined as having detectable self-interests on the
basis of categories that were themselves enforced by the scientific and
humanistic discourses of Enlightenment reason, those others were then
directed to overcome them in order to prove themselves enlightened.
The mental gymnastics that this requires contrasts spectacularly with
the absence of any such work for those already firmly ensconced in
self-proclaimed positions of neutrality.

It is this history that ensures that freedom can still be discussed
without any focus upon the power of some people to appropriate and
exploit others. As Kappeler observes:

> What made possible the translation of *service* into the language of
> freedom and democracy is the concept of the 'individual' as 'owner
> of the property in his person': that most 'political fiction' that 'a
> worker does not contract out himself or even his labour, but his
> labour power or services, part of the property in his person'. The
> answer to the question of how property in the person can be con-
> tracted out is 'that no such procedure is possible'. What is hired or
> brought is a person – even if it is only for a limited time and not for
> a whole lifetime. It is part of the brilliancy of this political fiction
> that its legitimizing thrust is aimed at submission – the alleged vol-
> untary submission of the persons contracting out their labour – with
> never a word lost about the legitimacy of the mastery – the purchase
> and use of other people.[9]

Considerations of wealth and power thus take place in a discursive
arena in which the economic, social and political advantages of the

bourgeoisie are merely a fortuitous precondition for a more democratic society. The enlightened bourgeois individual, as one who is unencumbered by any specific interests can then be advanced in liberal democratic theory as unique and precious for his disinterested articulation of 'human' aspirations and concerns. The fact that those defined as possessing *particular* interests (arising from their classed, raced or gendered locations in society) are saddled with 'particularity' precisely because liberal democratic theorists have declared themselves to be 'universal', is a conceit that Kluge and Negt challenge in their analysis of the Habermasian public sphere.

Kluge and Negt castigate both Habermas and Kant for prescribing a bourgeois public sphere and then concealing its class-specific composition beneath rhetoric of universal and general truths. They point out that Kant's classical public sphere and Habermas's bourgeois public sphere were founded on the systematic exclusion of every non-bourgeois individual and group in society. Thus by considering only the classical bourgeois 'public' sphere, Habermas is forced to justify the exclusions of the propertyless (the working classes, non-Europeans, women and children) whilst at the same time citing this public sphere as one that established and encourages democracy. As Negt and Kluge point out, such exclusions are all the more striking given that Habermas himself noted the violence of Kant's rigorous exclusions of people from the 'public' sphere. Thus, Habermas notes that in order to maintain the connection between property ownership and access to the pubic sphere:

> Kant must – with considerable violence of thought – exclude one substantial group of humanity after the other as inadequate to his 'true politics': children, store clerks, day laborers, even the hairdresser.[10]

Negt and Kluge's identification of the violence of exclusion offers a devastating critique of the ways in which perceptions of 'civility' are attained. For, as any student of patriarchy and imperialism soon discovers, declarations of 'civilised' values are invariably accompanied by physical violence (necessity to subdue the uncivilised) and intellectual violence (necessary to deprive others of any semblance of cerebral equality). Unsurprisingly while commentators such as Habermas stress the evolutionary credentials of the bourgeois public sphere, others are more interested in examining this history from the point of view of the excluded.

The growing power of the bourgeois public sphere was achieved through violent exclusion and a parallel process of steady privatisation.

As Enlightenment man stretched his body and his mind over previously unregulated territories, the number of subjects who needed to be placed at a physical and conceptual distance from the public sphere steadily increased. As Juliana Schiesari observes

> what humanism constructed was a range of others to the entity 'man,' whose dignity was praised and who was given exclusive rights over the public realm. These 'others' were subject to the privatized enclosures of domestication (women in the home, children in nurseries, the mad in hospitals, dogs in their kennels, sheep in their enclosed pastures) or banished to the edge of civilization (noble savages). A definition of humanity coterminous with the public sphere meant the deployment of massive exclusionary procedures to maintain that sphere as a masculine privilege.[11]

A deadly irony followed from this, for even as those 'others' were excluded from the 'public sphere' their lives and interests became a matter of utmost 'public interest'. This passionate interest in the excluded was, as it is now, couched in discourses that stressed rational objectivity. In practice this has meant that those situated outside of the public sphere are defined as needing to prove their commitment to the very principles that have ordered their exclusion.

In our own times the obscuring of privilege proceeds alongside narratives that stress the need for 'participation' and 'empathy' between all subjects. Participation is hailed as a cherished ambition of bourgeois institutions, while the extent to which equal participation is problematised by pre-existing exclusions and inequalities is pushed to the margins. As Kathryn Church[12] demonstrates in her examination of the legislation consultation between mental health professionals and survivors, the blindness of liberal democratic theory to pre-existing structural inequality between individuals forces *everyone* in the consultation process to proceed as though differences in material, social and political power are largely irrelevant.

Kathleen Rockhill argues that this violence at the heart of the classical and bourgeois celebration of rationality is reflected in the profound sense of intimidation that the excluded experience in their encounters with bourgeois institutions. Even when the aim is to encourage participation the implied possession of rationality and discernment on the part of professionals continues to position those without expertise and membership in a precarious and explicitly subordinate locus. What Habermas identifies as an enlightened rationality underpinning liberal

democratic institutions is, for commentators such as Church, better viewed as a deliberate suppression of other people's life experiences. Her exploration of verbal interactions between mental health professionals and survivors reveals a prohibitive context for rational speech that is a world away from Habermas's gentle invocation of rationality as the product of a universal human desire for consensus.

In Church's account, the achievement of such a dialogue is shown to be grounded upon the wider intimidation and suppression of any expressions that might indicate awareness of and anger towards the immovable inequality at the heart of supposedly universally beneficial bourgeois norms:

> The legislation consultation was characterized by a tension between the emotional turbulence of participants' experiences and a code of professional etiquette which implicitly defines emotionality as irrational. Most speakers worked actively to preclude the personal and emotional from their presentation in order to speak from an intellectual systemic standpoint. They were obedient to the 'ideal of rational self-mastery' (Lichtman, 1982:271), which governs behavior in western industrialized capitalist societies. This reason is not trivial: rationality 'is the basis of the liberal political demands for equality of opportunity and the right to self-determination' (Weedon, 1987:80). At the same time, where it enables only certain people and possibilities 'rationality' may be included with other 'categories of moral absolutism' as a form of state domination (Corrigan, 1980).[13]

It is the very absence of visible signs of conflict or emotion on the part of the powerful that defines them as in charge while emotions and expressions of conflict are both assigned to and prohibited from the less powerful.

The elite refusal to contaminate higher education with any uncivilised and confrontational evidence of class difference is accompanied by a predictable insistence that students learn to see beyond the particular and embrace universal human interests. In short, those students who are saddled with a classed, raced or gendered 'particularity' are taught that whatever insights they may have will never amount to more than a contribution to an already designated universality. The ability to rise to the heights of cultural and critical excellence can be measured by the extent to which an individual is able to transcend all particularities and address at last humanity as a whole. The problem here is that this

transcendence has already been defined as one that must first overcome and denigrate certain particularities (gender, class or race 'difference') while ignoring other particularities (male, white, middle class 'norms') entirely.

As Valerie Walkerdine relates conquering the rigours of academic customs involves also the acquirement of a painful class bigotry:

> There was no way ... that my success could have done anything other than take me out of my class, for to have stayed within it, I would have to reject school and being clever. However, inside that history is a suppressed history which could barely speak itself. The latter repressed and forgotten, is a history of pain and struggle through which I was constituted as a pedagogic subject. What is suppressed is another knowledge which had to be countered as wrong and which I had to learn to abandon. In rejecting this, my mother too had to be rejected and classified as stupid.[14]

The materially and socially unequal members of society who encounter bourgeois institutions are thus encouraged to demonstrate their mastery of bourgeois values and practices – to demonstrate in short their *similarity* and implicit acceptance of bourgeois ideologies. Naturally, those occupying privileged positions in bourgeois institutions are not obliged to attempt any reciprocal journey into equivalence for that would by definition be a journey towards irrationality and disadvantage.

It is this brutal exclusionary logic that is nourished and protected in liberal democratic institutions and practices that leads Kluge and Negt to name Habermas's public sphere as 'bourgeois' and reveal the careful protection of the bourgeoisie that permeates the public sphere. The 'special' training that the bourgeois insist is necessary to denote a capacity to engage in the public sphere is, as Negt and Kluge demonstrate, nothing less than the demand that all those who enter the public sphere learn and obey the rules and customs of bourgeois discourse and values. The much-lauded process of the rational differentiation of the spheres of art, science and morality becomes in Negt and Kluge's account simply the means by which the bourgeoisie were able to extend their ownership over influential social and political arenas. Thus, the 'special' expertise that was claimed by the professionals who emerged from the differentiated sites of law, science and philosophy enabled the bourgeoisie to regulate and control admission to influential social and political arenas.

In the same way, as Kathryn Church and Negt and Kluge direct their readers to the level of coercion operating in our supposedly democratic institutions:

> All bourgeois forms of the public sphere presuppose special training, both linguistic and mimetic. In public court proceeding, in dealing with officials … it is expected of all parties involved that they be concise and present their interests within forms of expression fitting the official context. As a rule they must be grammatically correct [and meet the expectation for] economy of thought and abstract flexibility … This is one of the most important exclusionary mechanisms of the bourgeois public sphere … the bourgeois public sphere's mechanisms for excluding and destroying experience are situated in those very areas where it believes it is operating to idealistic and humanistic principles.[15]

Having established the bourgeois underpinnings of Habermas's proposed public sphere, Kluge and Negt proceed to sketch out a far broader conception of the public sphere in order to investigate its potential for instigating radical social and political transformation.

For Kluge and Negt the transformative value of the public sphere lies in its connection to human consciousness and experience. And it is precisely the wholesale suppression and exclusion of human experience that for them marks the bourgeois public sphere as an authoritarian and decaying institution. In their reading, the suppression of any material history of the development of bourgeois institutions and practices and the refusal to implicate bourgeois modes of production with its public arena, reduces human experience to a mere 'technicality' in the bourgeois public sphere.

Above all, the bourgeois presentation of the private interests of individuals as a matter of utmost public interest transfers the specific interests of capital into the 'public' arena. Kluge and Negt, building upon Ferruccio Rossi-Landi's discussion of capital, argue that rather than pursuing universal ethical objectives the bourgeois public sphere merely makes public the private power of the bourgeoisie:

> 'What we call private is so only insofar as it is public. It has been public and must remain public in order that it can be, whether for a moment or for several thousand years, private'. 'In order to be able to isolate capital as something private, one must be able to control wealth as something public, since raw materials and tools, money

and workers are in reality part of the public sphere. One can act in the market as an individual, one can buy it up, for instance, precisely because it is a social 'fact'. The interdependent relationship between that which is private and the public sphere also applies to the way in which language, modes of social intercourse, and the public context came into being socially and publicly. Precisely because the important decisions regarding the horizon and the precise definitions of the organization of experience have been made in advance, it is possible to exert control in a purely technical manner.[16]

Kluge and Negt wrench the Habermasian public sphere away from its preferred connection with laudable Enlightenment ideals and ground it instead in the less ennobling contexts of commodity production:

Bourgeois society's awareness of its own experience and the organization of that experience is almost consistently **analogous to genuinely existing commodity** production. The value abstraction (above all the division of concrete and abstract labor) that underlies commodity production and has the world in its grip provides the model and can be recognized in the generalizations of state and public activities, in the law. Although anarchistic commodity production is motivated by private interest, in other words by the opposite of the collective will of society, it develops universally binding patterns. **These patterns are mistaken for and interpreted as products of the collective will, as if the actual relationships, which have only been acquired retroactively, were based upon this will.** (emphasis in the original)[17]

By refusing to grant the Habermasian public sphere its historical amnesia regarding its economic foundations, Kluge and Negt are able to place material interests at the heart of liberal democratic theory and invest their proposed counter-public sphere with the humanitarian interests that the bourgeoisie insist is their domain. Kluge and Negt's counter-public sphere is, as such, the reservoir for all the human experiences that are denied legitimacy or presence in the bourgeois public sphere. This 'proletarian' public sphere is unlike the official bourgeois public arena, not reducible to a single version of experience or a singular commitment to clear universal truths.

Negt and Kluge have been criticised for using what many see as hopelessly dated Marxist terminology.[18] However, Kluge and Negt recruit the categories 'bourgeois' and 'proletarian' principally to isolate

the interests of capital in the bourgeois public sphere. In this sense neither the experiences of the proletarian nor the bourgeois individual can be said to be realised in the bourgeois public sphere since its overriding loyalty is to the interests of capital. Kluge and Negt argue that while this may well serve the *interests* of the bourgeoisie the interests of capital cannot go so far as to reflect the experiences of any actual bourgeois individuals.

For Kluge and Negt, the 'proletarian' public sphere is that which is not served by the interests of capital: factory workers, the low paid, the homeless, the rural poor and all the other people who are exploited by the capitalist drive towards profits. In the same way as Subcomandante Marcos,[19] who extended the identity of the Zapatistas to anyone excluded or objectified by the globalised free-market economy, Kluge and Negt extend the Marxist definition of the proletariat to refer to anyone and any space 'outside' the dominant capitalist economy. Thus, they stress that the different perspectives of the bourgeois and proletarian public spheres are not born out of a different relation to democratic consensus but from a different relation to production. The proletarian counter-public sphere is, as such, any space that operates against the interests of capital whether consciously or not.

For, Kluge and Negt do not propose that the proletarian public sphere operates in a clear opposition to the bourgeois public sphere or that it is necessarily conscious of its own legitimacy:

> One can also define this [proletarian public] negatively, in terms of the endeavours of the ruling class to extinguish attempts at constituting a proletarian public sphere and to appropriate for itself the material on which this sphere is based – in other words, the proletarian context of living. The mechanism used in this process are isolation, division, repression, the establishment of taboos, and assimilation.[20]

However, employing such 'unfashionable' Marxist terminology also enables Kluge and Negt to stress that their commitment is not so much to the delineation of a counter-public sphere but to the overthrow of the existing bourgeois public sphere and the related capitalist economy. Thus, they emphasise that while validating and acknowledging 'different' voices and experiences is essential, it is equally essential that they are not put to use in the bourgeois public sphere. The dynamic oppositional force of the excluded must not, in other words, revive the decaying bourgeois public sphere but must seek to supplant it.

The Habermasian lifeworld becomes, in Negt and Kluge's reading, one that is hopelessly bereft of the life experiences of most of society. This austere and impoverished life world becomes the grey comparison with Negt and Kluge's disruptive proletarian public sphere. All the people excluded and despised by the strict regulatory logic of the Enlightenment public sphere are released into the proletarian public sphere to both demolish the universalising pretensions of Enlightenment celebrations of reason and to offer us dynamic alternatives to the austere confines of rational public space. Thus, in Negt and Kluge's delineations of public life, 'reason' is dismissed and 'experience' is ushered in to propel us towards a social and political order unlike anything imagined or realised by the bourgeois public sphere.

Like Habermas, Negt and Kluge were interested in democracy and saw the public sphere as the crucial arena for extending democratic principles over all areas of society. Their argument was not directed against Habermas's thesis that it was the public sphere that would secure democracy but rather with Habermas's specifically bourgeois public sphere. Negt and Kluge's purpose in *Public Sphere and Experience* was to demolish the universalising pretensions of Habermas's bourgeois public sphere by emphasising that while this public sphere did exist in material and concrete forms its commitment to any human lifeworld was negligible, based as it was on the private interests of bourgeois individuals.

For Kluge and Negt, the systematic exclusion of proletarian experience from the bourgeois public sphere meant that proletarian experience really was immeasurably different from bourgeois experience and as such provided the key to founding a wholly different world. Like Adorno before them, they identified the long triumph of reason in philosophy and science as a tradition that had lost all credibility culminating as it did in the death camps of Nazi Germany. However, if Negt and Kluge wanted to persuade their readers that a disruptive proletarian sphere really could supplant the existing bourgeois public sphere, then they had to tackle Adorno's bleak summation of life under a triumphant capitalist hegemony. Thus, in *Public Sphere and Experience,* Negt and Kluge affirmed Adorno's scathing rejection of capitalism but attempted to rescue his defeated proletarian from inside the 'iron system'[21] from which Adorno argued there was no escape.

Negt and Kluge's proposed proletarian public sphere challenged Habermas's bourgeois public sphere by explicitly laying claim to a direct connection and commitment to human experience. While Habermas depicted the material world as a site from which rational thought

constituted a transcendent ascent, Negt and Kluge proclaimed their attachment to the material world as the site towards which we all must descend in order to 'ground' theory in human experience. The direction towards human experience was, in other words, to proceed downwards into the proletarian public sphere.

And this is where the danger begins; because whether the proletariat, or working-class subject, is being recruited as the obstacle or the basis for the development of universal social democracy the working-class subject herself *living in this present* can be transported away either back into tired representations of dull stupidity or into utopian dreams of human liberation. Contemporary western theory has itself proved to be remarkably indecisive when it comes to deciding whether the working classes are a force for democracy or conservatism. Theodor Adorno's gloomy appraisal of the hegemonic power of capitalism and its devastating attack on creativity and culture gave way in later life to a cautious optimism, while both Kluge and Negt were to abandon the notion of a proletarian public sphere, with Kluge, in particular, shifting his argument towards a notion of public life more in keeping with that proposed by Habermas.

What is at issue here is not so much that theorists should be scolded for changing their minds but the extent to which the working-class subject operates in theoretical discourse as a moveable feast. Arguably, what theorists are able to avoid is the acknowledgement that equating language with freedom is a comment upon our own freedom, as writers and not necessarily any indication of freedom for those engaged primarily in 'non-intellectual' forms of employment. For while we are free to imagine new worlds and different political orders we are equally free to bestow 'reality' upon all those people who do not or cannot represent themselves. When Negt and Kluge identified the proletariat as the locus for political and social change they stepped straight into that space in which anything is possible because the proletariat does not, in these discussions at any rate, answer back.

Throughout *Public Sphere and Experience* the sterile reality of the bourgeois public sphere is contrasted with the vibrant potential of the proletarian lifeworld, which even as it is manipulated and suppressed by the dominant order, offers glimpses of a possible sentient social and political world. In this sense, the proletarian public sphere is only proletarian for as long as the bourgeois public sphere continues to exist, since it is the site of the regulation and suppression of human experience itself. Accordingly, in their text, Negt and Kluge split the world into the sensory (proletarian sphere) and the pragmatic (bourgeois public sphere)

and dedicate themselves to establishing their mutual incompatibility. However, while the proletariat and the bourgeoisie are trapped in their respective lifeworlds, the intelligentsia emerges as the only group able to understand both the bourgeois and the proletarian public sphere. Negt and Kluge argue that it is the intelligentsia's ultimate affinity with the proletarian public sphere that heralds the demise of the bourgeois public sphere and the capitalist economic system. And it is this claim that we will turn to next.

5
Thinking Subjects

At first glance Negt and Kluge's vibrant disruptive proletarian sphere is the very antitheses of Adorno's[1] gloomy summations of brute stupidity on the part of the masses. However, what connects Negt and Kluge's proletarian public sphere with Adorno's depiction of mass culture is the idea that the masses are confined within a strictly material world. Like Adorno, Negt and Kluge credit the 'culture industry' with the absolute power to distort and repress consciousness on the part of the workers. Ironically, by granting the 'culture industry' such power upon the entire workforce, Negt and Kluge end up presenting the workers as even less capable of critical self-consciousness than Adorno.

For, Negt and Kluge are only able to overcome Adorno's depiction of a state of virtual social and political paralysis by positing a rigorous distinction between the intellectuals and the masses. Negt and Kluge's energised reading of late capitalism is one that restricts the capacity to think beyond existing social and political reality to the intellectuals, while leaving the masses suspended in a condition of mental confusion and incoherence. Not surprisingly, the effect of Negt and Kluge's painstaking dissection of the difference between workers and intellectuals is to reinforce the tradition of intellectual difference that Adorno to a large extent undercuts by his all-pervasive pessimism at the ability of *anyone* to counter the social and political system. In short, what lifts Negt and Kluge's text away from Adorno's cultural prison camp is not a different evaluation of the masses, but an altogether more advanced faith in the revolutionary potential of the intellectual.

Thus, in Negt and Kluge's account it is the intellectual who will perform the necessary critical work to lift the proletarian sphere away from being merely a site of experience and attain at last a real and concrete form. Accordingly, while the proletarians and the bourgeoisie are

trapped in their respective life worlds, the intelligentsia emerges as the only group able to understand both the bourgeois and proletarian public sphere. Unfortunately, this assumed convergence between intellectual and proletarian interests is one that preserves intact and unchallenged the very foundations of the modernist dream that has produced such a powerful consensus among Western cultural theorists, namely, the fortuitous emergence of the Western 'thinking' subject.

For, Negt and Kluge's thinking subjects are essential to breaking the stable coexistence of a rational bourgeois public sphere and an experiential proletarian public sphere. It is this historically acquired ability to theorise that enables the intellectual to see through and beyond the existing capitalist system. Thus, while Kluge and Negt register their debt to Adorno's vision of a highly effective culture industry, they bestow upon the intellectual the specific ability to see beyond the production circuit and into the value that resides at the heart of the proletarian sphere. (Of course, this is an ability that Adorno fully subscribes to, since he, as the author of *The Culture Industry: Enlightenment as mass deception*, is presumably not deceived. Consequently, although the 'iron system' of capitalism 'hammers into every brain ... in this society' it has at least stopped short of fooling Adorno.)[2]

This specific ability of the intellectual to retain not only critical self-consciousness but insight into the conditions of both the powerful and the powerless is an assumption that unites Kluge and Negt with Adorno. However, while Adorno performs a deliberately personal condemnation of the capitalist system and all that it entails, Negt and Kluge extract from it the more specific figure of the intellectual and find in it the means of escape. In particular, it is the intellectual's ability to see the entirety of her contemporary society that most crucially distinguishes the intellectual from both the bourgeois public sphere and the proletarian public sphere. This difference may well be located in the intellectual's different location in the production process, but it nevertheless confirms traditional notions of cerebral superiority. Consequently, the basis of this differentiation between intellectual and proletarian activity relies upon the resurrection of that familiar dichotomy, namely, that of a thinking as opposed to a non-thinking subject.

Ironically, having upbraided Kant for insisting that it is only the property owners who were welcomed into the bourgeois public sphere – lacking as they did the material deprivation that would prevent them from exercising 'rational' and 'impartial' judgement – Negt and Kluge too nudge the workers out of the crucial formative construction of their

own proletarian public sphere by insisting that their material dependence on their labour deprives them of the ability to objectively understand their own condition. In many ways Negt and Kluge's formulation is even more extreme than Kant's, because the worker is not simply excluded from a bourgeois public sphere but is excluded from consciousness of a sphere that, although it bears their name, is not *as yet* present in a fully developed concrete form. For, now the proletarian public sphere exists on the margins of bourgeois society embodying the promise of a future society not yet born. In other words, the proletariat herself becomes symptomatic of a future that is not yet here and her much-vaunted realism becomes the stuff of raw, unfinished material.

In the same way as Adorno's thoroughly subjected subject, Negt and Kluge's worker too, as one who is particularly embroiled in the means of production, is as such the last to see her way out of capitalist logic. The worker cannot see her own condition for what it is because she is, as a producer of commodities and as one confined to the factory floor, deprived of the necessarily detached viewpoint of her activity that would enable her to 'think' rather than simply 'do'. Negt and Kluge's worker takes her place alongside Antonio Gramsci's 'active man' (who 'has no theoretical consciousness'),[3] as one who has been successfully prevented from assessing her own condition:

> To put it simply, the scientist or scholar is capable of subjectively placing behind his cognitive activity a sense of necessity that is not directly rooted in his economic situation. The worker is, under the conditions of his socialization, unable subjectively to form an image of the objective cognitive pressure that his context of living exerts upon him or to convert it into cognitive activity.[4]

The proletariat, as one who is utterly embedded in the capitalist social and political system, is reduced to simple corporeality. Thus proletarian consciousness becomes, in Negt and Kluge's text, recognisable precisely by its absence. Caught in the interstices of the capitalist system the proletariat is an amorphous 'mass' of experience, sensuality and incoherent passions:

> the masses live with the experiences of violence, oppression, exploitation, and, in the broader sense of the term, alienation. They possess material, sensual evidence of the restriction of possibilities in their lives, in their freedom of movement. Accordingly, the resistance to this restriction has a sensual credibility: 'This is a threat to us as human beings.'[5]

'Concrete experience' may well apply to humankind in general but it is, according to Negt and Kluge, most properly applicable to the 'masses'. Even worse, the workers' 'experience', hostage as it is to the capitalist order, cannot in the present system even be called their 'own' experience since they lack the means to either understand or recognise it. The reasons for this, Negt and Kluge stress, are not to be found in any reprehensible notions of innate inferiority but in the practical assignment of physical space to the workers.

The workers are deprived of insight because they are systematically deprived of the practical means to assess their own condition. Starting with the bourgeois schooling that the working-class child receives, in which her language and material existence is cast as 'marginal', and ending with her labour on the factory floor, the proletariat is structurally excluded from the resources that could enable her to connect the material world with her experiences of it. The worker is then the site of alienation *par excellence* – a producer who lacks any insight into her own production. Society, work, even herself is 'experienced' as an inevitability over which she has no control:

> For the overwhelming majority of workers, the place where they spend the greater part of their waking hours is marked by strictly delineated and limited room for movement. They are not capable of perceiving the compartmentalized space within the factory as a totality. Whereas other groups, such as foremen, clerical workers ... are virtually obliged to gain an overview, the productive activity of the worker is harnessed to individual component of the factory's overall machinery. This constitutes one blocking element, which in and of itself, prevents the experiencing of the external factory setting as a whole. The machinery which confronts the worker only in fragments, takes on the form of a mystified objectivity precisely because it is not perceived as a totality. It is a small step from this limited experiential base to the mystification of commodities and capital, which is experienced as a blind mechanism.[6]

Interestingly this ability, on the part of the intellectual, to see the wider implications of social and political life relies upon the privileging of sight that was so crucial to the modernist obsession with classifying and ordering the material world. The idea that maximum vision translates directly into a broad comprehension is a specific conceit of the enlightenment tradition in which among other things readily observable phenomena, such as alien 'tribes' and skin colour were deemed to

reveal an internal truth about people, or, in the language of the philosophical elites, to reveal the different intellectual, social and cultural stages which humanity – properly divided – could be understood to have attained. Arguably, vision, no matter how wide the view, can be as much an obstacle to *insight* as a precondition for it.

Be that as it may, for Negt and Kluge's purposes it is the hindrance to full vision that prevents the proletariat from fully grasping his or her subjection. The bourgeois public sphere, in the same way as capitalism for Adorno, has effectively blockaded all possible routes for the workers to objectively understand their condition. The masses accordingly, act, feel and react but have not yet developed these elemental passions into reflective thought and analysis. Indeed, the closest the worker can get to any semblance of cognitive activity is through her *un*conscious attempts to make sense of her situation.

Fantasy emerges as the only non-corporeal activity that the worker is able to engage in. However, since fantasies are inspired by real life and given that the worker is unable to understand the conditions of her existence, it follows that any fantasies she may have will be of little use when it comes to actually changing her material conditions. Significantly, Negt and Kluge while granting fantasies a universal status, spend no time discussing the content of *intellectual* fantasies. In short, as the site of simple material existence, the proletariat as Adorno indicated it should, must simply wait for 'others' to assess and classify her experience. Precisely because she 'owns' experience she is in turn dispossessed of any useful cognitive function. The worker's position in the production process is one that disqualifies her from any semblance of material or cerebral autonomy.

Moreover, the proletariat is, in Negt and Kluge's text, a thoroughly transparent category enabling them as intellectuals to confidently assess not only her level of consciousness but also her level of unconscious development. Thus her fantasies can be subjected to the same careful assessment that informs their readings of her conscious attempts to understand material reality. In Negt and Kluge's reading, while the proletarian public sphere is extolled as the essential replacement for the decaying bourgeois public sphere, the proletariats themselves are clearly neither equipped nor ready to bring this about. Precisely because they inhabit the existing contours of the proletarian public sphere they are as such 'blinded' and immobilised by it. Moreover, the lack of theoretical awareness on the part of the workers means that the proletarian public sphere has not as yet shaken off the destructive influences of the bourgeoisie. In other words, in order for the proletarian

public sphere to be fully proletarian, it must evince no signs of bourgeois oppression and be instead fully conscious of its opposition to the existing capitalist social and political system. The proletarian public sphere is, in this sense, an uncompleted sphere reflecting the level of ongoing development of the masses who as developing subjects, are not as yet ready to replace the bourgeois public sphere.

Thus, both the proletarians and the proletarian public sphere exist in Kluge and Negt's text as the unconscious and disorganised sites that will, when properly conscious and organised, replace the existing bourgeois public sphere. The experiential passions of the masses do not, as they do for Kant and Habermas, disqualify them from public life but rather function to provide the necessary antidote to the dehumanising reign of capitalist economics and bourgeois cultural values. Accordingly, Negt and Kluge's intellectual far from being repelled by the masses, views them with interested sympathy, observing that the workers 'attempt … to understand the surrounding world' but are thwarted by the absence of any existing 'forms for expressing their own interests'.[7] This in turn prompts them towards the reassuring familiarity of stereotypes or into the waiting embrace of distracting tabloids and the like. None of this however, Negt and Kluge remind us, should obscure the fact that

> there is, however, also a real impulse underlying this: **the attempt to grasp circumstances as they really are**. Yet this impulse is contradictory as well, for although it does indicate the correct path for understanding reality, this path is negotiated by means of oversimplifications; in other words, by means of an unrealistic, ideological picture of the world. (emphasis in the original)[8]

This inability on the part of workers to gain a coherent understanding of the world also enables us to understand why radical acts, such as wildcat strikes, are ultimately doomed to fail, predicated as they are upon an unrealistic and incomplete assessment of the situation. In short, it is the masses' desire for 'simplification' that hinders their efforts to understand the material world.

It is precisely this simultaneous desire for simplification and emancipation that impedes the workers and prevents them from either understanding the world or possessing the means to change it. It is however, an impasse that the intellectual is uniquely equipped to overcome since she too is fractured by her technical expertise that ultimately alienates her from the sensory and experiential world that the bourgeoisie has

successfully relegated to the proletarian public sphere. Thus the proletariat may well be merely a disorganised site of bodily impulses and unprocessed experiences but she nevertheless indicates the limits of rationality and in the process gives rational expertise itself an entirely new purpose. The worker's lack of consciousness emerges as the principal context for the proposed intellectual rescue since consciousness *is* the vital contribution of the intelligentsia. The intellectual emerges as the worker's principal ally precisely because she has mastered bourgeois discourses but has no loyalty to the bourgeois social and political system.

Rationality then, far from enabling the dominant culture to exclude the experiential masses, becomes the tool with which they are brought into public life. In other words, Negt and Kluge argue that the capacity for rational analysis may yet serve some purpose but only if it is directed towards the liberation of the working classes. Rationality is thus placed in the paradoxical position of being the tool with which a rational society can finally be overcome:

> Strategies for overcoming this blockage (the workers' contradictory desire for simplification and emancipation) can be found, above all, in the intelligentsia's method of work. Differentiation, complexity, interaction, totality, and so forth, as conceived by the great theoreticians of the labor movement, are the conceptual emancipatory forms of the intelligentsia, not of the working class ... the very quality that distinguishes intellectuals – their artificially forced capacity for abstraction – is a tool for grasping alienated social realities ... The type of labor performed by the intelligentsia is ... not helpful in a direct way. It would be helpful only if it were collectively transformed and rebuilt within the experiential context of the working class.[9]

The overthrow of capitalism, in other words, needs the workers to accept the organising skills of the intelligentsia and the intelligentsia to situate their labour inside the proletarian public sphere. This in turn necessitates a level of comprehension on the part of the workers and the intelligentsia that their modes of living are not as yet capable of offering a viable alternative to bourgeois hegemony.

Of course, in order for such an alliance to emerge, there has to be significant dissatisfaction with the present system and sufficient autonomy from it to reject it. It is this ability to understand and reject the system that the intellectual acquires through her apprenticeship in bourgeois institutions. For, while the proletariat is depicted as lacking any route to self-consciousness or autonomy, the intellectual is, by

contrast, equipped with both the material conditions for independence and the cerebral abilities to both desire and instigate a wholesale revolution in social and political life.

Thus the common ground between the intellectual and the proletariat is that both are alienated from the material world that they live in. However, the crucial difference is that the intellectual is in possession of the objective skills to recognise this alienation and hence want to change it. For the intellectual, alienation arises from the clash between the 'tools' of scientific and educational training (objectivity, empirical proof, logic etc.) and the *motives* for learning which are anything but logical and objective, based as they are in the libidinal economy of the pursuit of pleasure:

> Specialized knowledge, which has been developed through bourgeois production relations, must demand something of the structures of the human being that he or she cannot perform: the *how* of idea and invention and the *motive* of curiosity and cognition must be produced according to the laws of a character that is defined by a libidinal economy and an economy of drives. By contrast the *tools* – such as logic, the objective scientific system of rules, the way in which an experiment is set up – consist of extremely reified 'hard' matter which by its nature goes against the laws according to which living labor functions.[10]

It is the inability of the ruling classes to totally dictate the conditions and experiences of intellectual work that gives the intellectual the scope for pleasure and liberation that is so lacking in the worker's labour tied as it is to the reproduction of alienated commodities. For, while the proletariat driven by economic necessity is trapped inside an endless production of things, Negt and Kluge's intellectual, by contrast, produces self-consciousness and critical awareness.

Moreover the capitalist system's dependency upon innovation and technology prevents them from exercising the measure of control over the intelligentsia that it employs over the workers. This is, according to Kluge and Negt discernable in the very different degrees of control at work in the factory and the university. Thus, while the factory functions as a disciplining and oppressively hierarchical organisation, the university, by contrast, possesses the potential to operate with some measure of autonomy from its material contexts. The different levels of surveillance and control at work in the factory and the university are then reflected by the intellectual's ability to affect her institutional setting

as opposed to the proletarian's 'blind' immersion into commodity production.

Echoing Adorno, Negt and Kluge arrive at the conclusion that the university as the chief producer of knowledge and thought is by definition ill-equipped to serve the interests of bourgeois capitalism. Since both the desire for knowledge and knowledge itself are, according to Negt and Kluge, incompatible with bourgeois rationalism it follows that any bourgeois efforts to control intellectual production or the business of the university are destined to fail. Thus Negt and Kluge note that the practice of offering bribes and incentives to intellectuals for the most part fails because it is based upon the erroneous assumption that intellectuals are motivated by capital. Thus the university itself functions as both a servant of the ruling classes and as an opponent, and its main export – intellectuals – articulate the consequences of this struggle between service and disobedience to the dominant culture. The intellectual slips out of the confines of bourgeois public space because she is both armed with the necessary tools to understand the system and sufficiently free to reject it.

In Negt and Kluge's text it becomes something of an irony that the ruling class is unable to understand to control the intelligentsia precisely because the intelligentsia is more proficient at understanding the wider implications of bourgeois values and rhetoric. In short, what the intelligentsia possess is the freedom that both the bourgeoisie and the proletariat lack being, as they are wholly determined by the capitalist economy. Even worse for the ruling classes is the irony that it is precisely through the experience of bourgeois 'higher' education that the glaring discrepancy between the material world and bourgeois values becomes visible. Consequently, this discrepancy between the material world of capitalist exploitation and the real conditions of life for the majority of people makes the intellectual conscious of her own limitations as just a 'thinking' subject.

Thus Kluge and Negt's intellectual does not experience the condition of developing into a 'thinking subject' as a blessing so much as a curse. But the intellectual, in recognising her alienation from the corporeal world, understands that it is only through a thorough immersion in the proletarian public sphere that a proper resolution of thought and action can be achieved. Just as the proletarian public sphere needs the organisational and theoretical skills of the intelligentsia to lift it from mere corporeality, so too the intelligentsia needs the proletarian public sphere if it is to have any hope of reconnecting itself to the material world.

This conception of the bourgeois capitalist world as one that has performed a disastrous bisection of 'the mind' from 'the body' becomes in radical theory best represented in the actual bodies of workers and intellectuals. Thus in Antonio Gramsci, as in Negt and Kluge, the intellectuals personify 'the mind' and the workers symbolise 'the body', and the revolution itself becomes nothing less than the reunification of these two fatally severed halves:

> The popular element 'feels' but does not always know or understand; the intellectual element 'knows' but does not always feel ... The intellectual's error consists in believing that one can know without understanding and even more without feeling and being impassioned (not only for knowledge itself but also for the object of knowledge): in other words that the intellectual can be an intellectual (and not a pure pedant) if distinct and separate from the people-nation, that is without feeling the elementary passions of the people, understanding them and therefore explaining and justifying them in the particular historical situation and connecting them dialectically to the laws of history and to a superior conception of the world, scientifically and coherently elaborated – i.e. knowledge.[11]

The alleged dichotomy between barely conscious masses and knowledgeable sapient intellectuals has enjoyed a lengthy history in Western theory. In radical theory the dream of an egalitarian future hinges on nothing less than the dissolving of this difference between workers and intellectuals in order to reunite the fractured subjects of capitalism. However, the question that is raised by attempts to depict the workers and intelligentsia as divided by a cerebral as opposed to a 'materialist instinct' is just how convincing is this reading of both 'the body' and 'the mind'? Or, to put it another way, how persuaded are we by the argument that intellectuals are able to bridge the gap between the experiential and cerebral world and thus organise a new egalitarian society? In short, is Negt and Kluge's depiction of intellectuals and workers credible? For, arguably it is their idealisation of intellectual labour and parallel simplification of proletarian consciousness that jeopardises their rigorously scientific analysis of late capitalism.

Negt and Kluge grant the destructive consequences of late capitalism with the paradoxical capacity to create the conditions for a fundamentally different society. Unfortunately, depicting the advent of a new society on the self-evident basis of material masses and cerebral intellectuals goes some way towards undermining any claims for

philosophical innovation. Indeed, the notion of the intellectual as one who embodies an insight and wisdom that most of humanity lack, arguably constitutes one of the most persistent and unchallenged assumptions of social criticism across the political spectrum.

For what is striking about Negt and Kluge's thesis is the extent to which radical social change is dependent upon traditional notions of intellectual distinction. The proletariat may well be placed at the centre of the political stage but this centrality in no way dislodges or modifies existing elitist notions of the nature of 'popular' consciousness. The proletariat, in Negt and Kluge's account, differs from liberal and conservative doctrine only insofar as she is recruited as central to the task of revolutionary change rather than defined as unqualified to participate in the solemn matter of state politics. In other words, Negt and Kluge accept that the workers really do lack any form of useful consciousness but draw entirely different conclusions from this apparent sociological fact. This desire on the part of leftist theorists to make the proletariat the material reference point for radical programs has proved to be remarkably successful at distracting attention away from the questionable basis of such a reading of the proletariat in the first place.

At the heart of Negt and Kluge's radical intervention into Habermasian liberalism is their systematic refusal to entertain any notion of the need to rethink the traditional status of the intellectual. Instead they simply move the traditional intellectual into a different physical location as if that were all that were needed to transform intellectual labour into radical work. As Marx pointed out, it is a bourgeois reflex to 'ascend' from the material world and the tracts of liberalism testify to the overwhelming liberal distaste for the odour of sexuality, poverty and material deprivation. However, rejecting this for a thorough immersion in the material world, and signalling this by recommending a descent into the proletarian public sphere, at no point dislodges the fantasy that the intellectual is able to choose her object, context and grounds of enquiry as merely so much passive material.

Moreover, as Negt and Kluge unwittingly demonstrate, it soon transpires that intellectual labour in the proletarian public sphere is a matter of using precisely those bourgeois skills of abstract rationality that have proved to be so alienating for the intellectual in her everyday life. In the proletarian public sphere those bourgeois acquired learning skills can be put to use precisely because the proletarian public sphere *is*, as Matthew Arnold and his accomplices concluded, a seething mass of raw uncultivated human experience. Consequently, the degree of subversion that Negt and Kluge consider themselves to be dealing in, by

rejecting bourgeois institutions in favour of the proletarian public sphere, stops decidedly short of subverting any traditional notions of both the higher consciousness of intellectuals and the ignorance of the working classes.

Significantly, while the materiality of the masses is at no point complicated by any sign of political consciousness, intellectuals, by contrast, already exhibit promising signs of materiality. Indeed, in Negt and Kluge's account, the intellectual does not even need the proletarian public sphere to realise the discrepancy of life under bourgeois capitalism, since her cerebral encounter with real political events provides the bridge between abstract knowledge and the material world. While the proletariat languishes in a condition of pure materiality the intellectual surges ahead making vital theoretical connections about the material world. Crucially, as well as blinded by the conditions of her own experience, the proletariat is also unable to offer any directly supplementary role to the intellectual because the intellectual has accomplished the reunification of rationality and experience by herself. Meanwhile the proletariat, as a non-subject, cannot converse or engage equally with the intellectual but can exist only as a vital background, as context.

The proletariat is thus revealed as the context for the development of the intellectual – a development which will of course restate the materiality of the proletariat. While the proletariat is mere bodily matter the intellectual it seems can encounter the material world through the dialectic of her learning and the environment in which she puts it to use. In this formulation the proletariat is the passive metaphor for the material world that the intellectual can recognise as in direct conflict with bourgeois values of freedom, tolerance and fairness:

> It is certain that the immediate transfer of the experiences of the liberation struggles – from Vietnam to Iran – occurred more rapidly via university students than in other spheres of society ... **All human beings share a desire for consciousness and meaningful immediacy, but it can begin to be articulated only through the traditional, not the technocratically reformed, educational system.** (emphasis in the original)[12]

The idea that 'the people' are best defined by their limited ability to pursue abstract and theoretical thought is an assumption common to many on both the left and the right. And, while this is often attributed to the reprehensible determination of the powerful to exclude the powerless from those institutions that 'teach' this quality, strikingly little

attention is given to how exactly exclusion from elite institutions deprives the people en masse from the capacity to think. Instead of examining or analysing this particular assumption, the intellectual left, (and right) for the most part, take the emphatically corporeal status of the people as an uncontroversial foundation for their programmes and analysis.

Negt and Kluge's affirmation of the corporeality of the people is accompanied by their restatement of the liberal notion of intellectual 'disinterest'. Their departure from liberal thought occurs in their contention that intellectual disinterest must be overcome by aligning themselves to the interests of the proletarian public sphere. Significantly, although they expose Habermas's public sphere as reflecting bourgeois interests and the proletarian public sphere as currently expressing a confusing tangle of bourgeois and proletarian interests, they credit the intellectual with no other interest than the properly disinterested one of creating a better society for everyone. In short, Negt and Kluge's intellectual retains the right to declare that *intellectual interests* are ultimately a matter of universal benefit and as such cannot even properly be called interests. But it is only by suppressing the history of intellectuals and by underestimating the extent to which intellectuals continue to be implicated in sites of social and political power that Negt and Kluge are able to make such a claim.

The preoccupations of philosophy, and later the study of literature, with the explicitly *political* implications of artistic and intellectual knowledge laid the grounds for Negt and Kluge's intellectual as one who exists at a certain distance from the material world. However, positing this distance as one that needs to be overcome makes the unconvincing claim that intellectuals *ever* exist at a recognisable distance from the material world. Such an assumption mistakes the possibility of material comfort and privilege on the part of some intellectuals as evidence of the material autonomy of all intellectuals. Moreover, it repeats the questionable notion that a privileged individual is somehow less a part of the material world than the economically disadvantaged. Arguably, the extent to which the economically advantaged are able to pursue an ever increasing consumption of the material world should lead us to precisely the opposite conclusion which is that economic wealth grants the affluent the power to experience (in the form of consumption and appropriation) the world in its social and physical forms. In other words, we are in no way obliged to accept that the material world really does possess an inherent connection with the conditions of poverty and alienation.

Pierre Bourdieu,[13] like Negt and Kluge, insisted upon the need to include economic contexts in any discussion of society. Negt and Kluge's scathing indictment of Habermasian liberalism for its refusal to admit economic privilege as a context for liberal democracy mirrors Bourdieu's insistence that cultural privilege is connected to class privilege. For, while the intellectual can be absolved from any charge of direct class privilege, or even class interest, this can only be achieved by accepting that narratives of intellectual supremacy somehow never translate or mediate with existing political and economic structures. And as Bourdieu argues, to accept that cultural privilege cannot be read alongside class privilege is merely to participate in a long tradition of refusing to subject claims regarding the disinterested origins and pursuit of 'culture' to any serious analysis:

> Paradoxically, intellectuals have an interest in *economism* since by reducing all social phenomena, and more especially the phenomena of exchange, to their economic dimension, it enables intellectuals to avoid putting themselves on the line. That is why it needs to be pointed out that there is such a thing as cultural capital, and that this capital secures direct profits, first on the educational market … but elsewhere too, and also secures profits of distinction – strangely neglected by the marginalist economists – which result *automatically* from its rarity … from the fact that it is unequally distributed … the profit of distinction is the profit that flows from the *difference*, the gap that separates one from what is common. And this direct profit is accompanied by an additional profit that is both subjective and objective, the profit that comes from seeing-oneself and being seen-as totally disinterested.[14]

Bourdieu's challenge to the liberal celebration of intellectual 'disinterest' was to explore and expose precisely what interests govern mainstream intellectual labour.

Moreover, Bourdieu insisted upon the need for radical theorists to confront the implications of the systematic exclusion of the majority of people from powerful intellectual arenas. Thus for Bourdieu, the overriding necessity confronting intellectuals, who wish to challenge existing power structures, is to start by admitting the fact of educational exclusion rather than immersing themselves in facile celebrations of popular representation. He argued that the honest intellectual response to the glaring lack of democratic representation in Western societies is to

openly admit to the deliberate exclusion of most of the public from any familiarity or ease with political and philosophical discussions:

> The observation that the inclination and aptitude to express interests, experiences and opinions in words, to seek coherence in judgements and to ground it in explicit and explicitly political principles depend directly on educational capital (and secondarily on the weight of cultural capital relative to economic capital) has something deeply shocking about it ... I only fear that those who are so attached to their 'democratic' or even 'egalitarian' habits of thought that they cannot tell the difference between an observation and a wish, a constative proposition and a performative judgement, will read these analyses – which at least credit the most deprived with the fact of their dispossession – as subtly conservative assaults on 'the people', it's 'struggles' and its 'culture'. To acknowledge that the most deprived are, contrary to all populist illusion, also deprived of the political 'means of production' is to deny to 'the iron law of oligarchies' the universal validity that conservative thought ascribes to them ... The flagrant inequality of access to what is called personal opinion is a challenge for the democratic conscience, for the ethical good will of the do-gooders, and also more profoundly, for the intellectualist universalism that is at the heart of the scholastic illusion.[15]

Bourdieu's unflinching recognition of the fact that most people are not only excluded from influential debates through unequal educational access but experience their exclusion as a crippling lack of familiarity and confidence with the dominant state structures, I think, constitutes an invaluable advance over those who would look to the 'common people' for 'common sense', irrevocable stupidity or as a receptacle for some kind of ancient inarticulate wisdom. However, arguably by focusing on the cynical universalising rhetoric of a class that dispenses only stringently controlled access to its public sphere, Bourdieu risks overlooking the fact that the acquisition of knowledge and expertise can and does take place outside the dominant institutional arenas.[16]

Certainly, any realistic assessment of social knowledge must take account of the fact that knowledge exists even where it is not recognised or 'publicly' acknowledged. The connection between economic deprivation and cerebral deprivation is one that has led to a dangerous universalisation of the thesis that the working classes are by definition lacking in any signs of cerebral sophistication. Knowledge itself is often

casually reduced to a simple matter of the number of years any person has spent at academic institutions. And while the benefits of gaining time away from the monotony and low economic benefits of wage labour should not be dismissed, neither should the multiple ways that people learn, outside bourgeois institutions be overlooked. In other words, we need not only to account for the extent to which class advantages and disadvantages remain fully operational within bourgeois educational institutions, but also acknowledge the fact that there are other ways in which people learn to interpret and analyse the world that take place outside the arenas of bourgeois education. Declaring there to be a definitive connection between the ability to interpret the world and one's place in the educational hierarchy merely simplifies both intellectual labour and the thinking capacities of those not defined as intellectuals.

Furthermore, Negt and Kluge's attempt to find a relationship between the intelligentsia and the working classes overlooks the fact that connections and tensions already exist between bourgeois institutions and those excluded from them. The very significance of being uneducated is achieved precisely by the implicit and explicit assumption that college and bourgeois institutions are the *only* sites in which the ability to think and 'be clever' can occur. The existence of intellectuals – whatever their own particular beliefs and aims – is unfortunately intimately tied to the removal of any intellectual function for the rest of society and the working classes in particular.

It is this denial of the capacity of the working classes to contribute *intellectually* to society as a whole that makes entry into educational arenas for the working-class individual primarily a matter of class repudiation. Equally worrying though is the pressure upon the working-class intellectual to provide testimony for the specific materiality of her background. Carolyn Steadman, in her challenge to such reductive representations of working-class people, cites Marx's 'preface to a Contribution to the Critique of Political economy' as an example:

> The attribution of psychological simplicity to working-class people … derives from the positioning of mental life within Marxism … it is in the 'Preface' itself that Marx mentions his move to London in the 1850s as offering among other advantages 'a convenient vantage point for the observation of bourgeois society', and which indeed he did observe, and live within, in the novels he and his family read, in family theatricals, in dinner-table talk: a mental life apparently much richer than that of the subjects of his theories. Lacking such possessions

of culture, working-class people have come to be seen within the field of cultural criticism, as bearing the elemental simplicity of class-consciousness and little more.[17]

The intellectual left and right come together in their exposure of the liberal pretence that the worker is represented in all their talk of decency, equality and fairness only to diverge in their plans for what this lucrative empty figure of the worker could mean for a new society. My point here is not to suggest that there is an equivalence at work in the specific visions and agendas of the political right and left, but to argue that as long as the left retains the figure of the 'common people' as a blank thinking space as the basis for its egalitarian vision then intellectual equality is destined to remain a necessary but impossible dream.

For, the consequences of Kluge and Negt's desire to 'arrive at a relatively simple differentiation' between the different subjects of capitalism which is, they argue, 'possible at a more highly organized level of the productive forces',[18] is to reduce the proletariat to a simplistic corporeality. A striking consequence of granting the proletarian an exclusively bodily status is that she is deprived of any temporal existence in the world. In other words, as pure bodily material the worker cannot learn from her experiences unless the intellectual rescues her from her material condition. This refusal to grant the worker any sense of her past, present or future is an inevitable result of the fondness for casting her as the site of 'experience', even as experience itself apparently teaches her nothing. Something similar can be noted in the routine depiction of the non-West as a vast unchanging primal site pulsating with experience, but for the most part lacking in any useful cognition.

Richard Hoggart's depiction of English working-class communities in the 1950s is a striking example of this denial of time and change to working-class existence and experience. As Steadman notes, his assertion that 'the streets are all the same; nothing changes' reflecting the fact that most people lacked, 'any feeling that some change can, or indeed ought to be made in the general pattern of life,' constitutes an astonishing dismissal of any sense of engagement with, much less opposition to existing social and political realities.[19] It is this denial of the effects of history to the worker that enables commentators such as Adorno to refer to the perpetual loyalty of the masses to authority. The proletariat, even as she is recruited as one who must usher in social and political change, is depicted as the most unchanging of all subjects.

Significantly, Negt and Kluge's intellectual experiences her 'alienation' in a crucially different way to her working-class counterpart. For, while

the worker is alienated to the point of unconsciousness of her alienation, the intellectual is able to recognise her alienation and strive to overcome it. Thus, while the workers fulfil the sense of alienation as that state of being which deprives people of the consciousness necessary for them to be autonomous subjects, the intellectuals are able to recognise, and hence change, their material alienation. The intellectual, in doing so, signals that she is already a subject and as such an indication of what will be when class differences disappear. The proletariat on the other hand, despite, or rather because of her all pervasive materiality was never present as a subject in the first place. The proletariat, herself as the material context for a future that is not yet here, becomes so material that she loses any resemblance to a subject at all, functioning instead as at best an embryonic subject.

Of course, Negt and Kluge are not suggesting that intellectuals should retain their cerebral difference indefinitely either; but by giving intellectuals a conscious understanding of the present, they indicate *who* it is that can be entrusted to usher in a new society. The workers may have the most direct self-interest in overturning capitalism but, as Negt and Kluge reiterate throughout their text, all such attempts to overthrow or sabotage the capitalist system have so far resulted in failure. The intellectual is as such vital to the workers if capitalism is to be properly replaced by a radically different order imaginable only by those capable of distancing themselves from the constraints of present-day existence. In short, Kluge and Negt rework the traditional celebration of intellectual disinterest into a call for the absolutely essential role of the detached intellectual for imagining and organising a new society. Unfortunately, this retention of the intellectual's supposed autonomy ensures that Negt and Kluge's intellectual is aligned not simply with the working classes but with the liberal-humanist tradition as well.

For, as Bourdieu observes, the achievement of intellectual autonomy was inextricably tied to the assertion of a concrete intellectual distinction:

Having freed itself by stages from immediate material preoccupations, in particular with the aid of the profits secured by direct or indirect sale of practical knowledge to commercial undertakings or the State, and having accumulated through and for their work, competences (initially acquired through education) that could function as cultural capital, they were increasingly inclined and also able to assert their individual and collective autonomy vis-à-vis the economic and political powers who need their services (and also vis-à-vis the aristocracies based on birth, against which they asserted the justifications of merit and increasingly of the 'gift').[20]

In other words, intellectuals substituted the struggle against wealthy individuals with the struggle against the altogether more impersonal and consolidating forces of an emerging bourgeois hegemony. And the achievement of intellectual autonomy and subsequent demarcation of a specifically 'intellectual' sphere introduced the idea of intelligence as a material foundation and justification for this autonomy. Intellectual autonomy thus has profound implications for society as a whole which could now be classified in terms of an imagined and soon-to-be imposed intellectual inequality.

And, as Bourdieu rightly observes, the invocation of intelligence as a 'natural' difference between people should be subjected to the same challenges that progressive criticism applies to claims regarding a supposedly natural racial difference:

> The racism of intelligence is the means through which the members of the dominant class aim to produce a 'theodicy of their own privilege', as Weber puts it, in other words, a justification of the social order that they dominate. It is what causes the dominant class to feel justified in being dominant: they feel themselves to be *essentially* superior.[21]

Negt and Kluge's determination to find a use for intellectual labour rejects the consequences of disinterested thought even as it retains the notion of the intellectual as a fundamentally enabling subject. But without extending their challenge to the disinterested intellectual himself, Negt and Kluge end up with a hero whose political pedigree dates back to a supposed *particular* commitment to universal truths. Not surprisingly, this model of the disinterested intellectual has comfortably served opposing political aims. For commentators such as Negt and Kluge it was precisely the deliberate suppression of bourgeois interests in an allegedly 'public' sphere that led them to reject it. However, by rejecting the bourgeois public sphere as a thoroughly interested public sphere Negt and Kluge then proceed to use the same model of the valuable non-aligned intellectual as the starting point for a new properly universal public sphere.

For this reason, analysing the purpose of what is clearly a powerfully seductive model of intellectual labour becomes politically essential. Arguably, 'grounding' intellectual work upon the supposed ignorance of the masses far from signalling a radical departure from bourgeois cultural ideologies, constitutes instead a continuation of bourgeois notions of the 'raw and uncultivated' masses that served as the justification for educational programmes favoured by commentators such as Matthew Arnold.

And the question this raises is simply this: Can Negt and Kluge use the 'raw materiality' of the masses for radical ends or does such an employment of the working classes itself serve to limit the radicalism of their theory? In order to address this question, we need first to make a detour into the non-European world. For, it is there that the 'blind materialism' of the masses finds its counterpart in the vast 'undeveloped' expanses of the non-Western world.

Part 3 Impossible Subjects: Proletariats, Savages and Historical Materialism

6
The Savage and the Proletariat

At the centre of Marxist accounts of the transition to communism is the figure of the worker and her (or more often his) relation to the intellectuals who will direct her towards a different world no longer powered by the exchange of commodities and the exploitation of proletarian labour. Marxist accounts of the existing capitalist-economic system locate human labour as the fundamental generator of political consciousness. Thus rather than attributing the inability of most people to fully understand the relations between humanity and their social and political world to any inherent limitation on their part, Marxist accounts point to the inevitable suppression of political consciousness endured by those engaged in exhausting and exploitative wage labour. Unlike liberal accounts there is not in this sense any implicit judgement upon the people, but rather a condemnation of the political system for denying most people the capacity to lead fulfilling lives.

That is why in Marxist accounts the point of transforming society is frequently connected with a *return* to an original universal humanity. Thus, Marx describes how his model of historical development, from feudalism to capitalism and on to communism, is at the same time a movement *back* to a once unruptured unity between humanity and its own real human nature. Humanity here is evoked by the representation of it as only present when there is a complementary balance between human needs and human labour, and it is this that private capital and private property prevents. Communism, by contrast, suggests a visible equilibrium between the economic structures of society and human needs which are reflected in the universal satisfaction of human needs rather than the exploitation of the workers to satisfy the needs of the bourgeoisie. Thus, Marx states that

> *Communism* is the *positive* abolition of *private property*, of *human self-alienation*, and thus, the real *appropriation* of *human* nature, through and for man. It is therefore the return of man himself as a *social*, that is, really human being, a complete and conscious return which assimilates all the wealth of the previous development ... It is the true solution of the conflict between existence and essence, between objectification and self-affirmation, between freedom and necessity, between individual and species. It is the solution of the riddle of history and knows itself to be the solution. (emphasis in the original)[1]

However, this 'return' to an original humanity is dependent upon the processes of capitalist development and in particular the development of science and technology to ensure that humanity does not return to its pre-capitalist 'primitive' past.

Thus Marx argues that capitalism must fulfil its historical role before it can be overthrown by a radically different social and political order. Accordingly he warns his readers that however tempting it may be to abolish capitalism, any premature dismantling of capitalist society endangers the society that is destined to succeed it. Consequently, Marx dismisses arguments in favour of toppling capitalism, that are based on the 'will of the people', as dangerously idealistic, and proposes instead a proper attention to material conditions:

> As long as the productive forces are insufficiently developed to make competition superfluous, with the consequence that competition is always reappearing, the subject classes would be willing the impossible if they 'willed' to abolish competition and with it the State and law ... until conditions have developed to a point where they can produce this 'will' it exists only in the imagination of the ideologists.[2]

In short, both existing laws and revolutionary aspirations fail to express the 'will' of real people – because in the case of the former they are really only the expressions of the interests of the ruling class and for the latter the conditions that would create this 'will' are not yet actually in place. In both cases the real living conditions of humanity are the very ones that prevent humanity from living as the social beings that they really are. The foundations of living men become a foundation which proves that 'life' is not being lived whilst the absence of the appropriate economic conditions ensure that the 'will' for a different social order also cannot yet exist.

Attending to the actual economic (and therefore social) conditions of humanity reveals that although the capitalist system generates the conditions for its future disintegration, it is not yet ready to be overthrown. Thus, while the disintegration of capitalism is advanced as both a historical inevitability and a necessity, it is equally important that capitalism itself reaches its natural crisis point. Accordingly, Marx views the existence of workers' revolts and resistance as a protest against the inhumanity of economic conditions under capitalism, but stresses that they have to mature into the desire to create an altogether different society rather than simply destroy the present one:

> If the proletariat destroys the political rule of the bourgeoisie, that will only be a temporary victory, only an element in the service of the *bourgeois revolution* itself, as in 1794, so long as in the course of history, in its 'movement', the material conditions are not yet created which make necessary the abolition of the bourgeois mode of production and thus the definitive overthrow of bourgeois political rule.[3]

Marx's attention to history was based upon his belief that the key to social change lay in the dynamic passage from one form of production and society to another.

While Marx was a passionate advocate of a socialist revolution, he was less concerned with outlining how exactly a post-communist society would work – since he viewed that as an issue for the people that overthrew the capitalist system. However, precisely because the present and the past do *not* provide evidence of the 'real' nature of man, because their economic organisations prevent him from expressing himself as a complete human being, it follows that it is only in the future that 'real' men can be imagined to exist. The rigorous study of human history and economic history in particular that Marx advocates is concerned to record man's historical struggle to establish a society that will at last satisfy his nature.

Consequently materialism is simply the correct attendance to the fact that man is a material being and creates and structures the material world for his own purposes. For Marx, the mistake of idealist philosophy was to imagine that ideas could be divorced from the bodies of 'men'. Idealist philosophy, in other words, consolidated the alienation of the economic relations of capitalism by consenting to the brutal splitting of humanity's mental life from its material conditions of existence. In short, idealist philosophy, for Marx, is missing its subject – humanity – and far

from being liberated by its lack of material foundations is instead locked in an endless conversation with itself.

But it is, Marx argues, *only* by studying the practical lives of human beings that we can ever hope to produce imaginative and conceptual analyses that have any relation to either humanity or the world. Consequently, the objection directed towards philosophical idealism is not that it aspires towards universal conclusions, but that it possesses no mandate for them from the actual reality of human existence. By contrast, applying ourselves to an extensive and detailed study of human development leads us to world history without transcending the living conditions of humanity:

> This conception of history depends on our ability to expound the real process of production, starting out from the material production of life itself and to comprehend the form of intercourse connected with this and created by this mode of production (i.e. civil society in its various stages), as the basis of all history; and to show it in action as State, to explain all the different theoretical products and forms of consciousness, religion, philosophy, ethics, etc. etc. and trace their origins and growth from that basis; by which means, of course, the whole thing can be depicted in its totality ... it has not like the idealistic view of history, in every period to look for a category, but remains constantly on the *ground* of history.[4]

Here, Marx provides an early example of the substitution of works of science and philosophy for the study of humanity. The theoretical knowledge that informs what we now regard as the social sciences are not independent spheres denoting humanity's successful flight from the material world, but on the contrary owe their entire existence to the material world and the human beings that make it. And through a detailed study of humanity the 'will' to change our living conditions can be detected within our historical development as a species, which, in turn, is a narrative of human nature since humanity is a fundamentally historical entity. In this sense, communism is that which returns us to what we are which is something that we have never been able to be. Communism is as such the latent 'will' residing in the ongoing development of humanity.

Marx argued that far from being a matter of philosophical speculation, the nature and destiny of humanity was accessible through a painstaking study of human society throughout the ages. Rather than requiring the inspirational flights of fancy that characterised idealist

philosophy, Marx insisted that the social world needed instead to be brought under the rubric of science. Accordingly, he applied himself to the task of producing an empirical work that would consider, 'the development of the economic structure of society as a natural historical process'.[5] Human society was thus likened to a living organism constantly adapting and changing to external circumstances. But unlike the natural world, Marx suggested that the reasons for economic development themselves should be grounded in human beings.

For Marx, the most crucial aspect of human nature and the social world lay in their visible capacity for change. In other words, the very fact that humanity did live under vastly different conditions proved that the material world was itself subject to change. Thus, although Marx based his work upon the living conditions of humanity, this in itself required far more than simply attending to humanity in its present condition. For, if the most crucial aspect of the material world and of the human subjects that produced it lay in its ever-changing forms, then the materialist philosopher was obliged to consider not just this society but all previous societies and all those yet to come. England may well have been the 'laboratory' for his scientific analysis but understanding England required an understanding of 'world history' which in contrast to Hegel's investment in an omnipotent Spirit[6] would be one that was drawn from the record of human production and the economic relations that governed it.

By insisting that history was nothing more or less than the relations of humanity under their changing modes of production, Marx dislodged the traditional philosopher from his vantage point situated high above the material world. For, as Marx pointed out, Hegel's philosophy was one that removed people from their history and claimed for itself a 'history' that was situated outside the material world in both space and time:

> Already with Hegel, the *absolute spirit* of history has its materials in the *masses*, but only finds adequate expression in *philosophy*. But the philosopher appears merely as the instrument by which absolute spirit which makes history arrives at self-consciousness after the historical movement has been completed. The philosopher's share in history is thus limited to this subsequent consciousness. The philosopher arrives *post fetum*.[7]

Marx challenged German idealist philosophy for its assumption that the realm of ideas can exist independent from humanity and the

social world. The Hegelian ascent from the living bodies and relations of humanity into philosophy was, as Marx pointed out, one that not only forgot *where* it ascended from but ascended only to evaporate into pure speculation since it rejected any connection with the material world and the people in it:

> Man exists so that history shall exist and history exists so that truth can be revealed. In this critically debased form there is repeated the old speculative wisdom, according to which man and history exist so that *truth* can become *conscious of itself. History* thus becomes like *truth*, a separate entity, a metaphysical subject of which the real human individuals are only mere representatives.[8]

For Marx, it is precisely because humanity is identifiable by its active need to produce itself socially that history can be said to exist. In this sense, the emphasis in materialist accounts upon the need for 'men to 'intervene' in history is not a call for a new approach by men to the material world, but a reference to what he already by necessity does.

Indeed, the Marxist emphasis upon the active nature of 'man' is precisely the reason why every aspect of his social and natural world owes its animation to him. Thus, industry is the external evidence of human labour and nature is recognisable only insofar as it provides man with the means to realise his material existence:

> The first thing of which the labourer possesses himself is not the object of labour but its instrument. Thus nature becomes one of the organs of his activity, one that he annexes to his own bodily organs, adding stature to himself in spite of the Bible. As the earth is his original larder, so too it is his original tool house.[9]

This translation of the realms of science, nature, industry, religion and philosophy into matters of bodily existence means that nothing can be discussed without the inclusion of man himself as the sole active basis for its existence. Thus any conception of history is meaningless unless it is regarded as the product of the human relations that produce both the material and conceptual world:

> *History* does *nothing*, it 'does *not* possess immense riches', it 'does *not* fight battles'. It is *men*, real living men, who do all this, who possess things and fight battles. It is not 'history' which uses men as a means of achieving – as if it were an individual person – *its* own ends. History is *nothing* but the activity of men in pursuit of their ends.[10]

The problem is that while history can be described as the changing social, economic and political relations of humanity throughout time, the same cannot be said for what survives in the present as a record of this activity.

History does function to some extent independently of human relations, precisely because history is a particular form of memory and retrieval produced by particular people using particular conventions and addressing particular concerns. As Michel-Rolph Trouillot points out:

> Silences are inherent in history because any single fact enters history with some of its constituting parts missing. Something is always left out while something else is recorded. There is no perfect closure of any event, however one chooses to define the boundaries of that event. Thus whatever becomes fact does so with its own inborn absences, specific to its production. In other words, the very mechanisms that make any historical recording possible also ensure that historical facts are not created equal. They reflect differential control of the means of historical production at the very first engraving that transforms an event into a fact. [11]

Marx, on the other hand, treats the documents of the past as providing the would-be historian with all that she needs to complete and refine the narrative of the past. Unfortunately, it is precisely his determination to locate material humanity at the core of all theoretical knowledge that prevents him from attending to the actual exclusions of humanity from that work. For, by emphasising the fallacy of philosophical idealism with its rejection of the material relations of human beings, Marx overlooked the extent to which this very tradition of rejecting the material world had left its imprint upon the 'history' of humanity. And, precisely because bourgeois ideology insisted upon representing and defining the material world as that debased sphere from which women, the poor and the 'uncivilised' were yet to transcend; it followed that their omission from the historical record would be the most profound.

Moreover, because for Marx the technological development of literary production itself proves the ongoing development of humanity, the status of all those who were not involved in the technological revolution in the West becomes important only insofar as they proved that humanity *has* progressed:

> *Production in general* is an abstraction, but a sensible abstraction in so far as it actually emphasises and defines the common aspects and

thus avoids repetition. Yet this *general* concept, or common aspect which has been brought to light by comparison, is itself a multifarious compound comprising divergent categories. Some elements are found in all epochs, others are common to a few epochs. The most modern period and the most ancient period will have [certain] categories in common. Production without them is inconceivable. But although the most highly developed languages have laws and categories in common with the most primitive languages, it is precisely their divergence from these general and common features which constitute their development.[12]

In other words, those who have not progressed on to new forms of communication constitute the common ground for humanity while those who have reveal its ongoing development. The subordination of those situated outside the industrial and commercially expanding West find themselves installed with Western narratives as primitive points of common origin.

However, the clarity of this model of human development is problematic, not least because, if progress is a matter of discarding obsolete forms in favour of new and better ones, then how are we to account for the authority and resilience of forms that we are supposed to have surpassed? Marx's solution to this 'difficulty' was to define humanity's appreciation of older forms of artistic production in terms of nostalgia. Thus, Western audiences do not value classical Greek art for its intellectual stimulation but for its ability to evoke a society and consciousness that has long since gone. 'Our' appreciation of older forms of production can thus be safely contained within a model of development that gives the developed and enlightened members of humanity the freedom to enjoy the work of their forebears. All cultural production thus becomes legible within a model of technological process, with the deceased (the Greeks) and the living (non-Europeans) positioned in their usual role as humanity in its infancy:

> Does not in every epoch the child represent the character of the period in its natural veracity? Why should not the historical childhood of humanity, where it attained its most beautiful form, exert an eternal charm because it is a stage that will never recur? There are rude children and precocious children. Many of the ancient peoples belong to this category. The Greeks were normal children. The charm their art has for us does not conflict with the immature stage of the society in which it originated. On the contrary its charm is a

consequence of this and is inseparably linked with the fact that the immature social conditions which gave rise, and which alone could give rise, to this art cannot recur.[13]

Marx's incorporation of Greek texts into a medium that expressed the early consciousness of humanity was clearly essential, if his model of humanity achieving evermore developed forms of production and consciousness was to be convincing. For, it is precisely his insistence upon the progression of humanity that produces his equally emphatic belief in the backwardness of those who have yet to produce or experience industrial or technological development. And whilst Marx was certainly no advocate of needless human suffering, it is his adherence to the notion of a stage model of human development that enabled him to accept the cruelties of development tied as they were to the eventual emancipation of humanity.

It is this reliance upon the extreme removal of any humanity from economic relations in capitalism that leads Marx to identify any other form of trade and production as undeveloped, precisely because they lack the brutal clarity of capitalist relations of production. The inexorable conditions of economic production under capitalism are thus to be understood as both more brutal *and* more developed than any preceding forms and relations of production. The harsh economic reality of production needs to be the *only* reality that humanity confronts, since anything else merely diverts humanity from their essential task of destroying capitalist relations. Accordingly the 'genuinely trading nations' that Marx located in the ancient world can be contrasted with bourgeois society – as societies that are 'extremely simple and transparent'.[14]

Marx relied upon his belief in the ongoing development of humanity for his optimism that humanity would find the means to overthrow the degrading and exploitative conditions of the capitalist system. Thus, his differentiation between bourgeois society and 'Oriental States' locates the alienation of capitalism as the terrible but necessary precondition for human progress:

> They are founded either on the immature development of man individually, who has not yet severed the umbilical cord that unites him with his fellow man in a primitive tribal community, or upon direct relations of subjection. They are the result of a low-level of development of the productive power of labour, and of the correspondingly limited relation between men within their sphere of

material life, both between man and man, and between man and Nature ... The life-process of society, i.e. the process of material production, will not shed its mystical veil until it becomes the product of freely associated men and is consciously regulated by them in accordance with a settled plan. This however requires a definite material basis or set of conditions which are themselves the spontaneous product of a *long and painful* process of development. (my emphasis)[15]

Tom Bottomore and Maximilien Rubel, in their consideration of the influence of Marx on subsequent sociological thought, argue that Marx was not interested in existential philosophical questions but was concerned to replace them with those of science. Consequently, to label him a 'historical materialist' is to miss the point:

He was not concerned either with the ontological problem of the relation of thought and being, or with the problems of the theory of knowledge. Speculative philosophy of this kind was what Marx *rejected* in order to substitute science for metaphysics in a new field of knowledge. (emphasis in the original)[16]

But this installation of a 'scientific' methodology *in place* of a previous metaphysical orientation in the social sciences was a philosophical act (whether intentional or not) of immense significance. For, grounding the social sciences upon the new rationalism of empirical science was the means by which the European social sciences claimed for themselves an unrivalled point of origin for the common nature of humanity. At a stroke all previous beliefs and views and grounds for knowledge could be shown to be the embryonic anticipation for European scientific rationalism, while those societies yet to embrace scientific rationalism could be safely classified as still living under the anonymous shadow of a pre-history. Thus, while Marx toppled Hegel's idealism in favour of the material realities of 'men's' lives, for those 'men' living outside Europe no such seismic overhaul was forthcoming.

Marx's faith in empirical science as the most effective repudiation of philosophical idealism continued the battle to assert the supremacy of a scientific methodology that had begun in the Renaissance. The idea that the technical and scientific advances on the part of Europeans was a reflection of their higher consciousness, and, more importantly, evidence of the possibility for humanity as a whole to emerge from the

disorganised chaos of a primitive and infantile past survived intact into the nineteenth century. It is at work in Marx's juxtaposition of the emerging clarity of capitalism with the 'mystical veil' of pre-industrial relations – a clarity that marks the break between an ad hoc and confusing relation between the economic and social relations of humanity, and the overwhelmingly visible dislocation between these spheres that gradually emerges under capitalism.

Marx's emphasis upon 'observation' reflects his sense of humanity emerging from the darkness of confusion and superstition into the clear relations of capitalist production. Acquiring sight is of course far from painless, since what humanity (in the form of the proletariat) sees in capitalism is the painful clarity of oppression and misery. Capitalism marks an essential turning point for humanity insofar as it reveals the limits and costs of a society that is based upon exploitation and in the process redirects human interests and history towards an egalitarian society.

By identifying capitalism as a thoroughly historical development, Marx emphasised the myriad differences between different nations with comparable histories. It was precisely his excavation of differences in the developments of human societies that both endorsed science as a more accurate and realistic methodological tool than philosophical speculation *and* enabled him to dismiss any charges of harbouring pretensions to universal or 'supra-historical' truths. It was the very neutrality and dispassion of science that for Marx made any such charges preposterous. By staking his theory upon the progressive movement of history, Marx committed himself to the task of accounting for history within the methodological terms that he insisted made such a task possible. This in turn meant that all previous societies not only had to be incorporated into human history, but had also to be shown to be in some way connected to the development of industry and capital.

It is here that the power of bourgeois society as a definitive origin for humanity as a whole becomes clear, as all other societies become compressed into the same vast space and time of 'prehistory'. Accordingly, the non-European world and the ancient world meet across time precisely because time does not properly begin until a critical level of development and organisation occurs within bourgeois society:

In broad outline we can designate the Asiatic, the ancient, the feudal and the modern bourgeois modes of production as progressive epochs in the economic formation of society. The bourgeois relations of production are the last antagonistic form of the social

process of production … At the same time the productive forces developing in the womb of bourgeois society create the material conditions for the solution of that antagonism. With this social formation, therefore, the prehistory of human society comes to an end.[17]

The implications of this sweeping attribution of a 'pre-history' to the 'Asiatic' world in Marx's theory were immense. For, by relegating all the peoples of the non-European world to an anonymous 'pre-history', Marx effectively denied them the status of human beings, since history was, as he argued, nothing less than the record of men's social relations. The Asiatic world as a site of pre-history did not even possess the alienation that could suggest the desire to overcome it but embodied rather the dull obedience and simplicity of a pre-industrial consciousness. Europe as the site for an emergent and potentially revolutionary consciousness is thus contrasted with the baffling illegibility of the non-European world. And if Marx objected to Hegel's replacement of philosophy for man, then his own depiction of Asiatic humanity as living outside history and time performed something strikingly similar.

Gayatri Spivak[18] has pointed out that Marx and Engels' definitions of primitive communism and the Asiatic Mode of Production mark the outside of the Marxist description of the progression from feudalism to capitalism, since Marxism needs the difference of capitalism to work its dialectic. The extent to which Marxist theory was dependent upon a developed capitalist system to inaugurate its demise became all the more clear when a proletarian revolution broke out in Russia in 1917. In an overwhelmingly agricultural nation with a singular lack of industrial development the leading Bolsheviks were haunted by their failure to embody the necessary preconditions for a successful communist society.[19]

Fitting the model of historical development that Marx detected in 'history' to the world was a problem that led almost inevitably to the extension of the economic framework that Marx insisted should be the material context for humanity and society at large. After all, if the economic contexts were missing or at odds with those required by history to secure socialism, then clearly other explanations needed to be assembled in order to account for the actual limitations of the economic model itself. In short, in the absence of capitalism other contexts needed to be brought into play that could validate socialism. As Spivak notes:

> The question of revolution is situated within this broader requirement. Strictly speaking a revolution brings a new mode of production.

The relationship between the previous mode and the new one, however, must in actual fact be consonant with the feudalism-capitalism-communism/socialism series, this is one of the reasons why it is imperative to establish that Russia was already inserted into a developed capitalist economy on the eve of the Revolution. Gramsci introduces unequal development by way of 'The Southern Question'. And in a bold move, Mao Zedong had seen the need for a prescriptive *cultural* revolution, in the cultural encoding of the production of value, as it were, because the mode of economic production of value did not fit. In the context of the multinational Russian empire, Lenin thinks State; Stalin, Nation. In the context of the monolithic hierarchical mandarin China Mao thinks Culture.[20]

Mayfair Yang[21] documents how Joseph Stalin's revision of Lewis Morgan's three-stage theory of social evolution (the state of savagery, barbarism and civilization) in 1940 into five stages of 'relations of production', (primitive communism, slave society, feudalism, capitalism and socialism), became the official as well as the intellectual and popular view of universal human history in China in the 1950s.[22] Thus, Chinese history was reinterpreted according to the insights of 'historical materialism' by prominent Chinese historians.[23] As Yang points out, the casualties of this classification were China's minority peoples who were slotted into the early stages of this universal evolution and became 'living fossils' for those anthropologists anxious to prove the truth of Morgan's theory. A cultural and political distinction and inequality was thus created between China's minority people and more powerful groups like the Han who were accorded with a higher stage of evolutionary development.

Similarly, Yang argues, the centrality of class struggle in Marxist theory threatened to once again complicate the communist credentials of post-revolutionary China, since the theory of landownership was irrelevant in many local areas. However, rather than revise Marxist theory, Chinese officials and activists chose to define territories, such as Ding County in North China, as landowning areas in need of revolutionary change. Thus, despite the fact that in 1936 only 0.7 per cent of households in Ding County were landlords who hired labour and tenants farmed less than two percent of the arable land, Ding County was nevertheless defined as a 'landowning' territory.[24]

Clearly, the problems that Marxist theory has posed to those countries that have attempted to construct a socialist or communist society arose not so much from their exclusion from the correct historical

trajectory as from their inclusion. In other words, the problem was not so much that Marx was unable to find an adequate description or definition of the non-European world but that he included it in his 'history' in much the same place that Hegel had in his evocations of World History. Consequently, predominantly agricultural nations and the vast stretches of Asia and Africa remained locked in the same obscure pre-history that Hegel had insisted that they embodied.

In the West, Marx's problematical description of the Asiatic Mode of Production provided Western Marxists with further evidence of their own advanced historical sensibilities and their subsequent duty to intervene in the non-West. But, as Spivak observes, the efforts of Marx's followers to account for the Asiatic Mode are inevitably limited by the fact that the Asiatic Mode of Production is neither historically or geographically 'Asiatic' nor logically a 'Mode of Production'. Rather it is better understood as 'a descriptive/historical, not a logical explanation'.[25] And if Asia proved to be incompatible with the feudalism-capitalism-communism progression, then its incompatibility served to illustrate only its limitations and failings. The incoherence of the Asiatic Mode of Production, far from signalling the inapplicability of Marx's definition of capital for the whole world, provides instead the justification for its intervention in it. As Spivak comments:

> the general history of humankind as work, its origin placed by Marx in the material exchange or 'metabolism' between the human being and nature, the story of capitalist expansion, the slow freeing of labor power as commodity, the narrative of the mode of production, the transition from feudalism via mercantilism to capitalism, even the precarious normativity of this narrative is sustained by the changeless stopgap of the Asiatic Mode of Production which steps in to sustain it whenever it might become apparent that the story of capital logic is the story of the West, that only imperialism can aggressively insist upon the universality of the mode of production narrative, that to ignore or invade the subaltern today is to continue the imperialist project in the name of modernization in the interest of globalization.[26]

The potential contradiction involved in a theory that emphasises the materiality of human beings only to consign the peoples of entire continents to the outer reaches of humanity by the expedient practice of assigning them to a different time and space, reaches its fullest

expression in Gramsci, for whom the colonisation of America offered the opportunity for 'development' on a hitherto unprecedented scale:

> The Anglo-Saxon immigrants are themselves an intellectual, but more especially a moral, *elite*. I am talking, naturally, of the first immigrants, the pioneers, protagonists of the political and religious struggles in England, defeated but not humiliated or laid low in their country of origin. They import in to America, together with themselves, apart from moral energy and energy of the will, a certain level of civilization, a certain stage of European historical evolution, which when transplanted by such men into the virgin soil of America, continues to develop the forces implicit in its nature but with an incomparably more rapid rhythm than in Old Europe. (emphasis in the original)[27]

Here the actual inhabitants of America are not even present, enabling this 'virgin soil' to offer the potential for development at a rate previously unseen.

The obliteration of the native American Indians from the physical and intellectual landscape is such that History begins with the arrival of the Anglo-Saxon immigrants. But this is History with a difference since these 'new' arrivals bring with them the accomplishments of European civilisation without the impediment of archaic laws and morals to stand in their way. This supine and passive land is the fertile soil for those already schooled in the struggles of Europe. Lacking the customs and institutions that prolong these struggles enables human development itself to proceed uninterrupted. History, in this sense, while it does not begin in America can be completed by those already formed by the struggles within Europe.

Turning his attention to contemporary America, Gramsci registers his interest in the potential role that 'negro intellectuals' could play in bringing Africa into the present. Significantly, the Enlightenment practice of denoting Africa as currently living out an infancy (whether idealised or savage) that Europe has long since overcome informs his reflection as to whether the potential for transporting Africa into 'our' present is possible:

> One further formation in the United States is worth studying, and that is the formation of a surprising number of negro intellectuals who absorb American culture and technology. It is worth bearing

in mind the indirect influence that these negro intellectuals could exercise on the backward masses in Africa, and indeed direct influence if one or other of these hypotheses were ever to be verified: 1. that American expansionism should use American negroes as its agents in the conquest of the African market and the extension of American civilisation (something of that kind has already happened but I don't know to what extent); 2. that the struggle for the unification of the American people should intensify in such a way as to provoke a negro exodus and the return to Africa of the most independent and energetic intellectual elements ... This development would give rise to two fundamental questions: 1. linguistic: whether English could become the educated language of Africa bringing unity in the place of the existing swarm of dialects? 2. whether this intellectual stratum could have sufficient assimilating and organising capacity to give a 'national 'character to the present primitive sentiment of being a despised race, thus giving the African continent a mythic function as the common father land of all the negro peoples? It seems to me that for the moment, American negroes have a national and racial spirit which is negative rather than positive, one which is the product of the struggle carried on by the whites in order to isolate and depress them.[28]

Given the strict assumption of racial difference that underscored European social and political theory, one which relied in particular upon a conception of Africans as unintelligent beings, it is perhaps not surprising that Gramsci is somewhat unprepared for the emergence of 'negro intellectuals'. However, in Gramsci's reading, the potential challenge to the notion that Africa and its peoples constituted a primitive and undeveloped version of humanity is warded off by confining any intellectual development on the part of 'negroes' to their ability to 'absorb' American culture and technology. The fact that such an absorption would have involved an appreciation of the finer points of scientific racism[29] that might have proved to be incompatible with the high ideals of Enlightenment discourses is something that Gramsci neglects to consider. Certainly, the work of black American intellectuals in the early part of the twentieth century is hardly a record of a passive absorption of 'American' culture.[30]

In line with the notion that Africa needs to be led into its future via the rigours of development and capitalist expansion, Gramsci conjectures that the potential for the uplift of Africa is possible either by the 'use' of American negroes as capitalist ambassadors or by the return of

negroes to Africa in response to the 'unification' of America. America is, it seems, no longer a 'virgin land' but one that has implanted a history and a people with whom 'the negro' can and should be contrasted. The negro while he may attain the stature of an intellectual cannot, it seems, acquire the status of an inhabitant, much less a citizen. In fact, as Cedric Robinson points out, the very term 'negro' was one that was employed precisely in order to deny black people in America any claims to a history prior to slavery and thus deprive them of any access to the 'rights of man' that white Americans proclaimed as the basis of 'their' new state:

> The most significant obliterations of the New World's past was that which affected the African. The African became the more enduring 'domestic enemy', and consequently the object around which a more specific, particular and exclusive conception of humanity was molded. The 'Negro,' that is the colour black, was both a negation of African and a unity of opposition to white. The construct of Negro, unlike the terms 'African,' 'Moor,' or 'Ethiope' suggested no situatedness in time, that is history, or space, that is ethno-or-politico-geography. The Negro had no civilization, no cultures, no religions, no history, no place, and finally no humanity that might command consideration.[31]

The 'negro' was thus a useful classification that sought to place black people in America in an alienated relation both to America and Africa – an alienation that Gramsci uncritically accepts. Thus, the 'unification' of America involves 'the negroes' only insofar as it reminds them that this is not their home. Only the Anglo-Saxon immigrants possess the necessary degree of history to authorise their assumption of national power and identity.

And history, it seems, does indeed proceed without interruption from its European birthplace. For this history is one that has no interest in recalling that 'the negroes' were brought to America precisely so that industry, agriculture and technology could be 'developed'. The slaves that were brought to assist American development were necessary not just for their free labour power, but also for their indispensable knowledge of how to farm and mine these 'new' lands. Of course, the fact that the Anglo-Saxon immigrants needed the expertise of their slaves was a fact that threatened to reveal their depiction of Africa and its inhabitants as contemporary primitive ancestors as so much superstition.

The disastrous implications of the emphasis upon the different levels of 'development' and 'consciousness' between Europeans and all those defined as outside of Europe are reflected in Gramsci's tortuous presentation of the contexts for his observation that the American 'negroes'' capacity to rouse Africa from its pre-historical slumber is limited by their, 'present primitive sentiment of being a despised race'.[32] Thus, on the one hand, he attributes this to the aggressive struggle of whites waged against them and on the other to the *actual* primitive status of Africans. The fact that the aggressive struggle waged by powerful whites against the Africans was *based* upon the conviction that Africans were a lowly and primitive race is the missing connection that Gramsci is determined to avoid.

It is this inability on the part of radical theorists such as Gramsci to find a conceptual framework in which non-Europeans could be included as equal members in the history of humanity that makes the case of 'negro intellectuals' so suggestive. For, any hopes that he clearly did have for the emancipation of both them and the African continent were thwarted by the very logic of his own belief in the differential development of humanity. And this is of course no mere matter of history but a pervasive assumption underpinning much of what goes under the name of radical Western theory today. For, if the supposed end of Marxism as a relevant ideology has sanctioned the gleeful abandonment of class oppression as a meaningful banner to organise ourselves around, then the prospect of turning our backs upon a history of Eurocentric assumptions has proved to be far less agreeable.

Consequently, the notion that Europe as a modern civilisation could and should intervene in the development of a pre-modern non-Europe remains very much alive. Unfortunately, this sentiment, for the most part, is not based upon any sense that 'we' might bear some responsibility for the accelerated development of the modern world through our management of the non-European world throughout colonialism and imperialism. Instead the non-Western world appears still as a distant and alienated shadow of ourselves still needing Western guidance and assistance in order to maintain the very inequality that the West claims to be addressing. And if 'we' have subjected Marxism to criticism for its particular idea of how scientific rationalism could be used, 'we' have been considerably less keen to sanction our own abdication as those destined to lead humanity forward.

Postmodernism may have challenged the authority of science as a ruling discourse, but it has remained remarkably quiet about the extent to which the scientific and technological superiority of the West

continues to endow Europe and North America with the ideological justification for power and authority in the world. The repercussions of this installation of science as a neutral and rational tool for analysis and investigation that can be transported from the study of the natural world into the study of the human world, reverberates today in the dismissal of the non-European world as a theatre of unfathomable myth and superstition. Thus, even though Habermas constructs his entire project of enlightened liberalism upon its ability to transcend myth and superstition, he does not consider it necessary to elaborate upon what exactly he is referring to in his evocations of myth and mysticism.

This sly evocation of an unenlightened 'third world' contrast with which European rationalism can be favourably compared is achieved perhaps most crucially in the reluctance of prominent Western theorists to explain how exactly they are defining 'the world' that they take as their subject. Thus, as Ronaldo Munck notes, when asked about the relevance of his approach to progressive forces in the third world and whether these might contribute to the democratic transformation of the advanced industrial societies, Habermas replied:

> I am tempted to say 'no' in both cases. I am aware that this is a Eurocentric limited view. I would rather pass the question.[33]

Also keen to pass the question was Michel Foucault who also admitted to a silence on the question of imperialism.

The ability of prominent theorists of the social world to admit to silence on a vast proportion of that world is one that has been built upon the foundations of European social science itself. For it is precisely by designating the non-European world as an undifferentiated mass of unenlightened myth and superstition that investigation and incorporation of that world into Europe can be an optional practice for Western social scientists. Certainly, classifying the non-European world as still driven by myths and superstitions means that 'history' and 'development' can be discussed without including them in the frame. However, the social sciences are after all a study of 'humanity' and not simply Europe, and since 'Europe' itself attains its clarity through a contrast with a hazily sketched non-Europe it transpires that these unfathomable lands do after all have a place – one that is relentlessly 'outside' of 'history – a vast imaginative, reservoir for the European to refine and analyse himself. It is this that leads to the ubiquitous presence of the third world in the margins of Western

social science, a presence that enables the West to define itself as a progression *from* the vague entity that is the 'third world'.

The problem is of course that Europe too is built upon myths and superstitions which are every bit as resilient as those that are only supposed to take place in the pre-modern lands of the non-European world.[34] For, did not Marx, after all, speak of man's 'historical destiny' and of a human nature that was yet to exist in the material world, and did not evolutionary theory, as Henrietta Moore and Todd Sanders point out, begin as metaphysics?[35] And if economic rationalism and organisation is so different from those societies that still lack a rational context, then why does 'the market' – that pinnacle of European economic development – depend upon that most metaphysical of notions: the 'hidden hand'?

Moore and Sanders, in their discussion of the intersections between modernity and the occult in Africa emphasise that their investigation is one that does not view Africa as providing Europe with its mystical opposite. Thus their discussion of Africa does not begin in Africa but in 'modern' Britain where the introduction of compulsory education and the rise of popular science have failed to dent the public appetite for spiritualism in the forms of tarot cards, astrology, New Age Spiritualism and aliens:

> Why have beliefs in the occult and occult-related practices not died out? ... We might equally pose the question: when will western faith in grand teleologies of progress vanish, given there is a world – quite literally – of evidence that they lack explanatory value? Should it not concern us that western teleological models bear no obvious resemblance to our multiply-modern empirical world? And are western teleological beliefs about progress, development, rationality and modernity – those ready-made explanations for social change that provide answers to the Big Questions in life – really so different from the idea that occult forces move the world? What, after all, is the driving force behind 'progress' or 'development'? Could it be 'the market' and Adam Smith's 'invisible hand', or some equally enigmatic notion? When in short, will our own occult beliefs about the motor of our contemporary world be given up?[36]

It is perhaps not surprising to find that contemporary anthropology is currently embroiled in a critical reassessment of the relation between Europe, North America and the non-European world given that its own disciplinary origins are enmeshed with the project of direct and indirect colonial rule.

Anthropology from the start was directly embroiled in the question of what exactly constituted the difference between 'our' world and 'theirs' and more importantly through the practice of fieldwork was directly involved with this supposed 'other'. Radical anthropologists have wrestled with a disciplinary history that has offered various competing theories which have all managed to maintain the object of research whether frozen in time or brought up to date as useful only for contemporary European concerns. Thus when anthropologists in the 1950s and 1960s strove to undo the early-nineteenth-century anthropological 'discovery' of African witchcraft as evidence of a 'pre-logical' mentality, they did so by asserting that witchcraft was merely a way of 'making sense' of the social world and as such was a thoroughly rational response to the material world.[37] And while this did bring witchcraft into the social arena as a dynamic mechanism rather than a mysterious aspect of life, it nevertheless grafted a contemporary Western idea of society on to Africa.

As Michael Taussig points out, Evans-Pritchard's famous book on witchcraft and sorcery leads to the formula that 'sorcery explains coincidence' which presents sorcery only as a means of resolving questions, when in fact it is equally pertinent to think of coincidence and sorcery as raising questions about the social world.[38] As Taussig points out, the dominant reception of Evans-Pritchard's text as 'explaining' the 'mystical' Zande people reduced them to the simplicity of a puzzle, whereby complex rituals and beliefs could be explained by such concepts as 'envy'.

For Moore and Sanders, what distinguishes contemporary anthropological understandings of witchcraft is that witchcraft now is not simply seen as legible, but as intrinsic to modernity itself. No longer is Africa to be viewed as the only site that requires analysis and investigation but instead, they argue, *all* claims to rationality should be subjected to the same investigation. In short, Africa like Europe is part of modernity and its difference is no more or less significant than our difference from it:

Seeing modernity(ies) as a cultural project has allowed anthropologists concerned with witchcraft to refocus our discipline's analytic gaze back on ourselves and draw parallels between the operation of 'occult economies' (Comaroff and Comaroff 1999) the world over. In the process it has also freed up a valuable conceptual space for self-critique. The focus has shifted to certain dynamics of power, to how hidden forces shape the everyday world in specific cultural forms.

> Juxtaposing the west and the rest – considering witchcraft and conspiracy theories (la Fontaine 1992 ...) spirit possession in Asia (Geschiere 1998 ...), and American spin-doctors (Geschiere 1998 ...) as kindred beliefs about the world's workings – is important because it shows that 'witchcraft', and the particular dynamic of power it presupposed, are not just African phenomena. They operate in similar fashion the world over, albeit in different modernities and different culturally-inflected guises. Also, by rendering such beliefs and processes parallel, many recent scholars have suggested that 'occult economies' critique the varied modernities of which they form a part. The crucial point is that this particular project has allowed anthropologists to do what we have long excelled at: to render familiar the unfamiliar 'other', while standing our ordinary western world on its head.[39]

The benefits of this methodology are particularly obvious for those of us trained in cultural studies where cultural 'difference' is so often reduced to a casual gesture without any accompanying exploration into *what* those differences might be.

The contributors to Moore and Sander's exploration of witchcraft and modernity all combat notions of witchcraft as an archaic practice reflecting the pre-modern consciousness of Africans and point instead to its dynamic engagement in the modern world. Africa, in these readings, becomes part of the modern world and not simply a reference to a land that exists in a different space and time to ourselves. And in direct opposition to those who continue to ignore or simplify the heterogeneity of Africa they present instead evidence of the very different ways that the intersections between the occult and modernity have been embraced and resisted in Africa.

Moreover, by pointing out that the prevalence of witchcraft accusations and the perception of occult forces at work have been particularly evident in those African countries most targeted for structural adjustment policies[40] and World Bank directives, the contributors reveal that the occult is not merely resilient to the onslaught of rational liberalisation but is strengthened by it. Sanders relates how in the spring of 1999 the murder of six boys in Tanzania attracted international interest when reports leaked out that the boys had been skinned. The assumption in Tanzania that sorcerers as far away as Malawi, Zambia and the Democratic Republic of Congo were responsible for this trade – with their need for evermore powerful concoctions – ensured that the story remained at the forefront of media interest for the next three months.

As Sanders points out, while there was certainly evidence of a few cases of this grotesque form of murder, the sheer extent of media and popular interest in this story within the recently liberalised Tanzanian media pointed to an altogether wider sense of fear:

> What is particularly striking is how these few incidents in Southern Tanzania – inhumane, inexcusable, deplorable, without a doubt – rocked the nation and fired the popular imagi-nation; how they captured and crystallized, if for a moment, a nationwide sentiment that said somehow, something, somewhere, had gone intolerably wrong. When I visited Tanzania in the summer of 1999, urban and rural rumours had it that ruthless human skin traders were now searching out their victims not only in relatively remote villages, but also in the cities … it was here after all, in large urban sprawls, that people could be disappeared most easily, their skins sold for exorbitant prices, with little risk of detection. And even though, as far as I am aware, no skin-less victims have ever materialized in any Tanzanian city, rumours that they *had* ran rampant all the same.[41]

For Sanders the question that this raises is why now, in an era of structural adjustment and IMF-led 'reforms', is this perception of the power of the occult to wreak havoc so much a preoccupation for not just Tanzanians but many others across the continent. In order to answer this, Sanders argues that we need to understand how the conspicuous absence of any of the progress and prosperity that was promised by those who insisted upon an adherence to Western economic liberalism has encouraged doubt and insecurity. He points out that while the 'success' of Tanzania is expressed in the language of economics, the experience of structural adjustment is expressed by Tanzanians as one of spiralling poverty and individual uncertainty. And it is here that the market and the occult meet in that space of anxiety.

The anxiety that accompanies structural adjustment incorporates Western economic rationalism into the occult, precisely because the occult refers to many across Africa simply to the 'invisible' realm of social existence that is no less consequential than the 'real' 'visible' material world. He documents how the Ihanzu of Tanzania, like many people across Africa, divide their world into the manifest, visible world and the occult realm of the unseen, namely, that of witchcraft, ancestral spirits and god. These two realms, though distinct, are seen as connected insofar as the visible world is animated by the unseen forces of the invisible world.

However, because the unseen world is by definition inaccessible, there can be no definitive evidence of how exactly the unseen world is determining that of the material world. As Sanders points out, the result of this is that the operation of power between these two realms remains deeply ambivalent. The imposition of this capricious and invisible 'free' market thus becomes a particularly suggestive case of the unseen world directing the material world in a wildly unpredictable manner – for while a few get absurdly rich, others remain or become more impoverished. And it is this that ensures that the imposition of Western-led economic rationalism, far from stemming the power of the occult, instead revitalises it.

Sanders concludes that the answer to the fascination with human skins does not lie in some stubborn inability, on the part of Africans, to discard primitive superstition but lies rather in the magical workings of the 'free' market itself, where even its name denies the widening condition of 'unfreedom' that is produced by its presence:

> Why, just now, has human skin trading to occult ends so captured the Tanzanian popular imagination? ... the answer is surprisingly straightforward. 'Why not?', lamented one elderly Ihanzu woman, 'there are no limits to what people will do these days for money'. No limits indeed – which brings us to the crux of the matter. Tanzanians' frenzied musings over the marketing of human skins for wealth production are, I submit, musings over the (il)logical conclusion of unbridled liberalization – a world where *everything* is commodified through and through, a world where society, culture, history and humanity itself have fallen victim to the caprices of The Market. At issue here is 'a fear of the creeping commodification of life itself ... a relentless process that erodes the inalienable humanity of persons and renders them susceptible as never before to the long reach of the market ... These skins, corporal tropes of sorts, are being traded to far-off transnational places to the benefit of a few, at the expense of the many.[42]

Here, Sanders provides his own example of anthropological theory rendering the 'unfamiliar other' familiar, whilst recasting the obviously real as unfamiliar. Those who cite the free-market model as one that epitomises rationalism are revealed to be every bit as much dependent on metaphysics and superstition, as those who believe in the power of the occult.

Unlike Marxist theory, which posits capitalist rationalism as providing the exploited with the visible means to counter their oppression, this theory moves to collapse the differences between the supposedly primitive peoples of Africa with those of modern citizens in the West. Modernity, in this reading, is a decidedly universal experience even if modernity itself takes on a bewildering variety of forms. The African continent is, in this sense not awaiting the arrival of modernity but is living through it, only in different ways to those in the West. By rejecting Marxist teleology Moore and Sanders are able to incorporate difference without any accompanying suggestion of a difference in humanity:

> Since modernity has not led to the wholesale convergence of societies and cultures, it is plain that there is nothing particularly 'natural' or inevitable about it. Modernity is not simply the logical outcome of an inevitable unfolding of structures and ideas. Rather, modernity turns out to have been cultural all along. The notion of multiple modernities, then, is useful 'to remind ourselves that our pretended rationalist discourse is pronounced in a particular cultural dialect – that "we are one of the others"' (Sahlins 1993). It allows us to problematize modernity: to see it as a deeply cultural project, to treat its claims to rationality not as natural, universal truths but as particular discourses about truth that require explanation.[43]

Whereas before Africa was placed firmly outside the history of the West, here it is incorporated into 'Western' history it and with that inclusion comes another set of problems. For unfortunately, the entirely laudable desire to challenge the supposed differences between the West and the non-West runs the risk of ignoring or underestimating the extent to which the global 'we' masks particular exclusions and inequalities. In other words, the radical gesture of posting a 'we' and a world in which 'we are all others' is also the potentially dangerous one of overlooking the differences in cultural and economic power that complicate this 'we'.

For Moore and Sanders, the potential danger is more one of retaining the 'other' as a different being which is what leads them to consider not so much opposition to free market capitalism as the non-Western world's ambivalence towards it:

> Could it be that anthropologists are telling a popular liberal tale through 'others' and, in the process inadvertently reinscribing the

very 'us' – 'them' dichotomies we seek to dismantle? It seems most unlikely that, in all the cases and places, people are resisting or critiquing the technologies and conveniences of modernization, and they are certainly not shy of the capitalist relations needed to acquire them. Instead, what many are after 'is the indigenization of modernity, their own cultural space in the global scheme of things' (Sahlins 1999). In the end we need to pay close attention to witchcraft in specific social settings and historical settings rather than assume monolithic meanings. In rightly dismissing one of modernity's central master narratives – that of unilinear progress – we should not be duped into uncritically accepting another (Englund and Leach 2000).[44]

The problem here is that the terms 'we' and 'them' are deceptively complex and to reduce their discussion to a question of whether we are using them to denote similarity or difference is to replicate the very tradition of Western Cartesian rationalism that Moore and Sanders are attempting to undercut. A more productive move would surely be to accept that there is not a stable 'us' and 'them' in need of theoretical clarification but rather political solidarities that cut across national and racial divisions. In other words, the class, race, gender and national 'differences' that the dominant order maintains in order to safeguard beneficial foundations for the division of labour and concentration of profits are not differences that everyone either in the West or the non-West accept. Put simply, sometimes there is a 'we' that connects the West and the non-West, whether as ruling elites or as oppressed majorities, and when that happens 'they' are *our* national counterparts.

Moreover, because Moore and Sanders' investigation of Africa pivots on the experience of modernity, which even if it is global now was certainly not global prior to colonisation, then any assertion of similarity is inevitably a similarity that places the Western subject first and *then* includes the African subject in the frame. In other words, refusing to approach Africa as an alien continent, however progressive it may be in intention, does not and cannot in itself solve the problem of economic inequality. Indeed, it is the very emphasis upon similarity that exposes the crucial differences between the West and the non-West – ones that cannot be solved by philosophical egalitarianism alone. Sahlins' bland evocation of a world of others is problematic precisely because it suggests that a global 'we' can be discovered or posited when it would be more accurate to conclude that a global 'we'

needs to be created: one that can oppose and undo the dominant world order. In short, there is not a stable 'we' residing out there that can be marshalled against a history of racism and imperialism, but rather a 'we' that is being tenaciously built against another 'we' of global patriarchal and corporate power.

Nevertheless, the efforts of contemporary anthropologists to rethink the Marxist distinction between the peoples of the West and the non-West constitute a valuable corrective to the ethnocentrism underlying Marxist historiography. However, if the relation between European Marxist theory and the peoples and intellectuals of the non-West have proved to be problematic then so too does its proposed relation between the working classes and revolutionary intellectuals. And it is to this relationship that we will now return.

7
Proletariats and Urban Intellectuals

Marx ruminated upon the role and character of the proletariat in his scathing criticism of the German social classes where he contrasted the political idealism of the French classes with the dull parochialism of their German counterparts.[1] For Marx, it was the lack of ambition and passion on the part of all the German classes that prevented them from sharing the drama of class struggle that was evident in France, where:

> every class of the population is *politically idealistic* and considers itself first of all, not as a particular class, but as the representative of the general needs of society. The role of *liberator* can therefore pass successively in a dramatic movement to different classes in the population, until it finally reaches the class which achieves social freedom.[2]

It was through his distinction between the universalising ambitions of the French classes and the uninspiring 'modest egoism'[3] of their German counterparts that Marx produced his definition of the proletariat. The proletariat is introduced as a transformative agent whose sole purpose is to destroy the entire ruling political system and replace it with one that is no longer predicated upon economic inequality:

> There must be formed a sphere of society which claims no *traditional* status but only a *human* status, a sphere which is not opposed to particular consequences but is totally opposed to the assumption of the German political system, a sphere finally which cannot emancipate itself without emancipating itself from all the other spheres of society, without therefore emancipating all the other spheres, which

is, in short, a *total loss* of humanity and which can only redeem itself by a *total redemption of humanity*. This dissolution of society, as a particular class, is the *proletariat*. (emphasis in the original)[4]

The proletariat, then, exists as the inevitable casualty of capitalism whose losses are so comprehensive and profound as to make the only possible desire to be one of destroying the bourgeois capitalist system. Moreover, because capitalism itself has created this desire on the part of the proletariat to destroy its own living conditions, this signals not simply the end of capitalism but the end of the proletariat. This joint expiry of the proletariat and capitalism returns humanity to an original historical unity that is produced by *both* the growing political consciousness of the proletariat and the growing instability of the capitalist economic system. And it is this conflation of the proletariat with history that enables Marx to credit his history with the imprint of 'real men'; a claim that is unfortunately constantly undercut by his emphasis upon the working classes themselves as wholly alienated beings. Consequently, Marx's emphasis upon the denial of humanity *to* the proletariat does not prevent the implications of the proletariat as a class that *lacks* humanity.

However, for Marx's purposes the crucial point is that the proletariat's *only* experience is deprivation and loss so that existence becomes *all* that it has. The proletariat, stripped of any connection to the freedoms and profits that the bourgeoisie acquires for itself, is forced to live *without* any of the conditions for a humane and productive life. And because the proletariat cannot pursue a productive life under capitalism it follows that she can only attain a meaningful life in a different time to that of the present. Thus, the proletariat 'lives' in order to demonstrate to *others* that for human beings material existence alone does not constitute 'life'.

For, the proletariat's exclusive materiality is precisely what causes its comprehensive alienation – deprived as it is from any chance of making intellectual sense of its conditions and experiences. As such, the proletarian rejection of capitalism is not based on political analysis but springs from an experience more akin to filial despair. This informs Marx's attribution of emotional self-interested protest to the proletariat in the early stages of its development where it operates as a nihilistic and obscure entity representing the increasingly visible cost of bourgeois capitalism.

The problem is that the proletariat is assigned the task of ushering in a new and humane society even as she is defined as that class which has

experienced nothing but alienation and misery. Indeed, in Marx's reading, under bourgeois capitalism the proletariat as a viable human subject is categorically absent, since to exist in the present necessitates some degree of compatibility with bourgeois capitalist society. But, the proletariat functioning as the 'negative' representative of the present order cannot be a subject until she has destroyed both herself and the accompanying capitalist system. In other words, the implications of granting the proletariat a passion for the final and universal emancipation of humankind is that she cannot achieve this whilst functioning as a credible human subject.

However, for Marx, the fact that the proletariat is essentially an instrument for radical change and as such cannot be theorised as an actual human subject is of little import. Consequently, *what* the proletariat is, is far more crucial a matter than what the proletariat *thinks* herself to be, as Marx makes clear:

> It is not a matter of knowing what this or that proletarian, or even the proletarian as a whole, conceives as its aims at any particular moment. It is a question of knowing what the proletariat is, and what it must historically accomplish in accordance with its nature. Its aims and historical activity are ordained for it, in a tangible and irrevocable way, by its own situation as well as by the whole organization of present-day civil society.[5]

Indeed, since conscious recognition of their condition and its wider implications, *by the proletariats*, would effectively undercut Marx's attribution of wholesale alienation *to the proletariat*, then actual understanding of what the proletariat is must occur elsewhere. Meanwhile, for the proletariat the truth of their existence and the conditions in which they live are better understood to be a matter of some mystery.

This attribution of obscurity and secrecy to the consciousness of the masses as to their real interests informs Negt and Kluge's reading of capitalist society[6] and underlies Adorno's reference to the proletariats' 'secret rejection'[7] of capitalism. Of course, for every secret there is a detective, and in the case of the proletariat it is Marx who is able to explain the proletariat's words and actions:

> When the proletariat announces the dissolution of the existing social order, it only declares *the secret of its own existence*, for it constitutes the effective dissolution of this order. When the proletariat demands the negation of private property it only lays down as a principle for

society what society has already made a principle for the proletariat and what the latter *involuntarily* embodies already is as the negative result of society. (my emphasis)[8]

Significantly, the proletariat springs to life only *after* her political education at the hands of the socialist and communist theoreticians:

Just as philosophy finds its material weapons in the proletariat, so the proletariat finds its intellectual weapons in philosophy. And once the *lightning of thought* has penetrated deeply into this *virgin soil of the people* the Germans will emancipate themselves and become men. (my emphasis)[9]

Consequently, what distinguishes the socialist and communist theoretician from the proletariat is her location in time insofar as she gleans the truth of proletarian existence before they do. And if Hegel's philosopher arrives *after* the event (i.e. after the material world) grandly bypassing history and people in order to arrive at universal conclusions,[10] Marx reads history in order to anticipate the future. Marxist theory, in other words, lays claim to an insight into the passage of time and history that, because it is grounded upon the 'soil' of the people and material reality in general, can simultaneously reject metaphysical speculation whilst claiming the right to know what it is that history 'ordains' the future to be. Consequently, presenting the economic relations of humanity as the prosaic foundations for human history and development does not prevent the socialist and communist theoretician from ascending into the realm of speculation.

The proletariat under the management of the theoreticians gradually learns that her condition is not accidental, inevitable or desirable but one that *no* human being should experience. Thus, the proletarian begins 'life' as a unconscious subject, mere material matter, proceeds to acquire sight and in the process wills the abolition of herself and the society that has made her. In other words, the proletarian *never* finds anything in her existence or consciousness that she would want to retain and so experiences *and* ultimately comprehends herself to be a subject that is, and should be, an impossibility:

The contradiction between the personality of the individual proletarian and the condition of life imposed on him, his labour, becomes evident to himself. For he ... has no opportunity of achieving within his own class the conditions which would place him in another class. ...

the proletarians, if they are to achieve recognition as persons, will be obliged to abolish their own former conditions of existence, which are at the same time those of society as a whole, that is, to abolish labour. They are, consequently, in direct opposition to the State as the form in which the members of society have so far found their collective expression, and *in order to develop as persons they must overthrow the State.* (my emphasis)[11]

By introducing a distinction between materiality and personhood, Marx effectively utilises the proletariat as a symbol of humanity rather than as a human subject. The slippage between society and the proletariat occurs precisely because the proletariat of Marxist theory is the unconscious embodiment of a *different* society; present in capitalism only as the evolving foundation for a new society. The proletariat, even as she labours under capitalist society, lives in a different time to that of the bourgeois capitalist and the socialist and communist theoreticians. However, the proletariat is supplemented by the theoretical solidarity of the socialist and communist theoreticians who are determined to create a society in which the proletariat can at last become a subject.

The question and the problem that Marx raises here is one of finding a way to both distinguish and connect the socialist and communist theoreticians from the proletarian class with which they are aligned (and from which many emerge). Marx himself, as with the proletariat, is less concerned with *where* the theorists come from than with *what* the theorists are. Thus, the history of the socialist and communist theoreticians is not one that traces their location so much as their evolution from utopians to revolutionaries:

Just as the economists are the scientific representatives of the bourgeoisie, so the socialists and communists are the theorists of the proletariat. As long as the proletariat is not sufficiently developed to constitute itself into a class, as long therefore as the struggle of the proletariat with the bourgeoisie has not acquired a political character, and while the productive forces are not yet sufficiently developed, within bourgeois society itself, to give an indication of the material conditions necessary for the emancipation of the proletariat and the constitution of a new society, these theorists remain Utopians who, in order to remedy the distress of the oppressed classes, improvise systems and pursue a regenerative science. But as history continues, and as *the struggle of the proletariat takes shape more clearly, they have*

no further need to look for a science in their own minds; they have only to observe what is happening before their eyes, and to make themselves its vehicle of expression. (my emphasis) [12]

For Marx the question of *how* the theorist/intellectual acquires her advanced insight is one that can be answered relatively simply: she acquires it through her active involvement with working-class struggle which transforms her introspective analysis into a supposedly simple translation of what she sees before her. Interestingly, Marx did not conclude that the very obviousness of history and of working class struggle might make the theorist redundant well *before* the actual transition into communism. Instead, by retaining the notion of the theorists as those who 'express' who and what is before them, Marx effectively postpones any termination of the theorists until after the defeat of capitalism and thus retains a distinction between the theorists and the working classes even as he indicates that the realm of speculation, idealism and material reality are speeding ever closer together.

Theorists, such as Gramsci and Negt and Kluge, who succeeded Marx and drew upon his prescriptions were not surprisingly quick to accord themselves the ability to see what the proletariat by definition could not. Negt and Kluge focused in particular upon the ability of the theorist to 'see' with greater acuity than the masses and like Marx insisted that such observational skill needed to be directed toward the liberation of the working classes if it were to be of any use in the material world. This sense of intellectual usefulness being entirely dependent upon its alignment and commitment with the working classes led Negt and Kluge to restate Adorno's celebration of intellectuals as those whose labour was of no benefit for bourgeois capitalism.[13]

Negt, Kluge and Adorno's ready admission of their own inability to serve the interests of bourgeois capitalism was advanced in order to secure a connection between intellectual labour and radical politics; one that happily assented to being disinterested and superfluous to the needs of bourgeois capitalism. Thus all three theorists celebrated evidence of imagination and creativity in artistic production, arguing that they are only deemed to be pointless because bourgeois notions of culture with their commitment to economic rationalism have no hope of understanding the expression of freedom, imagination and truth. Negt and Kluge concluded that rather than viewing intellectual labour as irrelevant we should recognise that it is *only* irrelevant to bourgeois rationalism. In other words, its very superflousness to the capitalist-economic system is, in fact, the reason why it is so vital to a different

political system. Thus, what exists as merely 'indirectly' useful labour can become, if immersed into the 'experiential content of the working class', vitally relevant. Such a claim is, of course, dependent upon the persuasiveness of their original definition of intellectual labour as antagonistic to the needs of bourgeois capitalism.

It is precisely this myth of intellectual abstraction from the material world that has enabled the issue of intellectual labour to be viewed on much of the Western radical left as merely one of *finding* a social and political use for intellectual labour. Unfortunately this task has not been accompanied by any equivalent attention to the issue of why intellectual labour can comfortably serve the dominant culture. For, contrary to Adorno and his followers, it seems to me that the material 'uselessness' of artistic/intellectual production (and parallel implied aesthetic usefulness) conceals its material purpose which is to reinforce notions that the class divide, for the most part, merely reflects the natural division of a higher sensibility and intelligence in society. In short, the very existence of 'intellectuals' affirms that society as a whole cannot be described as an intellectual society.

For Gramsci it was not finding a use for intellectual labour that was the issue since, for him, intellectuals were intimately connected to their specific social class in society. Thus, when it comes to defining what it is that differentiates the intellectual from the rest of humankind, Gramsci suggests that, rather than citing the possession of higher sensibilities, we should attend instead to their material location in society:

> What are the 'maximum' limits of acceptance of the term 'intellectual'? Can one find a unitary criterion to characterise equally all the diverse and disparate activities of intellectuals and to distinguish these at the same time and in an essential way from the activities of other social groupings? The most widespread error of method seems to me that of having looked for this criterion of distinction in the intrinsic nature of intellectual activities, rather than in the ensemble of the system of relations in which these activities (and therefore intellectual groups who personify them) have their place within the general complex of social relations ... All men are intellectuals, one could therefore say: but not all men have in society the function of intellectuals.[14]

By connecting intellectuals to their specific class backgrounds, Gramsci avoids Negt and Kluge's problematical depiction of intellectuals as

possessing a crucial degree of autonomy from social and political structures. And if Negt and Kluge view this autonomy as prompting the intellectual to immerse herself in the proletarian public sphere, Gramsci moves in precisely the opposite direction – tracing the material contexts of specific intellectuals back to the class from which they emerged.

In Gramsci's reading, intellectuals are the product of developing class relations and express the consciousness and interests of their specific class. Furthermore intellectuals are directly connected to the development of society itself towards ever more complex forms of knowledge and organisation. 'Traditional' intellectuals are, in this sense, displaced by the intellectuals that succeed them as the 'deputies' of the different social groups that emerge from the changes in the economic base. Moreover, by drawing attention to those 'crystallised' intellectuals who despite their class origin insist upon clinging to traditional norms and values he avoids depicting intellectuals as a homogenous category, entirely reducible to their economic position. For Gramsci, the allegiances of intellectuals with their social class are crucial to the establishment of social and political hegemony. Bourgeois intellectuals, in other words, provide the capitalist state apparatus with the intellectual support and sanction necessary to exercise power. Drawing upon Marx's reading of civil society as essential to the exercise of state power, Gramsci too brings cultural and political power together:

> The relationship between the intellectuals and the world of production is not as direct as it is with fundamental social groups but is, in varying degrees, 'mediated' by the whole fabric of society and by the complex of superstructures of which the intellectuals are, precisely the 'functionaries'.[15]

Gramsci's rejection of the independence of intellectual labour and his insistence that it is grounded in politics and ideology has pleased many commentators[16] who cite his organic intellectual as the correct answer to the argument that intellectual labour has no relation to or basis in politics. Moreover, unlike Negt and Kluge, Gramsci emphasises that intellectual labour is fundamentally universal – since all 'men' think – providing, some would say, further evidence that his theory is the proper antidote to elitist ideas of intellectual difference.

However, while Gramsci's intellectual engages in the universal human occupation of thought and is located in the material contexts of class relations, his resultant skills are, as he emphasises, anything but ordinary. Certainly, replacing the 'dilettantism' of idealist philosophy with an

intellectual equipped with 'historical sense' is no small replacement. Consequently, when it comes to outlining what skills the intellectual possesses by virtue of his economic and social position, we are presented with a figure more impressive than any enlightenment philosopher could ever dream of:

> The professional or technical philosopher does not only 'think' with greater logical rigour, with greater coherence, with more systematic sense than do other men, but he knows the entire history of thought. In other words, he is capable of accounting for the development of thought up to his own day and he is in a position where he can take up a problem from the point which it has reached after having undergone every previous attempt at a solution. He has the same function in the field of thought that specialists have in their various scientific fields. However, there is a difference between the specialised philosopher and other specialists which is that the specialist philosopher is much more similar to the rest of mankind than are other specialists.[17]

Thus, Gramsci, taking his cue from Marx, concludes that since man is history then clearly 'historical sense' is crucial if we are to understand where history is leading us. The intellectual as the mediator between 'man' and 'history' does not transcend humanity in order to express his difference but rather understands the *grounds* of humanity better than anyone else. So we could add that, although all men are historical not all men have in society the function of historians. This recruitment of emphatically material contexts for intellectual labour provides Gramsci, as it did for Marx, with the mandate for a transcendence that occurs by a *descent* into the material world rather than by an escape from it.

Gramsci's intellectual is one who employs a universal human practice (thought) but, by virtue of his position in society, does so with greater perspicacity than other people. Such an intellectual in his simultaneous possession of human commonality and difference echoes Marx's description of production as both common to humanity and an indication of the differential development of humanity across the globe. Gramsci's intellectual as such acts as a two-way mirror, simultaneously embracing 'humanity' whilst operating as an elite and highly developed section of it. And in a familiar philosophical move the most urgent and advanced skill is simultaneously 'common' to humanity whilst being present only in a few. Not surprisingly, this possession of a unique aptitude for a universal human practice, far from making the

intellectual less impressive than those who possess particular technical or scientific skills, gives it greater power and significance. For, by understanding history intellectuals prove that they are aligned to the collective concerns of humanity:

> One could also say that the nature of man is 'history ... human nature' cannot be located in any particular man but in the entire history of the human species.[18]

Significantly, the intellectual by demonstrating an ability to know history also demonstrates that those who are not intellectuals do not possess this knowledge. This denial of proletarian historical consciousness is thus revealed to be as intimately connected to the definition of intellectual labour as it is to the brutality of capitalist society. In short, Gramsci confirms that even radical intellectuals are indispensable for confirming the blindness of the masses.

Consequently, Gramsci, in the same way as Negt and Kluge, identifies the task facing intellectuals as principally one of organisation and clarification. In Negt and Kluge's account, while the proletariat may possess 'experience', it is left to the intellectuals to appropriate it and liberate us all from the tyranny of economic bourgeois rationalism:

> The proletarian public sphere is the aggregate of situations in which this human sensuality, which has been repressed and which has emerged distorted in relation to capital, comes into its own, in a process of subject-object relationships that are linked together, proletarian public sphere is the name for a process of collective social production whose object is a coherent human sensuality.[19]

The problem is that, despite Negt and Kluge's professed esteem for human experience and the proletarian public sphere as the repository of that experience, there remains a troubling lack of clarity surrounding how it is that the intellectuals interpret and organise these experiences. The chasm between the intellectuals and the proletarians is realised by their allusion to a 'coherent human sensuality', whereby the vibrancy of the proletarian public sphere is abruptly locked into place. Such a project depends upon their highly questionable proposition that the intellectual should be viewed as someone who is uniquely able to organise and interpret the proletarian public sphere because she lacks any conflicting experiences of her own. What is proposed here, of course, is that the appropriation of intellectual expertise does not amount to

the accumulation of any kind of experience. But, as Pierre Bourdieu points out, such a reading of the intellectual apprenticeship fails to notice that the very assumption of an incommensurable divide between the mind and the body amounts to nothing less than the *experience* of being, or becoming an intellectual.[20] Bourdieu's reminder that intellectuals themselves are deeply implicated in the hierarchical split between the mind and the body undermines arguments that posit the existence of 'intellectual disinterest' and insist upon the corporeality of 'the people'.

Not surprisingly, positing such an emphatic distinction between the 'people' and the intellectuals complicates any progressive attempts to outline what our collective interests and experiences might be. For in Negt and Kluge's account, the proletarians, in direct contrast to the intellectuals, cannot exhibit any sign of individuality or specificity since they are the site of collective human experience, while the intellectual cannot allow herself to fully submerge herself into the collective experiences of the proletarian sphere, otherwise she would be unable to organise the experiences inside it into 'coherence'. At the same time, it is *only* by maintaining the notion of the proletarians as a collective and the intellectuals as individuals that authentic collective man himself can hope to exist, since he is the synthesis of these two opposing realms. In short, what has to remain in place in order for the intellectual to retain her political purity is a definitive distance between what the proletarian public sphere is and what the intellectual task is.

If Negt and Kluge fail to explain *how* exactly the intellectual sifts through the experiences of the proletarian public sphere Gramsci, by contrast, is keen to outline precisely how such intellectual labor should proceed. Gramsci, like Negt and Kluge, also regards the ability to organise experience as the specific contribution of the intellectuals towards radical historical change. But while Negt and Kluge locate the organisational skills of the intelligentsia inside the bourgeois educational arenas, Gramsci locates them in the far broader terrain of world history.

In Gramsci's reading, intellectuals can provide an objective appraisal of not just their own class interests but perhaps more importantly the interests of the other classes and thus provide their contemporaries with the means for political consciousness. For without the guidance of the intellectuals' 'practical man', as an active subject, can affect history but will remain ignorant of the implications and significance of his own activity:

> The active man-in-the-mass has a practical activity, but has no clear theoretical consciousness of his practical activity, which nonetheless

involves understanding the world in so far as it transforms it. one might almost say that he has two theoretical consciousness (or one contradictory consciousness): one which is implicit in his activity and which in reality unites him with all his fellow-workers in the practical transformation of the real world; and one superficially explicit or verbal, which he has inherited from the past and *uncritically absorbed.* (my emphasis)[21]

Gramsci asserts that although the intellectuals provide the members of their class with the tools for breaking free from the ideological underpinnings of their own class, such unified class knowledge is nevertheless essential for the progression of history. Accordingly, 'History' requires the classes to operate without a universal, or even general, consciousness of their own significance, since such political awareness would undermine, if not destroy the hegemony that the 'class system' itself depends upon. Thus, even as the intellectual labours to undo the hegemony that obscures the broader significance of the class system this same hegemony constitutes the grounds for the orderly progression into the next historical phase:

It must be stressed that the political development of the concept of hegemony represents a great philosophical advance as well as a politico-practical one.[22]

As in Marx, it is the very critical simplicity of the class divide under capitalism that ensures that a revolutionary future can only be one that seeks to overthrow the entire class system. Communism as the negation of the capitalist social and political order is the product of two historical developments: capitalism and the broader underlying progression of humanity into a society that rejects every practical and ideological capitalist dogma. However these two contexts are not so much oppositional historical currents as currents that the intellectuals are destined to bring together in the form of critical analysis, thus aligning intellectuals to the higher consciousness of World History and the rest of society to active participation in that history.

This division of historical significance and function between the intellectuals and the masses is one that Gramsci urges us to view as both natural and essential to the development of humankind:

Critical self-consciousness means, historically and politically, the creation of an *elite* of intellectuals.[23]

Communism becomes the product of struggle in which the intellectuals and the masses are *equally* important since they represent the sum of human society itself – namely its brain and its heart. Past societies are thus rendered legible by the evolution of both the masses and the intellectuals who, while permanently out of step nevertheless *together* shift society forward:

> A human mass does not 'distinguish' itself, does not become independent in its own right without in the widest sense organising itself; and there is no organisation without intellectuals, that is without organisers and leaders, in other words, without the theoretical aspect of the theory-practice nexus being distinguished concretely by the existence of a group of people 'specialized; in conceptual and philosophical elaboration of ideas ... innovation cannot come from the masses, at least in the beginning, except through the mediation of an elite for whom the conception implicit in human activity has already become to a certain degree a coherent and systematic ever-present awareness and a precise and decisive will.[24]

This confident recruitment of a hierarchal divide between the masses and intellectuals, that is based merely upon the *natural* occurrence of individuals with particular powers of observation, organisation and perception and the equally *natural* existence of 'masses' who lack these skills transforms, or perhaps more accurately displaces, the traditional ideas of intellectual distinction from the naturalism of the bourgeois viewpoint into the naturalism of the historical narrative of Marxism.

Gramsci's removal of intellectual ability from 'the people' is what enables him to delineate exactly how they can be taught to transform their experience into knowledge, or more specifically 'political consciousness'. In accordance with his conception of the simplicity of the masses it follows that any program of education should eschew complex methods and adopt instead the more effective methods of repetitive slogans and propaganda. Thus, he concludes that all new cultural movements never tire of repetition indicating that 'repetition is the best didactic means for working on the popular mentality.'[25] But since the working classes and their intellectual deputies also constitute a higher development of all that has previously occurred it follows that unlike other cultural movements, this one proceeds on the understanding that the people's 'simplicity' is a condition that can be changed.

Consequently, alongside the need to instil the truths of Marxism to the populace Gramsci also insists that intellectuals devote themselves to

the intellectual uplift of the people. His depiction of the intellectuals as the 'whalebone in the corset' reflects the mutual dependency between the intellectuals and the masses both for legibility and even for existence. The intellectuals, in this sense, must serve the people because, in the final analysis, that *is* what defines intellectual existence and labour. Thus, intellectuals must

> work incessantly to raise the intellectual level of ever-growing strata of the populace, in other words to give a personality to the amorphous mass element. This means working to produce *elites* of intellectuals in a new type which arise directly out of the masses, but remain in contact with them to become, as it were, the whalebone in the corset ... But these elites cannot be formed or develop without a hierarchy of authority and intellectual competence growing up within them, the culmination of this process can be a great individual philosopher. But he must be capable of re-living concretely the demands of the massive ideological community and of understanding that this cannot have the flexibility of movement proper to an individual brain, and must succeed in giving formal elaboration to the collective doctrine in the most relevant fashion and the one most suited to the modes of thought of a collective thinker.[26]

In other words, the intellectuals ascend from the people in order to think as and for them all. And historical progress depends upon the stable reproduction of an original distinction between the leaders and the led.

For Gramsci the relation between the working classes as material subjects and the intellectuals as thinking subjects was one that owed its existence both to history and nature. The crucial intersections between history, nature and 'man' were ones that Gramsci, like Marx, attempted to assemble in accordance with scientific methods and principles. Consequently, elites and great individual philosophers are the result of a natural organic progression on the part of the masses since they 'grow' from them *and* are the necessary condition for any such development to take place. Accordingly, this distinction between the leaders and the people is itself the impetus for political change since they 'act' together as different parts of the collective organism of 'man'.

The proletariat is – as it is for Negt and Kluge – the bodily site of history and experience while the intellectual is the mind that interprets and organises that experience and history. Thus, the individual philosopher equipped with 'historical sense' is a collective thinker because he

has recognised his origins and dependency upon 'his' (or more accurately the worker's) body. Of course, this appropriation of the worker's body as constituting the authentic material history of humanity conceals the fact that the intellectual's body mysteriously vanishes from the scene. Ironically, Gramsci's insistence upon the need for intellectuals to connect their labour to the material conditions of existence absolves them of the need to pay any attention at all to their own materiality.

While for liberal commentators like Appiah and Gutmann[27] the individual expresses her uniqueness and extraordinary difference from the majority of people, for materialists like Gramsci the elite leaders and individuals are unique precisely because they are able to exceed the confines of individuality and live and think as and for the people. This formulation enables Gramsci to abolish the difference that he has created between the elites and the people by giving his leaders the power to live and think collectively.

Significantly, while Gramsci includes the idea of change and growth in all individuals, the problem remains that the 'changing' social relations that promote this development on the part of the individual are curiously devoid of any sense of movement. For, the changing social relations that Gramsci identifies as the crucial impetus for the development of our collective history, are the very ones that refuse any notion of change to the relations between intellectuals and the people. Thus, any shift in social relations is always dependent upon the intellectuals for their transmission to the people. Consequently, without intellectuals there would be no change in social relations because there would be no awareness on the part of the people that anything had changed much less what these changes actually signified.

It is this belief in the natural, or more accurately the 'historical', distinction between the roles of intellectuals and the people that *in itself* forms the basis for their coalition (or 'historical bloc') that leads Gramsci to insist upon the indissoluble divide between the popular mentality and the intellectual's historical sense. The quality of our 'collective life' becomes, as it does for Negt and Kluge, wholly reliant upon a reading of the people and intellectuals that insists upon a permanent difference. Thus, 'collective man' is only possible if we recognise the need for unity which can, of course, only occur if we accept the original distinction that is proposed between thinking and non-thinking subjects.

The contrast between the breadth of the intellectual's knowledge and the starkness of her task (dissemination of her knowledge to the people) is both striking and absolute. For it is by focusing his attention solely

upon the urgent need for the intellectuals to *share* their knowledge that Gramsci is able to entirely circumvent any suggestion that intellectuals may also learn *from* the masses. Moreover, it is precisely this strict exclusion of the masses from possessing any counter knowledge that enables Gramsci to attribute his advanced intellectuals with egalitarian credentials:

> For a mass of people to be led to think coherently and in the same coherent fashion about the real present world is a 'philosophical' event far more important and 'original' than the discovery by some philosophical genius of a truth which remains the property of a small group of intellectuals.[28]

As Gramsci makes clear, the emergence (or occurrence) of elites is not a development that is destined to herald an unequal society but instead the necessary precondition for a thoroughly egalitarian society.

For Gramsci the political party enables the distinctions between the intellectuals and 'the popular element' to constitute an alliance. Rather than a distant bureaucratic party out of touch with the people who it claims to represent, Gramsci recommends, instead, one that is fully aware of the need for a synthesis of the experiential (proletarian) and theoretical (intellectual) realms. 'Collective man' emerges as the product of a synthesis between the divided body parts of individual man:

> With the extension of mass parties and their organic coalescence with the intimate (economic-productive) life of the masses themselves, the process whereby popular feeling is standardised ceases to be mechanical and casual (that is produced by the conditioning of environmental factors and the like) and become conscious and critical ... In this way a close link is formed between great mass, party and leading group; and the whole complex, thus articulated, can move together as 'collective man'.[29]

In the same way as Negt and Kluge, Gramsci's identification of experience and the material world as the correct starting point for any discussion of humanity culminates in a description of material, 'collective man' that is rooted in the discourses of science, philology and anatomy. The resultant depiction of collective man as a giant organism (or machine) is one that has in true enlightenment style dissected the body of the people in order to reassemble it in accordance with history. Collective man emerges as a hybrid form – partly natural and partly man-made – in

other words, as the authentic symbol of the unification between theory and praxis that humanity *will be* when the intellectuals have successfully ignited the material bodies of the people.

The urgency behind Gramsci's prescriptions for intellectual labour and the role of the political party reflect the particular historical moment that he was living in. His passionate appeals to radical intellectuals to immerse themselves in the class struggle were formulated in the context of the fractured and divisive debates that were paralysing the Italian left as Mussolini rose to power.[30] For Gramsci, the fate of 'collective man' hinged upon the ability of intellectuals to connect their labour to the emancipation of the exploited workers and rural poor in Italy. Interestingly, despite Gramsci's focus upon the workers as the group most in need of organisation and clarity, it was in fact the Marxist intellectuals who consistently proved to be unable or unwilling to agree upon unified aims and policies. Consequently, although Gramsci depicted the intellectuals as uniquely equipped to bring order and purpose to the masses this could hardly have been based upon his own experience of working with (for) the Italian Communist Party (PCI) throughout the fractured and chaotic 1920s. Certainly, it is tempting to read his evocation of a tightly organised union between the masses and the communist leaders as one that was inspired by the actual failure of the Italian *intellectual* left to achieve unity and the ferocious expansion of fascist control over Italy.

For Gramsci, the electrifying union between the masses and the revolutionary vanguard was destined to be a dream that he elaborated upon while he endured his final imprisonment for state treason. For Victor Serge, on the other hand, it was an event that took place in Russia in 1917, one which prompted him to return to Russia and serve the revolution. Serge's initial reading of the Bolshevik Party was celebratory; he regarded the party in 1917 as 'the conscious instrument of the masses' and argued that

> the October revolution offers almost the perfect model of the proletarian party. Relatively few as they may be, its militants live with the masses and among them. Long and testing years ... have given it excellent activists and real leaders, whose parallel thinking was strengthened in collective action.[31]

Serge, like Gramsci, envisaged the genuinely proletarian party to be one that operated with the fluid mutuality of a biological organism. And while he stopped short of entirely collapsing the differences between

social groups and biological organisms, he nevertheless retained the crucial faculty of sight for those situated at the cerebral end of the organism:

> Within the party, the relationship between the mass of militants and the leadership may be compared to that obtaining between the working masses and the party itself. The party is the nervous system of the working class, its brain. The leaders and key members perform the role of brain and nervous system within the organism of the party also ... however politically conscious they may be, the rank and file of the party is unable to get to know the situation as a whole. Whatever, the personal worth of these comrades they must inevitably lack information, liaison, training and the revolutionary theoretical and professional preparation, if they are not within that core of party members who have been selected and tried by long years of struggle and work, enjoy the goodwill of the movement as a whole, have access to the apparatus of the party, and are accustomed to thinking and working collectively.[32]

This allusion to the unity of the workers and the revolutionary vanguard as together comprising an anatomical whole, with the intellectuals equipped with the vantage point to see what is ahead of them, connects Serge with Marx and Gramsci. This combined ability to view the full implications of the future and understand the principles upon which it will unfold leads Serge to perform the same synthesis between the intellectuals and the proletarians that occurs in the work of Marx, Gramsci and Negt and Kluge. The product of this synthesis is the expression of the proletariat's real and higher interests and with it the disappearance of the proletariat as a distinct being:

> Proletarian class-consciousness attains its highest expression in the leaders of the organised vanguard of the working class. As personalities they are great only in the measure that they incarnate the masses. In this sense, only they are giants – anonymous giants. In voicing the consciousness of the masses they display a virtue which, for the proletariat is, sheer necessity: a terrible impersonality.[33]

Serge recorded his subsequent disillusionment with the Bolsheviks that culminated in his exile in 1928, in his memoir and in his detailed accounts of the Russian revolution.[34] His criticism of the relation between Marxist theory and practice is arguably all the more compelling because

it is advanced alongside his insistence that the most crucial context for the demise of the revolution lay in the pressure of outside events that facilitated and nurtured the corrosive counter-revolutionary forces within Russia.

Serge is an invaluable 'witness' to the revolution precisely because he criticised it whilst remaining passionately committed to it. Thus, Serge's passionate criticisms of the ruthless secret police (Cheka) and the general outlawing of any innovation from the workers, peasants, and 'dissident' intellectuals, that culminated in the Stalinist purges[35] and above all the increasing fear within the party of any thinking that did not rigorously support the party are always placed alongside the conditions in which the Communists were forced to operate. These conditions ranged from general hostility, the sabotage of progressive initiatives such as nationalisation and food distribution, to the concerted international attempt to overthrow the Soviet regime. As Serge notes

> Alone and confronted by limitless tasks the revolutionaries of Russia have not known a single day in which they did not have to conduct the violent defence of their very right to exist, and that explains a great many things.[36]

Serge's refusal to identify Bolshevism itself as the source of the repression that intensified after 1917 has been noted by commentators such as Peter Sedgwick, who draws attention to Serge's insistence that Bolshevism *could* have created a different future.[37] However, what Sedgwick's distinction between Serge's account and more recent commentaries that identify Bolshevism itself as the source of the repression risk underestimating is, I think, the profound contradiction that Serge detected within not just Bolshevik practice but Marxist theory itself. The tension within Marxism exists in the interplay between its libertarian and egalitarian aims and its reliance upon bourgeois notions of what it is that constitutes 'the popular mentality'. It is a problem that surfaces to devastating incoherence in the concept of 'the dictatorship of the proletariat'.

For Marx, the dictatorship of the proletariat exists primarily as a necessary transitional stage between capitalism and communism; a necessity that enables him to depict it in uncompromising terms:

> Between capitalist and communist society lies the period of the revolutionary transformation of the one into the other. There corresponds

to this also a political transition period in which the State can be nothing but the *revolutionary dictatorship of the proletariat.* (emphasis in the original)[38]

The revolutionary dictatorship of the proletariat interrupts history and functions as the terrible but essential period of transition between capitalism and communism. The logic of Marxist readings of history leaves it no other choice than to grant the proletariat the right to take over the means of production, since it is the class that has been deprived of ownership throughout the period of capitalism. Arguably, the immediate questions that such a concept raises (How long will the revolutionary dictatorship last? What will the vanguard do while the proletariat assumes control of the state apparatus) are nothing compared to the more simple one of accounting for *how* the proletariat is supposed to take over the means of production.

For, the problem is that the socialist and communist theorists and activists depend upon a conception of the proletariat that binds their relation to them in a well-nigh insurmountable hierarchy. This hierarchy occurs most crucially in the difference and distance that is posited between proletarian consciousness and intellectual consciousness. Not surprisingly, the critical moment of revolutionary transformation is fraught with contradictions; for, it is here that the proletariat temporarily takes control and exercises her judgement. The fact that this is only a temporary interval before the dissolution of all social classes does little to indicate *how* exactly the proletariat can assume authority whilst at the same time willing its own dissolution.

This contradictory proposal – that the class that wills its own abolition is the very same class that must, in the interval between capitalism and communism, assume a 'revolutionary dictatorship' of the State is problematic precisely because the proletariat has been so definitively placed into a different time to that of the bourgeois capitalists and the socialist and communist theoreticians. More precisely, what has been denied to the proletariat is any sense of existence in the present. For a subject whose existence in the present is only a matter of becoming aware that she does not live and so must seek life in the future possesses no foundations *until* the future itself takes place.

It is here that the assumption that the proletariat lacks consciousness and only gains it through contact with the revolutionary vanguard finally exercises its implications upon the Marxist dream. For, assuming that the proletariat *has* achieved the requisite degree of political consciousness to

effectively challenge and overthrow the capitalist state also means accepting that the proletariat has recognised herself only as a force of negation and opposition. And if the proletariat has recognised that it is only in a different system that she can hope to be a subject, then *who* exactly are these people taking over the means of production. How, in other words, can a class of people exercise a dictatorship over the state at the very moment that they are on the verge of willing their own abolition?

Marxist theory, by denying the proletariat any sense of herself as a political actor and subject within capitalism, ultimately depends upon a thoroughly mystical figure for the crucial transition period before communism in which the proletariat will not only destroy bourgeois capitalism but also herself in order to secure her evolution into a genuine human subject. Of course, the potential contradiction within a theory that, on the one hand, embraces the masses as the foundations for a future society and, on the other, insists upon their need for leadership and guidance in order to *be* that foundation is not problematic under capitalism, precisely because the proletariat is not yet ready to assume her historically determined role.

Thus, in 1906 Lenin expressed his confidence that Marxism was uniquely equipped to adapt to the changing historical and economic contexts of working-class struggle.[39] Lenin's assumption that the vanguard are merely the vehicle for expressing the real interests of the masses enabled him to accord Marxism with the flexibility of the changing conditions of the working classes. Marxism here is a theory of practice precisely because its theory is entirely determined by the experiences of the masses and history itself is the evolution of the masses into the agents compelled to overthrow the capitalist system. Marxism, as such can never be at odds with the struggles of workers, because Marxism is merely the conscious expression of the workers' interests and struggles. And the Bolshevik party itself is in turn the embodiment of this fusion between the workers and the revolutionary vanguard who together bind theory and praxis together.

However, acting upon the apparently symbiotic relation between the party and the vanguard *after* the successful uprising against capitalism in Russia proved to be an altogether more difficult proposition. The strain was not obvious immediately and the extent to which Lenin, and other leading Bolsheviks, believed themselves to be the conscious instrument of the masses is evident in the early years of the revolution.[40] The immense obstacles that confronted the Bolsheviks as they sought to create a new society did not dissuade Lenin from advocating that the

party's role was to nurture and respond to the 'living creativity of the masses'. As Serge noted:

> Throughout a civil a war against the revolutions thieves, adventurers and profiteers Lenin ceaselessly appealed to the initiative of the masses; he tells the peasants: 'Do what you please with the land: undoubtedly you will make mistakes, but it is the only way to learn.'[41]

But in 1921, as famine tightened its grip on Russia and the rift between the middle ranking peasants and the proletariat deepened and as Lenin announced that they were 'now facing the most elemental struggle of all human society: to defeat famine',[42] the party became steadily less inclined to support the initiatives of workers and critical voices within the party became less a valuable and integral part of the party but more an impediment to the centralised organisation that was implemented to feed the cities.

And while Serge continued to attribute the steady growth of repression to the suffocating constraints and conditions that the Bolsheviks were forced to operate in, he does also point to another far more devastating schism, namely, that between Marxism as a science and Marxism as a practice. For, while Serge defends the revolution he also challenges the most fundamental assumption of Marxist theory, which is that it has managed to solve the problem of the relation between theory and praxis:

> I do not, after all my reflection on the subject, cast any doubt upon the scientific spirit of Marxism, nor on its contribution, a blend of rationality and idealism, to the consciousness of the age. All the same, I cannot help considering as a positive disaster the fact that a Marxist orthodoxy should, in a country in the throes of social transformation, have taken over the apparatus of power. Whatever may be the scientific value of a doctrine, from the moment that it becomes governmental, interests of State will cease to allow it the possibility of impartial enquiry; and its scientific certitude will lead it, first to intrude into education, and then by the methods of guided thought, which is the same as suppressed thought, to exempt itself from criticism.[43]

Certainly, Marx's utilisation of 'neutral' scientific principles and emphasis upon the ordinary matter of 'men's lives' obscured the fact that this was a methodology that *retained* the ability of a select number of theorists to diagnose the entire world and the peoples in it. It was the willingness of the Bolshevik party to utilise their supposedly advanced

historical consciousness to direct post-revolutionary Russia that Serge identified as directly responsible for the disintegration of the original proletarian revolution.

The confidence that both Marx, and later Gramsci, exhibited towards the revolutionary intellectual stemmed from their conviction that such an intellectual had for the first time in history successfully bridged the gap between theoretical knowledge and the material world. Consequently, this intellectual could be entrusted to both interpret the world and to change it. Significantly, in the time that has passed since Marx and Engels first outlined their materialist philosophy, the relation between Marxism and 'the masses' has proved to be at best problematic and at worst hostile. For those of us situated outside of the crucial orbit of revolutionary consciousness (women, non-Western and black people, peasants and rural workers), Marxism has been a compelling exposure of the misery and injustice of the bourgeois capitalist system. Less straightforward, though, has been Marxism's insistence that it is only through our exposure to the twin forces of capitalist economic deprivation and radical leadership that we can hope to overcome the capitalist bourgeois system. The struggles and reservations with Marxism that concern those of us situated at the periphery of the Marxist dialectic contrasts tellingly with the nourishment that it provides for white male Western theoreticians. The struggle constitutes nothing less than 'our' struggle to refute the crushing and debilitating verdict of 'false consciousness' and 'alienation' that Marx (and Marxism) attributes to us, albeit sympathetically.

For women and non-Westerners 'alienation' is the condition that both expels them from political consciousness *and* provides Marx (and his advocates) with their own material and intellectual grounding in the world. For, the white male working-class subject can at least progress to a position of leadership at which point he is compelled to dissolve both himself and all other class differences in the juncture between capitalism and communism. And yet, it would seem that even he cannot be left unaccompanied at this vital historical juncture. For, as Cedric Robinson points out, it is at this crucial intersection that Marx and Engels provide us with one of their most mystical descriptions:

> Finally, in times when the class struggle nears the decisive hour ... a portion of the bourgeoisie themselves goes over to the proletariat, and in particular a portion of the bourgeois ideologists, who have raised themselves to the level of comprehending theoretically the historical movement as a whole.[44]

Thus, this small section of the bourgeoisie at this late and 'decisive' stage nudge the proletariat aside precisely because the proletariat cannot ever be cognisant of the universal operation of history since such a recognition signifies the end of the proletariat itself. Which leaves the bourgeois-radical in much the same place that Marx carved out for himself when he first substituted the actual working classes of Paris for the proletariat of his theory. And it was this initial act of observation that both secured the working classes as alienated subjects and confirmed the location of the radical theorist as one who had successfully bridged the gap between philosophy and political activism.

The proletariat entered Marx's theory as a description of the exploited Parisian workers that Marx observed in Paris.[45] Marx wanted to find a term that could describe the urban Parisian poor and that he could employ in order to challenge and replace speculative idealist philosophy with a critical and material theory that was intimately connected to the harsh realities of the industrial system. The attribution of alienation to the proletariat was one that Marx initially attributed to himself as a marginalised and outcast radical intellectual and activist. However, if alienation connected him to the masses then it also proved to be a condition that Marx at least could do something about. For it was by attaching himself to the alienated proletariat that Marx was able to overcome his own alienation as a theorist and activist.

The point, of course, is not that capitalism does not produce widespread alienation but that Marx as a radical commentator and activist assumed himself to be capable of surmounting the powerful effects of bourgeois capitalism. In short, Marx confirmed the existing intellectual hierarchies of bourgeois capitalism but suggested that intellectuals could (and should) align themselves with the working classes and through that alliance usher in the next progressive stage of human history. And, not surprisingly, while this assumption has proved to be enormously suggestive for radical intellectuals, it has offered considerably less promise for those situated upon the material ground of Marxism.

The evidence of this was clear even in Marx's own lifetime when he set out to produce a questionnaire which he hoped would provide the necessary data for understanding the conditions of the working classes (suggesting, in fact that the proletariat was not quite the obvious subject that he had already depicted with such certainty). The exhaustive questionnaire[46] was published in the *Revue Socialiste* in April 1880 and 25,000 copies were reprinted and distributed to prominent socialist groups and anyone who wanted a copy of it. Unfortunately, as Marx's editors note, the results of this questionnaire were never published, not

least because the working classes themselves declined to produce the data necessary for intellectual understanding of their conditions and consciousness.[47] This episode is interesting because it reveals both the genuine commitment of Marx to immersing his theory into the experiential content of the working classes and the resistance or indifference of the working classes themselves to this task.

For those who succeeded Marx the tension between the radical intellectuals and the masses continued to plague their attempts to depict the harmonious development of a politically conscious proletariat. However, this tension could always be ascribed to the regrettable level of consciousness amongst the masses, so that any evidence of a disconnection between the intellectuals and the masses could be defined as the inevitable consequence of a difference in 'historical consciousness' between them. Any signs of a dispute between the intellectuals and the masses can thus be dismissed as little more than a mistaken 'impression' that the theory in question is wrong as Gramsci makes clear:

> There continually recur moments in which a gap develops between the masses and intellectuals (at any rate between some of them, or a group of them) a loss of contact, and thus the impression that theory is an 'accessory', a 'complement' and something subordinate.[48]

Noticeably, the efficacy of this hierarchical relationship between the masses and the intellectuals was not addressed by subsequent anti-colonial activists and theorists who sought to revise and transcend the racial exclusionism of Marxist theory. And it is this anti-colonial attempt to revise Marxist theory in order to reclaim 'the people' that we will turn to next.

Part 4 Radical Intellectuals and the People

8
Speaking for the People

Significantly, the idea that Marx *did* solve the hubris of elitist philosophical abstraction and idealism is one that radical Western work on imperialism and colonialism continues to invoke. Thus, Johannes Fabian[1] in his groundbreaking criticism of anthropologist's depictions of their objects as situated in a different time and space to themselves juxtaposes the conventions of anthropological theory and practice with that of a materialist and sensuous approach to the world that he discerns in Marx's materialist methodology. He begins by drawing attention to the explicitly political effects of placing people into a different time. As Fabian points out, it is precisely by presenting people as inhabiting a different time to our own that subjects can become objects; that is people frozen in time and as such accessible for empirical and scientific analysis. Most crucially, placing people into a different time rules out any possibility for communication between the analyst/observer and the observed/analysed.

For Fabian the only way to correct this tradition of imperial distance is for anthropology to contribute towards the creation of temporal equality:

> For human communication to occur, coevalness has to be *created*. Communication is, ultimately, about creating shared Time ... on the whole, the dominant communication model remains one in which objectivity is still tied to (temporal) distancing between the participants ... Beneath their bewildering variety, the distancing devices that we can identify produce a global result. I will call it a *denial of coevalness ... a persistent and systematic tendency to place the referent of anthropology in a Time other than the present of the producer of anthropological discourse* (emphasis in the original)[2]

Fabian contrasts this anthropological tradition of transforming non-Western peoples into objects for scrutiny with Marx's conception of material reality as first and foremost a matter for sensual involvement and not 'objective' and passive contemplation. Thus, he criticises Lévi-Strauss's assumption that the ethnographer could simply observe the society before her and decode its meaning for its arrogant dismissal of society as a dynamic and historical entity.

Fabian's impatience with Lévi-Strauss's methodology centres upon the latter's presumption that the ethnographer is producing particularly valuable work on 'other' cultures, because the ethnographer can through her cognitive skills override any local particularities and discern instead the universal patterns of a culture. In other words, the ethnographic project here succeeds through the imperialist notion that the ethnographer's main tool in defining and understanding 'other' cultures lies in her superior cognition and observation. Accordingly, the Western ethnographer can understand and define seemingly unfamiliar and alien cultures simply by careful observation:

> Observation conceived as the essence of fieldwork implies on the side of the ethnographer, a contemplative stance. It invokes the 'naturalist' watching an experiment. It calls for a native society that would, ideally, at least, hold still like a *tableau vivant*.[3]

As Fabian notes, this privileging of sight and observation is politically crucial because it attributes to the Western ethnographer the ability to interpret and decode any society that 'he' chooses to study. Moreover, this emphasis upon the ethnographer's perspicacity ensures that the non-West is 'seen' as a disorganised and alien puzzle legible only to a gifted few. Thus, in Lévi-Strauss's reading, non-Western societies resemble abstract puzzles that the ethnographer is uniquely equipped to solve precisely because he has located himself 'outside' of the society under scrutiny:

> There are serious reasons for dwelling on his [Lévi-Strauss's] way of turning apparent emphasis on the personal into affirmations of the trans-subjective, the ritual and the institutional: The researcher's personal encounter, we are told, *is* the objective working of science because it is posited as a sort of pure channel through which ethnology passes into ethnology and anthropology. Closer inspection of the many statements Lévi-Strauss makes about the nature of fieldwork reveals that the one notion which for him characterizes this activity

more than any other is *observation*. He does not seem to have much use for the qualifier *participant*, customarily attached to the term. Even less does he consider communicative interaction ... For Lévi-Strauss the ethnographer is first and foremost a viewer (and perhaps voyeur).[4]

Unsurprisingly, as Fabian reminds us, Lévi-Strauss's successful establishment of anthropology as a discipline uniquely equipped to understand the non-Western world coincided with decolonisation and the growing practice of absentee colonialism.

Fabian argues that the only way that we can escape the imperialist consequences of Lévi-Strauss's celebration of the Western anthropologist as a gifted surveyor and translator is by refusing to accept that we can (or do) occupy a superior vantage point. He urges us to take note of the fact that the Western celebration of observation is intimately connected to the discreet assumption that the Western observer is one who resides outside the mundane confines of other peoples' space and time. Consequently, the only way to overcome this is to situate the Western ethnographer back where she should be: *in* the world rather than a disengaged commentator *of* the world.

The antidote to Lévi-Strauss's omnipotent ethnographer can, Fabian suggests, be found in Marx's approach to the world. Fabian cites Marx for his insistence that it is not the act of observation that summons the material world but material engagement with it:

The major defect of materialism up to this day ... has been to conceive of the object, reality, sensuousness, only in the form of an object of contemplation, not as sensuous-human-activity, praxis not subjectivity.[5]

Marx's reading of the philosopher as an active and engaged critic of human society is for Fabian the necessary corrective to traditional celebrations of imperialist and colonial scholarly distance. But the more-radical potential that Fabian detects in Marx lies in what he identifies as his 'radical presentism' which, he suggests, allows for the theoretical possibility for a 'negation of allochronic distancing' which is, precisely the task that Fabian assigns to contemporary anthropology. This 'radical presentism' is the mark of a theory that refuses to place the 'Other' into a different time and space from ourselves and one that Fabian perceives to be at work in Marx's materialist methodology. Thus he points out that Marx scorned German historians for their fondness for 'prehistory'

which conveniently absolved them from the more difficult task of understanding contemporary society.

By contrast, Fabian notes approvingly, Marx argued that research into human societies should ignore mythical postulations and instead grant humanity a common origin and regard different social organisations as merely 'moments' which 'from the beginning of history, and ever since human beings lived have existed *simultaneously* and still determine history'.[6] This is, Marx concluded, the 'materialist connection among human beings which is conditioned by their needs and the mode of production and is as old as mankind itself.'[7] It is Marx's presentation of humanity as occupying the *same* time that prompts Fabian to regard Marx as an early opponent of such distancing techniques as those espoused by Lévi-Strauss.

However, recruiting Marx as an obvious refutation of traditional Western intellectual conventions is, as Fabian concedes, not entirely straightforward. Thus Fabian notes that Marx's concept of human 'needs' is worryingly vague while his reliance upon notions of phases, periods and stages hints at a possible hierarchical division of the world. However, Fabian argues that Marx's insistence that people can only be discussed as a collective unity that exist in the same time as each other is not necessarily contradicted by the presence of different developments across the world that can be viewed in chronological succession.

For Fabian, the crucial point that Marx grasped is that theoretical work has to proceed on the assumption that we all live in the same time and it is this that allows for the possibility of replacing the hierarchical devices that are used to explain the different human societies that exist in the world with ones that reflect the dialectical relation between us in our various societies. Consequently, Fabian concludes that

> if we can show that our theories of their societies are *our praxis* – the way in which we produce and reproduce knowledge of the Other for our societies – we may (paraphrasing Marx and Hegel) put anthropology back on its feet. Renewed interest in the history of our discipline and disciplined inquiry into the history of the confrontation between anthropology and its Other are therefore not escapes from empiry; they are practical and realistic. They are ways to meet the Other on the same ground, in the same Time.[8]

For Fabian the radicalism of Marx lay in his ability to see that differences in the world cannot be ascribed to people living in different times but rather living differently in the same time. In his reading, the

implications of Marx's insights exceed even himself since a 'radical presentism' enables the proletariat and 'the savage' to meet within the same time as victims of a dominant capitalist order:

> coevalness aims at recognizing cotemporality as the condition for truly dialectical confrontation between persons as well as societies. It militates against false conceptions of dialectics-all those watered-down binary abstractions which are passed off as oppositions: left vs. right, past vs. present, primitive vs. modern. Tradition and modernity are not 'opposed' (except semiotically), nor are they in 'conflict'. All this is (bad) metaphorical talk. What are opposed, in conflict, in fact, locked in antagonistic struggle, are not the same societies at different stages of development, but different societies facing each other at the same Time. As J. Duvignaud, and others, are reminding us, the 'savage and the proletarian' are in equivalent positions vis-à-vis domination ... Marx in the nineteenth century may be excused for not giving enough theoretical recognition to that equivalence; certain contemporary 'Marxist' anthropologists have no excuse.[9]

But the problem here is that it was precisely Marx's perception of humanity as living in the same time that informed his racial division of the world. The non-West was deemed to be inferior and less developed than the West precisely because it existed in the same time but lacked the same 'level' of economic and social organisation. Moreover, such was the significance of this lack of discernible economic and social development on the part of the non-West that Marx felt able to define the non-West as an area that had yet to enter history. Marx's assumption that radical history originates in bourgeois capitalism effectively placed the non-West outside of both history and time.

Consequently, the point is not that Marx's 'radical presentism' allows for the emergence of the shared condition of 'the savage' and proletariat but that his radical presentism licensed the differences that he identified in economic development between them. For, 'the savage', unlike the proletariat, had not attained the level of consciousness that was necessary for her to understand their connection. Indeed, 'the savage' could only ever be analogous to the proletariat after her adoption of bourgeois capitalist alienation at which point she would no longer be a savage at all. Unfortunately, Fabian's attempt to differentiate between Marx and contemporary Marxism overlooks the fact that *both* employ race as a measure of human inequality within time. Thus, Marx's emphasis upon material reality and the world as a diverse array of different

forms of society all living in the same time was imperialist precisely because he raised the question of human difference inside shared time and answered it with race.

Not surprisingly for non-Western and black radicals, while Marxist theory offered a compelling account of class, its conjectures upon race and empire proved to be far less neoteric. For Cedric Robinson, it was Marxism's location within the Western intellectual tradition that obstructed its universalist aspirations:

> The limits of Western radicalism ... relate directly to the 'understanding' of consciousness, and the persistence of racialism in Western thought ... it would have been exceedingly difficult and most unlikely that such a civilization would produce a tradition of self-examination sufficiently critical to expose one of its most profound terms of order.[10]

Robinson's examination of the work of W.E.B. Du Bois, C.L.R. James and Richard Wright explores why their support for Marxism was qualified and eventually abandoned and concludes that it was Marxism's inability to overcome traditional Western ideas of racial inequality that made black Marxism ultimately an impossibility. For, the Marxist insistence upon the white European proletariat as the authentic agent for revolution was not only contradicted in practice, by events in Haiti, Mexico, India, Cuba, Africa and Russia, but was also accompanied by evidence that while the working classes of Europe and America had challenged their ruling classes they had in defeat also turned towards bourgeois nationalism and racism.[11]

Unsurprisingly, such practical refutations of the Western proletariat's 'historical destiny' did not encourage black radicals to accept their inclusion into Western Marxist parties as conditional on their ability to embrace an allegedly universal 'class consciousness' and overcome their narrow and implicitly backward racial consciousness. The combined force of an unacknowledged white nationalism and hostility towards any signs of a retrograde 'black nationalism' did little to create the international solidarity to which the mainstream radical left aspired.[12]

Robinson draws particular attention to the American 'labor aristocracy' that far from uniting the white and black workers divided them, observing that

> the labor movement was most often at best ambivalent towards
> Black liberation and progress. The ideology of racism in combination

with self-interest functioned to pit immigrant and poor white workers against the Black workers and the slave. And after the Civil War, the same social consciousness divided the working classes – immigrant and white – from the ex-slave.[13]

Robinson cites Du Bois who far from observing the evolution of a common cause between the white proletariat and the ex-slaves discerned instead a connection *within* white America that conspired to maintain, both practically and ideologically, the role of the black American as a subordinate and marginalised subject.[14]

This leads Robinson to conclude that while Marxism continues to be 'a superior grammar for synthesizing the degradation of labor'[15] and exposing the instabilities and oppressions of the bourgeois capitalist system, it nevertheless inevitably fails the non-Western world and the non-white subjects of the West because it cannot overcome its racist foundations. Consequently, the numerous and supposedly historically impossible, revolutions and struggles that have enveloped the non-Western world[16] confirm not only the errors of Marxist historiography but also the reasons for the error: racism buried in the roots of Marxism itself:

The critique of the capitalist world system acquired determinant force not from movements of industrial workers in the metropoles but from those of the 'backward' peoples of the world. Only an inherited but rationalized racial arrogance and a romanticism stiffened by pseudo-science could manage to legitimate a denial of these occurrences. Western Marxism in either of its two variants – critical; – humanist or scientific – has proved insufficiently radical to expose and root out the racialist order that contaminates its analytic and philosophic applications or to come to effective terms with the implications of its own class origins. As a result it has been mistaken for something it is not: a *total* theory of liberation.[17]

Robinson identified the black radical tradition as one that was steadily overcoming the inevitable alienation that accompanied the black intellectual's' investment in Western Marxism.

However, in Robinson's account, the black radical tradition offers far more than a simple compensation or refuge from the particularities that plague Marxist understandings of world history. Thus, he concludes his investigation of the black radical tradition with the assertion that the African peoples *are* in the process of acquiring a 'world-historical consciousness'.[18] Accordingly, this 'Black collective identity' is the site

of the transcendent consciousness that Marx and his followers believed to be within their reach. Consequently, Robinson's dismissal of the universalism of Marxist theory and practice is one that relocates it as the *starting* point for black intellectuals. The black radical tradition becomes the higher plane to which Marx and his followers aspired but from which they were debarred, formed as they were on the racial exclusionisms of the Western radical tradition:

> Harboured in the African diaspora there is a single historical identity that is in opposition to the systemic privation of racial capitalism ... The resoluteness of the Black radical tradition advances as each generation assembles the data of its experience to an ideology of liberation. The experimentation with Western political inventories to change, specifically nationalism and class struggle, is coming to a close. Black radicalism is transcending those traditions in order to adhere to its own authority.[19]

Here black people as a unified group displace the European proletariat from the centre of the world historical stage so that their history becomes one of the gradual evolution towards 'world historical consciousness'.

Robinson's attack upon Western Marxism is not simply for its omission of the non-Western world from any equal engagement in 'world historical development' but for its ability to usher in progress at all. For the agent of Marxist theory is, as Robinson points out, not a universal proletarian subject but one divided between complex loyalties to the existing social and political hierarchies and oppositional aspirations for freedom and justice. Such a protagonist could hardly be expected to usher in 'human' emancipation marked as it was by racial privilege. Robinson does not dispute Marx's assumption that universal human liberation can only be achieved through the struggles of the most dispossessed and disenfranchised people on earth; rather what he contests is exactly *who* it is that these people are. Consequently, Robinson inserts the black subject into the now vacant seat of the white European proletariat and assigns to 'him' the compulsion and ability to struggle for a properly universal emancipation.

Perhaps not surprisingly, black radicals encounter the same dilemmas that assailed European radicals as they sought to explain the connections between the masses and themselves. However in black radical theory, alienation and the capacity for mistaken identification is placed firmly on the shoulders of the black intellectual who has inched 'his' way through

'history' only to find that it was not his history he was following but a destructive white European narrative. This discovery leads him towards the insight that it was his own tradition (history) all along that provided the clues and the nourishment that he needed for his future. Unfortunately, this discovery, on the part of the black radical intellectual, does little to disrupt the notion that the masses embody experience and the intellectuals thought, and consequently fails to explore the question of *who* is speaking for 'history' and 'experience'.

A central charge that Robinson levels at the Western radical tradition is that its theoretical production was the work of people who had little knowledge of or interest in the subjects of their theory; namely the working classes. He asserts that Marx, Engels, Lenin and Trotsky were all 'bourgeois idealists' in terms of their 'schooling and education' and that with the exception of Engels had remarkably little to do with working-class people. In particular, Robinson notes the absence of proletarian writings in their theories and concludes that this reinforces the impression that Marxism is, ultimately, a theory 'of' rather than 'for' the proletariat. Interestingly, Robinson does not consider the third option which would be of course a theory 'by' the proletariat since his focus here is trained firmly upon the failure of either socialism or Marxism to connect with the people that they take as their subject.

Robinson contrasts the black radical tradition with that of European socialism by identifying 'the proletarian writer' Richard Wright as evidence of the black radical tradition's progression away from its petty bourgeois origins. By concluding his genealogy of black radical thought with Wright Robinson seeks to abolish the distance and difference between radical black theory and black experience. Wright's confident assumption that he could convey the feelings and experiences of the black masses is presented by Robinson as evidence that he has, so that Wright's 'recognition' of the self-destructive anger and bitterness of the exploited black workers constitutes confirms that black radical theory can articulate the feelings of 'the people'.

Wright's perception of the psychology of the black masses enables him to transform Du Bois's lament regarding the 'double consciousness' of the 'Negro' into a celebration. The fractured psyche of the 'Negro' thus unites the writer and the people into a distinctive and necessary black nationalism. Nationalism, on the part of intellectuals, is viewed as an unequivocal act of identification with the people. However, even as Wright identifies nationalism as the bond between the intellectuals and the people he nevertheless directs the intellectuals to transcend their identification with 'the people'. Wright's instructions to his fellow

writers thus mirrors Marxist stipulations that revolutionary intellectuals need to identify with the proletariat in order to see beyond the present:

> Negro writers must accept the nationalist implications of their lives ... [T]hey must accept the concept of nationalism because, in order to transcend it, they must possess and understand it. And a nationalist spirit in Negro writing means a nationalism carrying the highest possible pitch of social consciousness.[20]

But, in contrast to Western Marxist readings of the proletariat as a blind historical subject 'the people' of nationalist discourse are those who reveal to their intellectuals what it is that constitutes the 'truth' of their condition. This truth may not be comfortable, as Wright makes clear in his depiction of the black masses as enraged by dispossession and partial entry into white American culture, but it is a truth that no radical black intellectual can afford to ignore.

In short, the racially oppressed and colonised people of nationalist theory are nationalists because they have lost their nation and with it their traditions and culture. And if the significance of this loss is overlooked by a small number of elite intellectuals then no such lack of clarity is present in the masses. This perception of the masses as embodying the raw emotional truth of colonialism and imperialism is what leads Amílcar Cabral[21] to assert that while imperialism did corrupt the intelligentsia, it failed to corrupt the masses. Frantz Fanon[22] too, lambasted the African national bourgeoisie for their intellectual mediocrity, economic bankruptcy and political immaturity and identified the peasantry as the revolutionary class since they, unlike their urban counterparts had not been corrupted by colonialism.

This search for and discovery of 'a people' who had escaped the influences of Western colonialism and could therefore exist as an uncontaminated opposition to colonialism and imperialism, was one that enabled radical intellectuals such as Cabral and Fanon to ground their work upon the people and from there formulate a future. The uncorrupted body of the people emerges as the site to which the radical intellectual must 'return' if he is to have any chance of defeating colonial rule. And 'returning' to the people means first and foremost 'returning' to what it is that 'they' identify with, namely, their severed national origins.

This desire to return to a lost, or more accurately 'interrupted', point in time prior to the colonial invasion proposes, of course, that such a return is possible even as it identifies the colonial intervention as one

that utterly destroyed the culture that it encountered. For contemporary critics of Western material and cultural dominance, like Ziauddin Sardar,[23] the expansion of colonial domination into a thoroughly invasive Western cultural imperialism that now seeks to transform the entire world into a supine market only serves to deepen the cultural losses that were first experienced by non-Westerners under colonial domination. For Sardar, what once existed as real living traditions and cultures have been displaced and distorted by facile and damaging representations. Furthermore, in Sardar's reading, the extent of the destruction is such that there is now no possibility of ever returning to the point at which non-Western cultures thrived unimpeded by external agendas.

Indeed, in Sardar's reading, the very term 'non-Western' culture suggests a profound paradox since it both signals the appearance of 'a' non-Western culture and the moment at which culture in the non-West was extinguished by the Western colonial powers. Sardar's reading of non-Western culture and history draws upon the work of earlier theorists such as Amílcar Cabral who also depicted non-Western culture as that paradoxical entity that entered history at the very moment that it was being extinguished and repressed. As Cabral explained

> colonialism can be considered as the paralysis or deviation or even the halting of the history of the people in favour of the acceleration of the historical development of other peoples ... The colonialists usually say that it was they who brought us into history; today we show that this was not so. They made us leave history, our history, to follow the progress of their history.[24]

For commentators such as Sardar and Cabral, this colonial expulsion of the non-West from history serves to identify the present task of the non-West which is nothing less than to re-enter history. Consequently, the pre-colonial past becomes an indispensable source of authority and legitimacy for the 'history-making' efforts of the present. And the pressing problem becomes one of identifying precisely what values and traditions existed in the non-West prior to colonialism.

For Sardar the project is the relatively straightforward one of retracing the body of knowledge that existed prior to colonialism. And what this material provides is authentic proof that the non-West is informed by fundamentally different values to those of the West:

> What makes the Other different from the west is a civilisational corpus of ways of knowing, being and doing defined by value parameters.

> These active principles have been in suspended animation often for centuries, under the onslaught of modernity and colonialism.[25]

For Sardar the battle between the West and non-West is primarily a struggle over 'culture' and not a struggle between two different cultures, since it is Sardar's contention that the West should be viewed above all as a site in which culture has been lost. Thus, the reanimation of non-Western principles and modes of living become the necessary condition for humanity to retain culture at all. Western culture is, in short, nothing more than a dubious and reactionary attempt to deny the *actual* existence of non-Western culture by distorting it through representations that are inevitably ignorant of the *real* meaning of the non-West. In this sense, Sardar extends Edward Said's 'Orientalism'[26] by concluding that the West's determination to represent 'other' people and 'other' cultures has infected the entire corpus of Western culture so that 'western culture' now can be recognised for its very *lack* of anything resembling culture.

For Sardar, this gaping abyss of cultural significance that permeates the Western world is one that only the non-West can rectify since it is the one place where culture still exists, in its real life-affirming form. The challenge is thus located between two antagonists – postmodernism and tradition – and the problem becomes one of representing this particular struggle while at the same time dismissing representation itself as a specifically Western conceit and preoccupation. For as Sardar reiterates throughout his book the value of non-Western culture is precisely its stubborn refusal to accommodate the Western desire to transform reality into representation:

> Watch a craftsman in a traditional society and see how his reality shapes his craft. The craft may be for sale but the reality isn't. Experiential realities have to be lived and experienced. They are not amenable to a culture totally submerged in the instant, spontaneity, hyperreality, self-delusions, anxiety and angst ... The realities of Other cultures are not for sale in the supermarkets of postmodern nihilism.[27]

Unfortunately Sardar's contention that 'experiential realities have to be lived and experienced', although it is directed against Western consumers also raises the altogether more difficult question of how these experiences can be understood by anyone who has not lived them, including of course Sardar himself. His contention that the craftsman

demonstrates the harmonious resolution of labour and humanity remains silent about the processes of both interpretation and representation that have enabled him to isolate the craftsman for his argument.

But perhaps it is not surprising that Sardar neglects to address this question, since his central claim is that non-Western traditions defy and evade all attempts to represent them. And it is this assumption that enables him simply to *assert* the truth of the non-West, non-Western peoples and their traditions. Thus, the craftsman serves to summon up an entire 'traditional society' and in the process single-handedly demonstrate the extent of the challenge to postmodernity. As such the craftsman is a positive symbol; one that proves Sardar's conviction that Western imperialism, whose latest guise is one of a postmodern consumption of ethnic difference, has finally met its match. The destructive legacy of Western appropriations and distortions of non-Western cultures, are, for all their postmodern ambitions, destined to fall beneath the immovable fact of non-Western difference. Tradition then is, in the final analysis, the real evidence of real history and real difference between the West and the non-West:

> While postmodernism may displace, fragment and even momentarily occupy Other cultures, the innate and powerful desire for historic meaning and identity in non-western societies cannot be eradicated. It is this urge of every culture to be true to its Self, to be self-confirming and self-propagating. It is this unfathomable urge – which has 'presence' as its prime value and forms the matrix of every idealism – that will lead to the return of dynamic tradition and give the twenty-first century its defining character. The invincible, life-denying forces of postmodernism are about to meet the immovable object of life-enhancing tradition.[28]

Sardar's craftsman is indeed present in his text as an 'immovable object' whose very lack of engagement with the present reflects only the extent to which he is 'enhanced' by tradition. The craftsman does not need to contest postmodernism since his very existence proves that there is an alternative so radical that it *cannot* communicate with the present postmodern order.

Moreover, it is precisely by connecting the craftsman to a timeless past and labour that Sardar is able to add weight and resilience to 'traditional society'. Postmodern culture emerges in this depiction as flimsy precisely because it is the culture of a specific age whereas the craftsman, like the society to which he is bound, predates postmodernism

and survives it. The craftsman is carved out of his present and dispersed into an endless and unassailable history. Not surprisingly, such mundane matters as the exploitation of apprentices in craftwork and the wider capitalist market that the 'traditional' craftworkers are engaged in are insignificant minutiae compared to what *being* a craftsman signifies. Clearly, embroiling this pure symbol of 'tradition' into the 'modern' world would rob the postmodern/native opposition of its moral clarity; a clarity that unfortunately occurs at the expense of 'the craftsman' who is extracted from any engagement in his present.

By insisting that the craftsman embodies the severest challenge to postmodernity, Sardar not only rules out any possibility that the craftsman may be implicated in capitalist relations but more importantly rules out any possibility that he may be actively resisting his economic conditions. Moreover, Sardar's 'positive' identification of tradition in the body of the craftsman fails to address the problem of the inherent violence in *all* representations, violence that he would prefer to locate only in Western consumerism and appropriations of the non-West. For, as Rey Chow[29] points out, the problem of representation is a problem that should concern all of us who are in the business of representing the world and the people in it:

> I want to highlight the native – nowadays a synonym for the oppressed, the marginalized, the wronged – because I think that the space occupied by the native in postcolonial discourses is also the space of error, illusion, deception and filth. How would we write this space in such a way as to refuse the facile turn of sanctifying the defiled images with pieties and thus enriching ourselves precisely with what can be called the surplus value of the oppressed a surplus value that results from *exchanging* the defiled image for something more noble.[30]

By including her own 'vantage' point as vitally relevant to her investigation into representations of the non-Western world, Chow is able to foreground the conditions that inform our 'engagement' with those we seek to represent and speak for. As she reiterates throughout her work, 'we' should perhaps begin our efforts to undo the imperialist and colonialist damage of the Western orientalist tradition by pausing to reflect upon our own entanglement with a tradition that sees fit to omit any analysis of how it is that 'we' came to represent 'them'.

Chow's unease at the willingness of radical commentators to assert what it is that the native *really* represents contrasts strikingly with Sardar's confident assumption that the non-West and its inhabitants

exist as emphatically obvious subjects. Thus while Sardar absents himself from the scene of his representation, Chow confronts us with the present disparity between the native and herself that is, of course, the very condition that has produced the possibility for representation in the first place. What Chow acknowledges and Sardar ignores is the actual difference and distance between those of us who represent others and those who are represented by others – an estrangement that connects 'us' back to the Western orientalist tradition itself:

> We need to remember as intellectuals that the battles we fight are battles of words. Those who argue the oppositional standpoint are not *doing* anything different from their enemies are most certainly not directly changing the downtrodden lives of those who seek their survival in metropolitan and nonmetropolitan spaces alike. What academic intellectuals must confront is ... the power, wealth, and privilege that ironically accumulate from their 'oppositional' viewpoint, and the widening gap between the professed content of their words and the upward mobility they gain from such words.[31]

Unsurprisingly, Chow's insistence that radical intellectuals confront their own intellectual investments and locations is a charged and contentious position in the field of postcolonial studies.

For Benita Parry, the critical work of theorists such as Rey Chow and Gayatri Spivak is nothing less than an elitist dismissal of the anti-colonial struggles. Thus, in a recent article Parry[32] challenges the 'ambiguous' status of anti-colonial theory within the field of postcolonial studies and argues that those who fault anti-colonial leaders for being too reliant upon idealistic versions of an idyllic pre-colonial past and too quick to speak for the marginalised 'subaltern' subject are forgetting the political subversion of the anti-colonial movements. She argues that even those independent movements most shackled by the global status quo did at least mobilise the masses and disrupt colonial authority.[33] Parry's interpretation of the debates surrounding the conditions for and possibilities of representation as constituting an attack upon the political achievements of the independent movements assumes, of course, that there is a choice to be made between advocating 'theory' and advocating 'radical political activism'.

Significantly, it is Parry's distinction between different types of postcolonial theory that enables her to circumvent the issue of authorial power in *any* theory. Accordingly, she distinguishes between her own materially grounded theory and what she regards as the unnecessarily

convoluted theories of writers such as Spivak. In this the commonplace distinction is sought between theorists who are needlessly esoteric (that is to say beyond the compass of 'the people'), as opposed to those theorists who do not indulge themselves with introspective ramblings about issues of representation and narrative power. Consequently, her distinction between theorists is discussed in terms of a perceived waste of time on the part of those who would stall the revoluition by devoting their time to the inconsequential matter of elite theory. Any undue attention to the problems of theorising 'the people' and radical change is thus attributed to a greater allegiance to 'theory' rather than 'the people' with whom revolutionary (i.e. less theoretical) writing is concerned. It is in this sense that Parry castigates Spivak for her 'exorbitant discourse' and subsequent 'related incuriosity about the enabling socio-economic and political institutions and other forms of social praxis.'[34]

Parry's attack upon Spivak's 'exorbitant discourse' maintains a familiar criticism of difficult theory as self-indulgent as opposed to native-friendly. In this reading, native-friendly theory simply requires the theorist to listen to 'them' and mobilise along the clear grounds of national autonomy. Above all, it is about *not* descending into peripheral areas that do not concern 'the native', such as analysing and questioning the ability of the postcolonial theorist to articulate native subjectivity. In short, providing that we are willing to do so, it is quite possible to identify with 'the native' and express progressive theory, because our own positions as theorists only becomes at issue when we fail to identify with 'the native'.

Therefore, it follows that we should not waste time deconstructing discourses that sanction notions of identifiable cultures, homogenous cultures, the benign difference of third world nationalism, the priority of national independence before wholesale reconsideration of post-colonial policies, or any other unhelpful and gratuitous deviations from the task at hand. Similarly, we must restate native intolerance for those discourses that would problematise the ability of postcolonial intellectuals to speak for the native on account of their elitist pretensions. Thus, Parry observes that, 'those engaged in colonial struggles would probably read such theorising with considerable disbelief.'[35] This as well as assuming that those engaged in anti-colonial struggles are a homogenous group, also circumvents the fact that for the many people who are specifically excluded from theorising about the world (through their limited access to academic and public spheres), *all* forms of theorising reflect the capacity of *some* people to interpret, define and imagine the world and its inhabitants.

However, in native-friendly theory an appropriately elementary argument is advanced. In this narrative we must continue to insist that everything is simple: natives can be brought to speech (by us), indigenous cultures can be resurrected (by us) and colonialism can be overcome by the ability of radical intellectuals to discern which traditions to revive and which to discard. Consequently, just as our agenda is clear and simple so too is 'the native'. The anti-colonial intellectual needs only to identify *with* 'the native' and her own position as one who interprets, speaks for and listens to this native becomes placed outside of the critical arena. This strikingly malleable native (present *both* as foundational evidence of the non-West and as the source from which a new order can be imagined), exists both as the proof of the author's concrete political commitment *and* as the means by which authorial power can be rendered unintelligible. But unless the connection between the reestablishment of indigenous culture and anti-colonial/ neo-colonial politics is raised we are left only with the choice of 'welcoming' Western imperialism or 'defending' non-Western cultures. There is no room in this dichotomy for the urgent need to analyse what it is that notions of culture validate, much less contest those readings that would have us believe that autonomous and coherent indigenous cultures exist in a state of temporal limbo and can be resuscitated by anti-imperialist intellectuals.[36]

A striking effect of Parry's determination to differentiate her work from that of theorists such as Spivak is that she is forced to suppress her own criticisms and reflections upon the anti-colonial struggles. Thus, having assigned herself the role of 'defending' anti-colonialism from intellectual 'misreadings' of it she is left in the position of 'admitting' to various limitations on the part of the anti-colonial leaderships. Thomas Sankara's 'narrowly utilitarian stance on the arts', Amílcar Cabral's 'mechanistic model of the relationship between material circumstances and culture' and the worryingly 'residual masculinism' present in many anti-colonial leaders and intellectuals become a swift corrective to the charge that she is guilty of idealising libertarian thought.[37]

And yet it is precisely the extent to which anti-colonial leaders and intellectuals themselves insisted upon the need to reflect and reinterpret their own ideas in order to safeguard the liberatory potential of independence that makes Parry's determination to defend them so questionable. Certainly, Parry's embarrassment at the potential irrelevance of political theory is not evident in the anti-colonial intellectuals and leaders that she devotes her energies to protecting.[38] Indeed, for Amílcar Cabral and Frantz Fanon the need to consider how to transform

the cultures of the newly liberated colonies lay at the very core of the political theory and practice of liberation. We are not, in other words, obliged to accept that by problematising the relation between radical theory and the material conditions of people's lives we are 'betraying' either the masses or the anti-colonial leaders who struggled for a just and radically egalitarian new world.

Arguably, Parry's concern at the 'political implications' of 'denying' the native speech is no more or less 'political' than are 'our' concerns at the 'political implications' of assuming that intellectuals can speak for the masses. At the very least, perhaps rethinking our understandings and representations of 'the people' would go some way towards changing our current political practices. However, for Parry, Chow and Spivak's open unease about speaking for the subaltern is nothing less than a wilful decision to not 'listen' to the subaltern. Parry's objection to Spivak's identification of subaltern silence is that it gives, 'no speaking part to the colonized', and in doing so undermines and blots out the history of native agency. For Parry, this oversight does more than simply overlook history; it reflects Spivak's real allegiance to institutional power. All the more ironic then that Parry turns to a text in order to demonstrate that the subaltern has spoken. For it is by offering us a counter-reading of Jean Rhys' *Wide Sargasso Sea*[39] that she intends to recover the native's voice and agency. Unfortunately, by refusing to reflect upon the implications of relying upon texts to solve the problem of 'the native's' or 'the peoples' historical agency, Parry in fact misses the opportunity to engage with the problems that Spivak's theory raises. Consequently, her suggestive criticism of Spivak's 'silent subaltern', as being the overly coherent and homogenous subject of a theory of unrepresentability, is diminished by her own unreflective investment in texts to affirm the material presence of 'the third world woman'.

Arguably, inattention to *how* and *why* 'natives' came to be important for their symbolic significance, rather than for their histories, is critical for any investment in 'non-western' native authenticity.[40] As María Elena García[41] demonstrates, the 'resistance' of 'natives' to calls to celebrate or recognise 'their' cultural traditions extends beyond the colonisers to the advocates of indigenous traditions themselves. García documents how in Peru the recent addition of the Ccara community to its jurisdiction meant that they received the fruits of a decade of organisation, on the part of linguists, anthropologists, writers, teachers and education theoreticians working both within the Peruvian state agencies and regional non-governmental organisations (NGOs). This coalition of activists, professionals and intellectuals was supported by various Europe-based

international organisations and indigenous leaders in neighbouring Andean countries. The principal aim of the activists was to promote the development of a unified Quechua identity among the highland Quechua people through the implementation of bilingual intercultural education in place of the former monopoly of Spanish.

The activists argued that the incorporation of indigenous languages and cultural practices into national language and educational policies would both empower the indigenous citizens and enable them to access national resources and thus contribute to the development of civil society. As García observes, the fact that these activists encountered the most vehement opposition to their bilingual education policy from the indigenous highlanders themselves demonstrates that the restatement of an ethnic identity is not necessarily something that the supposed beneficiaries appreciate. For the indigenous parents who protested at this initiative it was far from clear how beneficial it would be for their children to be politically relevant as 'indigenous' people. The ensuing breakdown in communication arose from the inability of the activists to recognise indigenous people's unease about an initiative directed 'at' and 'for' them by fellow citizens who demonstrated little inclination to pursue the same course of action. Certainly, the progressive validation of Quechua culture was undermined by the fact that many of the activists declined to involve their own children in this programme.[42]

Not surprisingly, the refusal of the activists to relinquish the dominant status of 'their' culture suggested that 'indigenous' culture would remain a less powerful culture within the nation after its official inclusion. The bafflement on the part of the activists sprang from their own uncritical assumption that 'the people' were more concerned with matters of 'culture' than they were with matters of political justice. Consequently, while the activists and intellectuals failed to recognise the connection between cultural and economic power and capital, the Quechua parents insisted upon their relevance. Certainly, it is something of an irony that the activists assumed themselves to be addressing the most pressing concern of the Quechua-speaking inhabitants only to find that the beneficiaries of their reforms were concerned to *extend* the implications of 'indigenous 'representation into the wider *non-indigenous* social and polit-ical arena. In short, 'asserting' the cultural (and by extension the political) validity of Quechua identity was a considerably less radical proposal for the indigenous people than it was for the activists and intellectuals who spearheaded the campaign.

Interestingly, the activists were unprepared for the *lack* of concern that many Quechua parents demonstrated with regard to the survival of

Quechua culture. Meanwhile, the adoption of 'an indigenous identity' has proved to be considerably less problematical for those who aspire to the possession of political power. As García observes

> indigenous identity is already being forcefully asserted by individuals designated by activists as future Andean indigenous leaders ... the emergence of Peruvian indigenous intellectuals is a crucial component of ethnic politics in the Peruvian countryside. Selected youths are sent to a master's program (based in Bolivia) for indigenous students from five Andean countries. At this transnational institute, students receive two years of training in bilingual intercultural education methodology and theory from primarily European, North American, and non-indigenous Latin American instructors. They are labelled indigenous intellectuals, leaders, and international representatives of indigenous peoples, and they continually appropriate, challenge, and modify these labels. Given that the Peruvian highlands are noted for a lack of indigenous identification, that the Peruvian students identify themselves as Quechua intellectuals is particularly significant.[43]

Of course, the political intentions of indigenous leaders may be radical ones that seek to improve the material conditions of the indigenous communities. However, the difference and distance that is created by the existence of 'qualified' indigenous leaders and 'the' indigenous people themselves inevitably complicates any intellectual claims to power that are based upon notions of cultural 'authenticity'.

And while it is possible to argue that such mobilisation is necessary in order to secure political emancipation the problem remains that mobilisation itself is based upon notions ('authenticity', 'identity') that can serve the interests of conservative agendas every bit as effectively as leftist ones. In short, what the conflation of 'culture' with political rights can avoid is the arguably more radical equation between political emancipation and the removal of poverty and race and gender-based oppression. For, the fact that these inequalities *have* been justified in terms of a supposedly immutable 'cultural difference' in no way obliges us to accept the argument. For accepting cultural difference as a primary factor in political representation and participation implicates 'us' in pre-colonial and imperial dichotomies that have proved to be remarkably effective at maintaining gender privilege in particular.

The turmoil that accompanied the construction of an ethnographic museum in Ecuador is a striking example of this clash between those who apply themselves to restoring and revitalising 'indigenous traditions'

and the indigenous people themselves. The creation of the museum (Mundos Amazónicos, 'Amazon Worlds') was the brainchild of a local NGO, (Sinchi Sacha, 'powerful forest'), which received funding from the Canadian government in order to fulfil its main objective which was to strengthen local cultural pride and to generate employment for local people thereby providing a sustainable economic alternative to forest cutting. But, as Patrick Wilson[44] observes, the resistance and scepticism of the local indigenous organisations to this project was a factor that Sinchi Sacha had not anticipated. Jésus González, one of the three core members of Sinchi Sacha, expressed his frustration and incomprehension at the ingratitude of the local indigenous groups:

> I think that this is the great pain that the Indians of the Huacamayos have, and it is for this that they hate us. And I am tired of it ... because we have given them their symbols – we the mestizos, the whites, the Mishus [Quichua for 'mestizo'], the colonisers. We have built them a museum ... We have given them the element so that they can have culture, man, culture! Do you understand? And for this they hate us more.[45]

Arguably, the tendency of non-indigenous individuals and groups to detect a state of cultural crisis within the 'traditional' communities arises from their insistence upon viewing indigenous peoples as the embodiment of ancient traditions. This desire to assess the *contemporary* position of indigenous peoples in terms of their enactment and practice of traditional cultures conveniently assumes that 'the indigenous people' are not interested in the intersections between 'their' culture and contemporary social, economic and political realities. The paternalism of Gonzalez's vision of cultural and economic inclusion is striking:

> Our position is to initiate certain processes so that the communities can have, shall we say, a dignified relationship with the markets, so that they can structure themselves – to see if we can culturally serve the community ... We have said, for example, that the base of understanding for the Amazon is in its art. If a community does not have a structured artisanship, the process of [cultural decay] is greatly accelerated. Therefore, we have viewed artisanship as the base of our participation – art and artisanship.[46]

But if Gonzalez and his associates were very clear about the benefits of this 'dignified' inclusion into the wider capitalist markets they were

considerably less prepared to investigate their own material and ideological investments in this re-creation of indigenous cultural identity. Consequently, while Sinchi Sacha insisted upon involving the indigenous organisations as practitioners of 'tradition' and 'culture' they failed to address the indigenous organisations' own interest in the intersections between their crafts and the wider global market. Moreover, the assumption that the successful participation and involvement of indigenous people in the ethnographic museum could be accomplished simply by enabling them to practice and rekindle 'their' traditions replicated the very assumption of indigenous simplicity and political naiveté that the indigenous organisations themselves were anxious to disprove. For, the overdetermination of 'the indigenous people' with cultural significance was a practice that indigenous people themselves were determined to challenge.

As Wilson comments, the indigenous organisations regarded the history of development in the Amazon as inherently political, including the existence of domestic NGOs such as Sinchi Sacha. Indeed, the influx of intermediary NGOs that had arrived in Ecuador's Amazon in the 1970s with the intention of revitalising the indigenous communities were seen by many as merely another form of exploitation on the part of non-indigenous organisations. The reluctance of the indigenous organisations in Ecuador to gratefully enact and 'perform' 'their' traditional cultures should serve as a warning to those who insist upon diagnosing 'the native' purely in terms of her ability to practice her 'traditional way of life', for as Wilson concludes

> what was oddly absent from the conflict over the construction of the museum was discussion or debate about its contents. Sinchi Sacha ... never questioned its authority to represent Amazonian Indians ethnographically or its capacity to represent them accurately ... While the Unión Huacamayos and FOIN did not contest the cultural content of the museum what they did resist was Sinchi Sacha's attempt to depoliticise the use of indigenous culture for economic ends. Indigenous organizations have devoted as much attention to resisting cultural as material domination. As a result, they present their movements as struggles over cultural meaning as much as struggles for material benefit.[47]

The disquiet at any evidence of co-temporality, on the part of those who recruit the native as a living embodiment of traditional culture, dates back to Lévi Strauss's discomfort at seeing a feathered Indian using

a Parker pen in the New York Public Library room where he was compiling his research for his *Elementary Structures of Kinship* of native Indian culture.[48] Similarly, Margaret Mead found the interest of Arapesh Indians in cultural influences other than their own 'annoying', because as James Clifford notes, '[t]heir culture collecting complicated hers'.[49]

For the purity of 'the native' is, of course, wholly reliant upon her remaining in her proper place and time. Her purity is, in other words, wholly dependent upon her refraining from interrupting the time and place of the observer/guardian with any claims that contradict their own readings and investments in her difference. And 'the native', then and now, is required to contribute to the Western world precisely by demonstrating her indissoluble difference from it. The fact that she may be required to demonstrate the consumerist excesses of the Western world merely shuffles her significance whilst leaving her function firmly in place. As Alcida Ramos comments

> The present day ecological movement shares with the natavistic and the romantic discourses two main features: the emphasis on the 'naturalization' of the Indian and the affirmation of his purity. A latter-day edenic discourse in search of a threatened Eden, the ecological movement at its most naive presentation (although relatively recent, the movement already shows considerable internal differences), takes the Indian as a monolithic figure, he is also threatened and needs protection. And thus the protector, preferably European, comes full circle in five hundred years: from invader to saviour.[50]

Unfortunately, the fate of real Indians (who undermine such assumptions of nobility and in doing so challenge those that devote their energies to acting upon their notions of 'Indianness') is to lose any ethnic/cultural/racial identity at all. Consequently, Indians who interrupt and contradict the desires and representations of others cannot be Indians at all but merely an aberration of both the 'white' and 'the' Indian: a noxious mixture of both confirming, if confirmation were needed, that the role of the Indian as an essential and eternal other was the most resilient aspect of her identity all along:

> For all the apparently sympathetic and benign inclinations the environmentalist rhetoric – associated with the less sophisticated side of ecological activism – displays towards the Indians, it conceals an element of paternalism and intolerance that can easily come to the fore whenever the Indians betray its expectations. If a good Indian is

a pure Indian – and here as usual, the definition of purity is given by whites – an Indian who falls prey to western seduction (selling lumber, making pacts with the military, striking deals with corporations) is denigrated and doomed to fall lower than the white wheeler and dealer. An Indian who has sold out is ... much less deserving of understanding or forgiveness than a white in the same situation. Assigned the absurd role of the guardian of humanity's reserves of 'purity', the Amazonian Indian becomes charged with the 'white man's burden' in reverse, whether he wants it or not.[51]

Predictably enough the 'un-Indian' interest in matters of wealth expansion and land ownership continue to 'alarm' those who look to 'the Indian' to retain some kind of conservationist ethic in a world of unbridled capitalist expansion.[52]

The point here, of course, is not that Indians *lack* any interest in their old traditions or that they regard their relationship to the land in the same way as Western commentators but rather that 'we' lack the mandate and the basis for any definitive knowledge as to *what* 'the' Indian is or should be. Furthermore, the fact that people inherit different cultural traditions does not mean that some people possess more or less 'culture', but rather different ways of interpreting and addressing the practical constraints and possibilities that confront us all. Thus, if the Basotho people of Lesotho find that asserting their Sesotho identity offers some protection against the annihilating effects of political and economic dependence upon their British colonisers and the subsequent white settlers that accompanied 'independence' then this does not 'affirm' the importance of 'tradition' to Africa any more than it affirms the *intersections* between culture, power and political equality.[53]

However, the troubled history of intellectual appropriations of 'the people', or 'popular' culture, is strikingly absent in Parry's discussion of anti-colonial history. Instead, all is clear, since the radical intellectual simply needs to supplement her intellectual labour (compiling the organic traditions of the pre-colonial past) with 'a total definitive identification with the aspirations of the masses' which are the rejection of both 'foreign culture' and 'foreign rule'.[54] Unfortunately, while it is obvious that entrenched systems and structures of domination need the organised unity of the workers and colonised to collapse, it is far from clear how a national or cultural identity will function as that unifying principle. The fact that nations and cultures are mobile mixtures of reality and invention (i.e. *constructions* that are made by people and put to use in the 'real' world) is not helped when one adds to that the

difficulties involved in determining *where* exactly a national or cultural identity begins.

In other words, do we track mass antipathy to 'foreign rule' further back to the Mogul dynasties of fifteenth-century 'India' or celebrate the contribution of Muslim culture to the rich heritage of contemporary India? And, are the Indonesians, the first recorded visitors to Australia, to be regarded as foreign impostors or as an integral part of contemporary 'aboriginal identity'? Given the lengthy history of conquest and settlement across the globe, it is little wonder that 'national' and 'cultural' identity turns out to be considerably more difficult to 'ground' upon notions of 'a' discrete primordial origin than its proponents would like us to believe.

For Parry, the answer to the problem of merging national identity with national liberation lies in the hands of the anti-colonial intellectuals and leaders. In her reading, the role of the intellectual is sufficiently self-evident as to *solve* the problem of both restating indigenous culture *and* transforming the political present. Thus, the correct response to those who question the possibility of 'returning' to a pre-colonial past is to remind us that anti-colonial intellectuals were thinking in terms of a 'retour' to living cultures that were 'always subject to the innovations of the people'.[55] Accordingly, intellectuals, like Cabral, who called for a 'return to sources', were

> not recommending the recuperation of a pre-existent condition, but anticipating Glissant's notion of 'retour': 'We must return to the point from which we started ... not a return to the longing of origins, to some immutable, state of being, but a return to the point of entanglement, from which we were forcibly turned away ...' Cabral's phrase should, therefore be understood as compiling the inventory of intelligible and still vital indigenous practices that are always subject to innovation and at no time more ingenious than during the popular resurgence of liberation struggles.[56]

Parry adds that faced with such an immense task of organising mass struggles, liberation theorists had to create a strong sense of national identity in order to produce a solidified opposition to colonial rule.

Unfortunately, the question that Parry raises and neglects to answer is whether the masses do possess a collective identity or whether they are being said to require evidence *of* their collective national identity. For surely, if 'culture' and 'the people' are as distinct and unified as Parry and Cabral imply then there is no need to construct and rebuild a

national identity. Moreover, if we are talking about the need to construct native culture in order to create a unified resistance to colonialism and its legacies, then this is surely to delve into those murky areas of 'representation' and 'manufacture' that 'native culture' is supposed to resolutely refute through its authentic realism. Parry's dismissal of such matters results in a striking lack of attention to the question of *who* decides *which* traditions constitute the pre-colonial past.

In much the same way as Marxist theory, the anti-colonial intellectual emerges as merely a facilitator of 'the people's' aspirations. The extent to which this facilitation is dependent upon subjective interpretations as to which traditions articulate 'the people' is obscured, as it is in Marxist theory, by a routine emphasis upon the intellectual service of the radical intellectual. Thus, the past can be 'compiled' and assembled in accordance with whatever surviving indigenous practices remain without any obvious need to ponder whether these practices are equally appreciated by 'the' indigenous people. Noticeably, the masses are not granted leave to reassess their 'own' practices, much less to decide to abandon them altogether. And any consideration of the extent to which pre-existing inequalities (notably ones based on gender)[57] complicate the homogeneity of 'the people's' traditions can be sidelined by our determination to speak for 'them'.

This perception of the radical intellectual as the anonymous facilitator of the people's liberation also permeates Sardar's work, and occasionally surfaces to reveal the crucial task that befalls the radical non-Western intellectual. Like Parry, Sardar's faith in 'the people', and his assumption that identifying with the people is a matter of political choice rather than an ongoing aspiration, enables him to present the intellectual as fulfilling a vitally specific role. For, as Sardar explains, 'the other', while it possesses and offers different 'ways of knowing', cannot simply be left unaccompanied and unmediated to express this non-Western viewpoint but needs 'the animation of thought, critically undertaken in the sincere belief that the value parameters matter and must be maintained'.[58] In other words, the natives, like the proletariats of Marxist theory, are the raw material in need of 'animation' whereupon they can resume and rediscover their ruptured connections with their forbears. Or, to put it another way, without this intellectual intervention the native will remain in the possession of 'different ways of knowing' but will have no idea how to relate them to the contemporary world. The intellectual here thus serves the same purpose as 'he' did for Marx, namely transforming the people's experience into knowledge and agency.

Sardar's optimistic recruitment of Muslim intellectuals for the task of securing a universal theory and practice of liberation mirrors Cedric

Robinson's identification of the black Marxist tradition as one that has evolved into the natural successor of the European socialist tradition. Thus, Robinson identifies the black Marxist tradition as properly universal because it is uniquely capable of delivering the universal principles that Marx and his followers imagined themselves to be acting upon, while Sardar looks to the Muslim intellectual to repair the destructive exclusions of European history and usher in a new reciprocal age. In both accounts history is depicted as a process in which the dispossessed are gradually overcoming their alienation in order to usher in a genuinely universal world order.

Meanwhile, for Benita Parry such optimism in the passage of history to deliver a humane future is tempered by the ferocious expansion of Western capitalism across the world and the parallel rejection of earlier libertarian anti-colonialism nationalism on the part of prominent 'post-colonial' intellectuals. Thus she points out that we need to consider

> how the consolidation of the capitalist world system since the 1980s has made it virtually impossible for any legally sovereign state to pursue either redistributive or egalitarian policies.[59]

Parry argues that we need to supplement our support for liberation struggles with a commitment to socialism in order to move beyond resistance to a transcendence of both the pre-colonial past and the post-colonial present. Thus, she distinguishes between anti-colonial manifestos which target colonialism and socialist programmes that move beyond a rejection of the colonial order to an imaginative and liberatory transcendence of the dominant capitalist system.[60]

As Parry documents, this determination to transcend the foundations of colonial society was evident in the African Party for the Independence of Guinea and Cape Verde (PAIGC), whose purpose, as Cabral explained, was, 'the destruction of the capitalist system … implanted by imperialism'.[61] Or, as Thomas Sankara, put it to a Swiss journalist, shortly after the coup which established Burkina Faso:

> You cannot carry out fundamental change without a certain amount of madness. In this case it comes from non-conformity, the courage to turn your back on old formulas, the courage to invent the future.[62]

Clearly, the anti-colonial leaderships of the newly independent African countries were not attempting to establish their new societies upon notions of 'traditional' pre-colonial traditions but were looking to create a *different* future for their citizens. And while this did involve

a re-statement of a non-Western dignity and cultural vitality that had been quashed under colonialism, it also meant, for many prominent leaders, embracing the insights of the Western radical tradition, notably Marxism. Thus, Cabral spoke of the need for an intellectual vanguard that could rouse and educate the 'man in the street', adding that '[t]he members of this organization must bring light to those who live in ignorance'.[63]

Significantly, although Parry notes the various limitations of prominent anti-colonial leaders and intellectuals she does not question the capacity of national liberation movements to express the will of the people. Or rather, she distinguishes between specific forms of national liberation struggles in order to isolate 'insurgent nationalism' as uniquely expressive of the people. Thus, she argues that anti-colonialism nationalism lacked the patriotic fervour of imperial nationalism. And yet even as she identifies insurgent nationalism as the spontaneous will of the people to overthrow colonial rule, she simultaneously defines it as a form of nationalism that was 'conceived' by liberation theorists who had to unite the people in order to displace and defeat the colonial state:

> Unlike its elite or bourgeois forms insurgent nationalism was conceived as a means of soliciting the participation of heterogeneous communities and classes in defeating and displacing the colonial state.[64]

But while there is obviously a very different intention at work in anti-colonial and bourgeois/elite nationalist efforts, there is nevertheless a simple connection; namely, that a specific group of people seek to unite 'the people' in order to make 'a' national community.

In both accounts mobilisation of the majority population is *sought* in order to realise a specific kind of society and citizen which means that in both accounts 'the people' are as much an idea as they are a material reality. In other words, what both anti-colonial leaderships and bourgeois dominance reveal is that 'the people' as they are now do not exist as 'the people', they need to be in order for 'the nation' to make sense. For, 'the people', as those who were solicited to participate in the struggle, did not, in this reading, necessarily perceive of the necessity for 'insurgent nationalism' themselves. Indeed, nationalism here is figured as an answer to the *problem* of mobilising a colonised society against colonial rule. Given this, the power and coercion that is needed to secure an oppositional unity towards colonial rule, must be subjected to examination rather than be assumed to be inherently and infallibly for the common good. For, the fundamental question that must be raised is

whether 'national' liberation will prove to be *equally* liberating for the disparate classes and communities that oppose colonial rule. And if some people remain less free than others after independence then what exactly does this say about the particular kind of cohesion that was being sought?

Significantly, questioning the capacity of nationalist theory alone to secure liberation remains a dangerous pursuit. For, as Barbara Harlow points out, the penalty for thinking beyond the nation was, for anti-colonial intellectuals and leaders such as Amílcar Cabral and Walter Rodney (and we can add here Thomas Sankara) assassination.[65] Moreover, their murders were not simply the action of hostile colonial powers but the work of their own former comrades.[66] Uncertainty regarding the ability of national liberation to deliver a just and progressive postcolonial society dominated the later work of both Fanon and Cabral. Thus, no sooner had they identified nationalist struggle as the means by which the colonial state should be overthrown than Fanon and Cabral both looked to abolish national sentiment in exchange for a wider more international vision. For Parry, this leap from nationalism to internationalism is evidence of the ability of nationalist struggle to articulate wider international goals. Accordingly she reminds us that

> amongst liberation theorists, Fanon was not alone in declaring that '[i]t is at the heart of national consciousness that international consciousness lives and grows (Fanon 1965), a dialectical formulation and a Marxist sentiment which neither categorically rejects anticolonial nationalism or proleptically embraces a contemporary cultural politics of transnationalism.[67]

Steve Pile,[68] too, argues that Fanon's attempt to theorise a way in which to move national liberation beyond the nation provides us with evidence that nationalist politics is not inevitably rigid and reactionary. For Pile, Fanon and other anti-colonial radicals had no choice other than to work with nationalism in order to defeat the colonial state, and their attempts to break out of the confines of nationalist rhetoric and principles indicates that nationalism itself is a pragmatic, if potentially difficult, necessity that nationalist intellectuals themselves grappled with.

Pile points out that Fanon spent his life wrestling with the dangers involved in a successful national liberation movement. Fanon argued for the necessity of socialism (specifically economic nationalisation) precisely because he feared that the new nationalist elites would replicate the oppression of their colonial predecessors and engage with the

old colonial powers thus maintaining and introducing new forms of colonialism. Thus, the problem for Fanon was that he regarded national liberation movements as essential for the creation of an independent and politically vibrant 'third world' whilst at the same time being deeply suspicious of the very grounds for unity that nationalism inevitably evokes – namely, blood, history, land and race. As Pile notes, Fanon scorned attempts to ground and unify struggles through seemingly natural spatial scales:

> Geographical spaces are troubling spaces. Fanon decries all regional and sectional parochialism, yet relies on national parochialism to forge an anti-colonial struggle and to identify the subjects of revolution. The land and the people are ambiguously placed in his revolutionary theory: they are both what needs to be freed and also the agents through which liberation is to be defined and achieved. Paradoxically, Fanon privileges the nation in his revolutionary theory, yet the nation is simultaneously the scale of oppression. In Fanon's abstract dialectics, freedom is doomed to vacillate between the land and the people, since the land and the people rarely coincide.[69]

Thus, even as Fanon asserts the practical necessity for third-world nationalist struggle, he moves on to the necessity of constructing new revolutionary subjectivities that will abolish the confines of a nationalist victory.

Like Marx on the eve of the abolition of the capitalist world, both Cabral and Fanon greet national liberation with a desire to eradicate the foundations of both the colonial state *and* the nationalist struggle that was necessary in order to extinguish the colonial state. Fanon looks towards new revolutionary subjectivities and recommends that 'the people' be free to abolish all forms of elite power, including those of their anti-colonial leaders, while Cabral emphasised that the anti-colonial struggle was only genuinely revolutionary if it *continued* to eradicate injustice and transform the postcolonial world.

It is this political restlessness on the part of leading anti-colonial radicals such as Fanon and Cabral that leads Pile to conclude that nationalism should not be dismissed as a reactionary ideology or practice. Thus, he observes that in Fanon's later writings the nation could be viewed as only a first and ultimately expendable link in a chain which connects people together. In short, the nation, conceived now as merely a tentative first step *into* the world, could be viewed as a link to wider connections:

Individual experience because it is national and because it is a link in the chain of national existence, ceases to be individual and shrunken and is enabled to open out the truth of the nation and of the world.[70]

Accordingly, we can regard Fanon as articulating 'useful ambiguities' that point to the potential for wider ambitions to reside within nationalist discourse. Thus Fanon identifies the responsibilities of native man to be 'global' rather than 'national', and adds that responsibility within the nation must extend to the other cultures that the nation does not represent but nevertheless exist. Pile concludes that Fanon's awareness of the difficulties involved in constructing political citizenship and responsibility around ideas of 'a' nation suggests that nationalist discourses *did* produce international aspirations among the more radical nationalist leaders and intellectuals:

> Fanon, I am arguing was edging towards a sense of spatial comradeship in which the politics of location co-ordinates not only your place in the world, but also a wider set of connections with others, who may be in very different places, or indeed, in the same space.[71]

But, in order to accept Pile's conclusion, we need to agree that the fundamental problem that Fanon, and other leading anti-colonial radicals, correctly wrestled with is how to reconcile the *real* diversity within and between nations with the equally *real* need to defeat colonial rule through organised nationalist struggle. Unfortunately what this 'dialectic' or 'radical ambiguity' assumes is that human emancipation can be debated *within* a model that diligently refuses to problematise its conception of 'the people' either in its implicitly (and often explicitly) male form or in terms of its definitive possession of revolutionary historical capability.

In fact, it is striking how more recent studies of anti-colonial nationalism apply themselves to the liberatory potential of nationalism whilst reproducing the masculinist and 'populist' assumptions of earlier anti-colonial intellectuals and leaders. It is in this spirit that Ntongela Masilela approves Cabral's 'correction' of Fanon's 'misreading' of history.[72] Thus, he argues that Fanon mistakenly identified the peasantry as the revolutionary class that would liberate the third world, a 'misreading' that was usefully corrected by Cabral's study of classes in Guinea which led him to realise that the principal revolutionary actors in the third world were the working classes. Such deliberations between identifying the peasants or the workers as the raw material for a new society have

proved to be remarkably successful in preventing any undue attention to the hubris on the part of intellectuals defining other people as the 'physical' motor for history.

The eerie emptiness of anti-colonial depictions of 'the people' under colonialism live on in recent commentaries that uncritically reaffirm Cabral and Fanon's contention that Africa *was* a continent that lacked history, ideology, imagination or personality until the time of anti-colonial struggle.[73] Significantly, both Fanon and Cabral agreed that the gravest danger facing Africa and the third world was not so much colonial power and authority as the absence of any form of revolutionary ideology that could combat and transform colonial institutions and ideologies. Thus, Cabral argued that

> the ideological deficiency, not to say the total lack of ideology within the national liberation movements – which is basically due to ignorance – of the historical reality which these movements claim to transform – constitutes one of the greatest weaknesses of our struggle against imperialism, if not the greatest weakness of all.[74]

While Fanon observed that

> colonialism and its derivatives do not, as a matter of fact, constitute the present enemies of Africa. In a short time, this continent will be liberated. For my part, the deeper I enter into the cultures and the political circles, the surer I am that the greater danger that threatens Africa is the absence of ideology.[75]

This postulation of ideological absence within the nationalist struggle was almost inevitable given that the ability of the colonised masses to overthrow colonial oppression had been so unanimously attributed to the desire of the colonised to reject colonial authority in favour of their own pre-colonial identities and traditions. And while many leading African and third-world intellectuals did contest the notion that Africa lacked history and ideology *before* the colonial invasion, they nevertheless accepted the notion that during colonialism Africa was expelled from History. Unfortunately, the argument that colonialism did introduce 'development' (that is to say 'History), into Africa and the third world is a regular reference in studies of African history.[76]

For Cabral, the 'cultural resistance' on the part of the people constituted one of the greatest victories of the African people. However, arguing that the *motive* for resisting and opposing colonial rule was the desire on

the part of the masses to *retain* their cultural traditions and identity meant that any desire on the part of radical anti-colonial leaders and intellectuals to *change* the identities and traditions of the colonised masses risked confronting the same mass resistance that had inspired them to reject colonial rule and authority. Consequently, if radical anti-colonial nationalist discourse desires radical new subjectivities and politics for the postcolonial nation then it either has to abandon its model of the cultural resistance of the masses or locate the agent for transformation somewhere else. Cabral and Fanon, in the same way as Marx, locate the origins of mass transformation within the popular struggle itself. Thus, the people in the process of collectively defying colonial rule become different subjects. Consequently, for Cabral a national liberation struggle *becomes* a cultural act that expands previous cultural assumptions and practices.

My point here is not that this does not happen but rather that the effect of this reading of the beneficial relation between the masses and their struggle is to avoid any focus upon the capacity of the anti-colonial leaders and intellectuals to change. Inevitably then, the pressing need for *all* of us to examine our own capacity to change and our own reliance on contestable 'cultural' beliefs and practices is nudged out of the frame. Restricting the exploration of humanity's capacity for radical change to 'the people' reduces them to the laboratory-like function that they fulfilled for Marxist theory. And the fact that this question should *equally* apply to those intellectuals and leaders who aspire to change the world is conveniently circumvented. Instead the duty of the intellectual becomes one of recognising that 'the people' must be given the freedom to rule themselves. As Cabral put it:

> We must constantly go forward to put power into the hands of our people, to make a profound change in the life of our people, even to put all the means for defense into the hands of our people, so that it is the people who defend our revolution ... Anyone who rules his people but fears the people is in a bad way. We must never fear the people.[77]

Clearly, Cabral and Fanon were firmly on the side of 'the people' exercising power in the postcolonial nation but what was absent in their discourse was any recognition that their instance upon the absence of ideology in Africa during colonialism made it that much more difficult to envisage *how* the people would construct a radically different postcolonial nation.

A popular answer to this problem has been to identify the texts of prominent anti-colonial theorists as themselves marking the origins of opposition to colonialism. Thus, Ntongela Masilela asserts that there is 'little doubt' that Fanon's *The Wretched of the Earth* 'implanted a revolutionary ideology in Africa'.[78] I am not disputing the power or influence of Fanon's text upon political struggle but I am querying the notion that the capacity of political texts to inspire political action proves that critical and political thought did not exist prior to the text. In other words, I am questioning Masilela's depiction of the *relation* between texts and 'the people' which seems to assume that texts function as some kind of autonomous motor for political thought upon a previously unconscious people.

By locating the origins of revolutionary thought and action within anti-colonial texts commentators like Masilela are able to insist that 'the people' continue to 'fulfil' their historical destiny through an obedient adherence to Classical African Marxism:

> The many breakthroughs that are still to come in Africa during the next centuries can only be on the basis of Classical African Marxism, for this materialist theory of history is Africa's living philosophy today. There can be no going beyond it until all the historical tasks it calls forth have been fulfilled by the African peoples.[79]

Of course, this depiction of the relation between the anti-colonial theoretical tradition and 'the people' comfortably assumes that radical anti-colonial theory can and does express 'the people'. Consequently, if we query such readings of 'the people' we are proposing nothing less than to remove 'the people' from both theoretical and practical consequence. The fact that theoretical investigations into anti-colonial constructions of 'the people' lead so easily into charges of 'ignoring' or undermining the *existence* of the people reflects nothing less than the ability of anti-colonial theorists to grant for themselves an exclusive understanding and attachment to those that they study, organise and seek to represent.

And yet the very fact that anti-colonial and nationalist theory is embroiled in *representations* of the people is apparent in the dissensions of those who dispute their presence in anti-colonial and nationalist theory. Women's objections to their inclusion in nationalist theory have, it seems, done little to halt the tedious bracketing of women's oppression as a regrettable shortcoming in an otherwise triumphant march towards 'human' liberation. For unfortunately, the search for a 'new society' and

'new' revolutionary subjectivities has been, for the most part, silent about the ability of the old society to privilege men and uncritical in its assumption that a revolution can be achieved without attending to the oppression of women. Little wonder then that women have long suspected that theorists such as Cabral and Fanon, who recommended the bloody and violent 're-entry' of third world peoples into history through armed struggle, were expressing their own desire to give birth to a 'new' patriarchal order. As Chow argues

> In order to conceive of community without women Fanon, like all revolutionary male thinkers bonds instead with 'the people': which is the figure that empowers him in this *competition between the sexes* for the *birthing* of a new community. Community formation thus takes on, at the theoretical level, the import of a sexual struggle – a seizing of power to reproduce and procreate. It is in this sense that the 'native' – etymologically linked to 'nation' and also to 'birth' – becomes the progeny of the male postcolonial critic. The exclusive bond with this progeny allows for the fantasy of undoing and out-doing woman.[80]

It is this sense that women are not simply marginalised in nationalist discourse but included in ways that entrench patriarchal privilege that concerns radical women and feminists who also aspire to create new revolutionary subjectivities.

9
Outsiders: Women and Radical Theory

Of the three traditions that I have discussed so far in this book, it is arguably nationalist discourse that has provoked the most stinging criticism from feminist commentators. The sense that nationalist theory is essentially a male narrative that contributes towards the stable reproduction of masculine privilege was summed up by Cynthia Enloe who argued that 'nationalism typically has sprung from masculinized memory, masculinized humiliation and masculinized hope'.[1] Feminist commentators, such as Mary K. Meyer have identified the extent to which nationalist rhetoric depends upon the bodies of women to represent the nation:

> Women or their bodies represent the sexualized/biological blood-ties that demarcate the nation, a word that comes from the Latin *natio<natus*, born, and *nascar*, to be born.[2]

But this is a decidedly specific female body; one which is above all a source of national regeneration. For as V. Spike Peterson points out:

> The nation-as-woman trope 'works' only if the imaginary body/woman is assumed to be (heterosexually) fertile. Imagining the beloved country as a female child, a lesbian, a prostitute, or a post-menopausal wise woman generates quite different pictures, which enable quite different understandings of community.[3]

In their analysis of popular metaphors that are used in nationalist speech and theory, Stephen Reicher and Nick Hopkins point out that after animal metaphors[4] by far the most prevalent are those that relate to gender. As Reicher and Hopkins observe, arguably the most work has

been put into naturalising gender relations within the family unit. However, while gender can be successfully naturalised when it is applied to relations between men and women the same, they argue, cannot be said of efforts to naturalise the family:

> Families involve more than two people and hence more than one set of relations: that between husband and wife; that between parents and children; that between mother and daughter; that between husband and mother in law and so on. The consequence is that family metaphors are particularly useful because they can be used to so many ends.[5]

Reicher and Hopkins cite the ability of both critics and advocates, of the British Government's colonial relationship with North America in the eighteenth century, to utilise the same familial metaphors for entirely different purposes. Thus, for Soame Jenyns the colonies' opposition to taxation indicated that the time had come to sever the 'parent-child' bond while for Edmund Burke the colonies had demonstrated their filial duty by averting famine in the mother country.[6] For Reicher and Hopkins, what is instructive about this manipulation of the 'parent-child' metaphor is that it is able to accommodate entirely different political arguments and objectives.

Unfortunately, however, the family model itself is built upon pre-given and hierarchical gender norms, which is precisely why it is so useful for nationalist theory. Consequently, the 'new' nation can be re-imagined within the comforting parameters of an undisturbed heterosexual gender hierarchy. Thus, when Juan Perón challenged the liberals' definition of Spain as Argentina's 'stepmother' by claiming it instead to be 'our mother'[7] he reinforced, rather than reconfigured the traditional family.

The extent to which the emphasis upon women as mothers dominates nationalist theory does not, as Luce Irigaray points out, constitute a radical rupture from the Western philosophical tradition:

> 'Motherhood' provides the focus for the definition of 'woman' which runs through the entire Western philosophical tradition. Whereas 'man' is recognized as separate and separable from 'father', there is no space within (male-centred) discourse for 'woman' disassociated from 'mother'.[8]

Clearly, the identification of the nation as female and of women in the nation as responsible for the reproduction of the national collectivity

gives women a powerful role in nationalist theory. In Rey Chow's reading, male anti-colonial attempts to theorise the nation have been marked by a sustained attempt to re-imagine the nation without any accompanying challenges to its patriarchal foundations. Consequently, women are central to the concerns of the male anti-colonial theorist and activist but must also be shown to be of distinctly secondary importance. Thus, as Chow points out, Frantz Fanon's apparent disinterest in the black woman ('I know nothing about her') was at odds with his laborious attempts to theorise women within pre-colonial and post-colonial nations. Chow tracks Fanon's ideas of national community back to Sigmund Freud's classic work, *Totem and Taboo*,[9] which was the culmination of his anthropological, sociological and religious studies of 'primitive' societies. Freud concluded that community participation is achieved through the sacrificial murder of the primal father, who is then elevated to the status of a god or 'totem', and by the institution of a law prohibiting incest. As Chow observes, this postulation of the properly masculine origin of the community is accompanied by a move to define women exclusively in terms of their sexual difference and to conceive of that sexual difference as a threat to the stability of the community. Women, as those who possess the power to destroy 'the community' can, in this reading, be legitimately deprived of power in order to guarantee the stability of 'the community'. For as Chow points out, Freud's text confirms

> the unmistakable recognition of female sexuality as a form of physical power. It is this physical power, this potentiality of transmission, confusion, and reproduction through actual bodies, that could break down all the boundaries and thus disrupt social order in the most fundamental fashion.[10]

Thus, Fanon's conception of black women as potential traitors of 'the' national community, far from signalling his commitment to the formation of radical new subjectivities instead, refers back to a masculine tradition of defining woman exclusively in terms of her biological difference and regarding this difference as constituting the gravest threat to the patriarchal foundations of 'community'. As Chow documents, Fanon's sympathetic accounts of the black man's existential angst, that at times leads him towards a desire to be white, contrasts tellingly with his severity towards any such aspirations on the part of black women.

Moreover, Fanon's descriptions of black women as deliberately manipulating black and white men, ensures that her sexual 'choices' can never

be ones that reflect her honourable inclusion in the nation. For, her desire for the black man (because of his social inferiority) or the white man (because of his social superiority) confirms that black women's sexuality is only intelligible within the confines of a masculine racial hierarchy *and* that it is only when black men and white men achieve parity that her sexual choices can be extricated from a calculated investment in the tragic estrangement between black and white men. For, it is this tragic estrangement that preoccupies Fanon towards the end of *Black Skin, White Masks* – one that he speculates can and will be overcome:

> On the field of battle, its four corners marked by the scores of Negroes hanged by their testicles, a monument is slowly being built that promises to be majestic. And at the top of this monument, I can already see a white man and a black man *hand in hand*. (emphasis in the original)[11]

Unsurprisingly, the hopes that Fanon coveted for a bright and fraternal future were dependent upon black women respecting the present plight of black men. Thus, if black men and white men could be imagined holding hands, no such innocent joy was attributed to the friendship of black women and white men. Indeed, black women who desired white men were guilty of postponing the resolution between men by contributing to the psychic alienation and insecurities of black men.

Consequently, contact and desire between black women and white men, displaced the proper union that was needed to repair and remake the postcolonial nation by casting black men 'outside' the nation. As Jacqui Alexander argues,

> women's sexual agency … and erotic autonomy have always been troublesome for the state … pos[ing] a challenge to the ideological anchor of an originary nuclear family … which perpetuates the fiction that the family is the cornerstone of society. Erotic autonomy signals danger to the heterosexual family and to the nation.[12]

In Fanon's reading, far from demonstrating their commitment to the common humanity of black and white men, the black woman and mulatto demonstrate instead their absorption of the destructive lessons of racism and imperialism. Thus, he explains that

> there are two such women: the Negress and the mulatto. The first has only one possibility and one concern: to turn white. The second

wants not only to turn white but also to avoid slipping back. What indeed could be more illogical than a mulatto woman's acceptance of a Negro husband?[13]

In other words, black women, in Fanon's reading, bear the consequences of the outrageous inequality of black men vis-à-vis white men. Consequently, his optimistic premonition of a black man and a white man holding hands confirms that the 'new' community that he had in mind was one that consolidated and extended the patriarchal underpinnings of the colonial order. Significantly, Fanon's insistence that black female loyalty to black men *is* their proper contribution to the struggle against racism survives today, and has proved to be a valuable source of power for those black men who wish to restrict sexual and political freedom to themselves.[14]

Running alongside the notion that black women can best demonstrate their commitment to the anti-colonial (or anti-racist) cause through their sexual choices is the evident neglect of any interest in the notion of women's relations with each other in prominent nationalist theory. While brotherhood exists and is celebrated as a founding principle of the nation, sisterhood is conspicuous by its absence. For as Peterson observes,

> while men are expected to bond politically with other men of the state/nation, the heterosexist state denies women's homosexual bonding, and the public-private dichotomy denies women's political bonding. Rather, as an effect of patriarchal households and the family wage model, women are linked to the state through their fathers/husbands; women are expected to bond only through and with 'their men'.[15]

Significantly, while male theorists and activists have for the most part neglected to consider the complex implications of male solidarity, women – by contrast – have been embroiled in a lengthy and often painful debate about the *possibility* for female solidarity.[16] Unfortunately, however, the necessary and productive work that has taken place within feminist theory and activism has been accompanied by an equivalent interest in women's differences by the dominant patriarchal culture. Thus, while feminists, for the most part, explore the differences between women in order to rethink how gender oppression can be defined and mobilised against the dominant patriarchal culture, the dominant culture for its part continues to utilise differences between women in order to affirm the impossibilities of sisterhood. Moreover, because women function in patriarchal discourse as a convenient shorthand for the

character of the nation, any differences that are asserted between Western and non-Western women invariably contribute towards the assertion of differences between specific cultures and nations. As symbolic metaphors for the nation or culture at large, any discussion of actual women in these nations remains optional. For as Zillah Eisenstein notes,

> because the nation fantasizes women in a homogenised abstracted familial order, women become a metaphor for what they represent, rather than what they are. First-world women of the west represent modernity; women of the third-world south and east represent tradition.[17]

Accordingly, Ziauddin Sardar's[18] discussion of the differences between a redundant and culturally depleted postmodern West and a vibrant traditional non-West is succinctly illustrated by the photograph on the book's cover. Rasheed Araeen's photograph, entitled 'Jouissance', depicts a smiling white woman offering a packet of cigarettes to a veiled Muslim woman. Three cigarettes protrude from the packet which advertise the name 'West' and the white woman functioning as a comforting guide to the route of Western depravity is smiling reassuringly at the Muslim woman her own cigarette already lit and in her hand. The Muslim woman's expression is ambiguous; her raised eyebrows could be signalling interest or shock or a combination of both; given that Sardar declines to discuss women in his text she is destined to remain an enigma. However, the photograph successfully encapsulates Sardar's argument precisely because women symbolise cultural difference whilst at the same time being entirely absent in any accompanying discussion of culture.

Such depictions of national and cultural relations through images of women confirm that women can be summoned to signify the supposed essence of 'a' culture even when the author is proposing that a synthesis or reconciliation between different nations and cultures is essential. Sardar's optimistic extraction of 'the Muslim intellectual',[19] as someone who is uniquely equipped to achieve this, is in this sense explicitly male. His utilisation of an image of women as embodying the essence of their cultures draws upon a well-worn tradition of insisting that women perform the crucial task of preserving 'the' national culture. As Peterson argues,

> because of their assigned roles in social reproduction, women are often stereotyped as 'cultural carriers'. When minority groups feel

threatened they may increase the isolation of 'their' women from exposure to other groups or the legislative reach of the state. Tress writes that in Israel, 'Zionist ideology considered women to be the embodiment of the home front'. While political transformations might require a 'new Jewish man,' the Jewish woman was to remain domesticated.[20]

It is this that ensures that male theorists and intellectuals can speculate about the positive need for nations and cultures to learn from each other whilst remaining suspicious of any evidence of cultural and political exchange between women. In short, what for men constitutes a progressive sign of intellectual maturity constitutes a dangerous case of cultural 'contamination' when it occurs between women. It is difficult not to conclude that many non-Western male theorists, like their Western counterparts, do not want women to exchange their ideas and experiences, since any such exchanges both disturb the convenient status of women as embodying 'a' cultural essence *and* threaten to challenge the foundations of patriarchal privilege. Not surprisingly, the antipathy of 'progressive' non-Western male intellectuals towards 'their' women 'encountering' feminism continues to irritate black women and women of color. For as Cherrie Moraga points out:

> Over and over again, Chicanas trivialize the women's movement as being merely a white middle-class thing, having little to offer women of color ... Interestingly, it is perfectly acceptable among Chicano males to use white theoreticians, e.g. Marx and Engels, to develop a theory of Chicana oppression. It is unacceptable, however, for the Chicana to use white sources by women to develop a theory of Chicana oppression.[21]

And as Uma Narayan points out, the critical charge of 'westernization' that is frequently levelled at non-Western women is not one that men are about to apply to themselves:

> This 'selective labeling' of certain changes and not others as symptoms of 'Westernization' reflects underlying political agendas. For instance ... Hindu fundamentalists ... characterize Indian feminist issues as symptoms of 'Westernization' even while they skilfully use contemporary media ... to propagate their ideological messages.[22]

The combined forces of a patriarchal insistence that virtuous women will gladly serve as visible representations of 'their' cultures and the

readiness of too many Western feminists and women to regard 'the Arab woman', in particular, as a thoroughly subjugated victim have produced what can seem to be intractable obstacles for those women who want to make alliances across national, racial and class divisions. The effects of race and racism have made alliances between women and men who experience that oppression (or indeed that privilege) far more straightforward than alliances based upon gender and sexuality precisely because it is an oppression that divides women. But, while patriarchy softens the brutality of racial and class oppression for men, women struggle to find any equivalent contexts that can enable them to connect or share their experiences.

The routine practice of contrasting women in order to demonstrate profound 'differences' between nations and cultures is particularly evident in times of war and, of course, particularly effective in the present political climate when 'the West' and 'Islam' are recruited as the contexts for military aggression. The veiled Muslim woman and the independent Western woman are cited as evidence of the difference between the West and non-West and function to cement the loyalties of women to 'their' men. The customary unease that surrounds the idea of women combatants in the West can thus be overridden by the opportunity to demonstrate the liberties enjoyed by Western women. Unfortunately, the gravity of the contemporary world 'order' enables the irony of patriarchal Western medias pre-senting 'their' women as evidence of the advanced credentials of Western societies to pass, for the most part, without comment. As Peterson notes,

> during the Gulf War the 'oppression' of Arab women (veiled, con-fined, unable to drive cars) was contrasted with the 'independence' of United States women (armed, at large, able to drive tanks), thus suggesting a 'civilizing' tone to the war against Iraq.[23]

Winifred Woodhull[24] documents how both Fanon and French colo-nialists identified Algerian women as the key symbol and object in assessing the nation. Significantly, although Fanon aligned the Algerian women combatants with the European women of Algeria who were arrested for supporting the national liberation struggle he obscured any common ground between them by referring to the Algerian female combatant entering the European district of the city in Western dress as 'completely nude'.[25]

For Mai Ghoussoub, the time has come to unravel 'the double knot' that binds together definitions of femininity and religion and religion

and nationality in Arab culture and politics. She contends that these 'fatal connections' have meant that '[E]very assertion of the second sex can be charged – in a virtually unanimous register – with impiety to Islam and treason to the nation.'[26] Arguably, women should be suspicious of attempts to circumvent the question of gender oppression, since there is little evidence that it has acquired any urgency *after* national liberation struggles, or, for that matter, after the successful bourgeois capture of the state throughout Western Europe and North America.[27] Thus, as Marie-Aimee Helie-Lucas argues, denying the importance of gender oppression in the present almost guarantees inattention to it once the nation has been 'liberated':

> It is never, has never been the right moment to protest ... in the name of women's interests and rights: not during the liberation struggle against colonialism, because all forces should be mobilised against the principal enemy: French colonialism; not after Independence, because all forces should be mobilized to build up the devastated country; not now that racist imperialistic Western governments are attacking Islam and the Third World etc. Defending women's rights 'now' (this 'now' being ANY historical moment) is always a betrayal – of the people, of the nation, of the revolution of Islam, of national identity, of cultural roots, of the Third World.[28]

For Woodhull the only way to overcome the differences between women across the globe lies in Western feminists aligning themselves with those women who are criticising the patriarchal constraints of their societies. Thus she criticises Barbara Harlow's essay[29] which analyses the French occupation of Algeria as an illuminating study that incorporates the work of North African feminists but does not support their critical attempts to evaluate the status of Arab women. As Woodhull observes,

> this leads Harlow to give undue approval, for example, to 'reforms' of women's civil status in Arab countries, reforms unequivocally denounced by the very feminists she cites.[30]

Presumably, Harlow's identification of 'progress' in Arab countries is intended to differentiate her work from those who are keen to dismiss the Arab world as a seething cauldron of fanaticism and oppression. However, as Uma Narayan points out, such efforts to 'respect' or 'positively' evaluate the non-West, particularly when they are accompanied

by a desire to criticise patriarchy in the West, contain other altogether less progressive implications. Narayan cites the argument advanced by Marilyn Friedman, who asserted that her 'respect' for women in other cultures compelled her to refrain from 'challenging' their lives unless she was explicitly invited to do so.[31] For Narayan this refusal to critically engage with women from other cultures denies third-world women the opportunity to enter the 'dialogue' as equal participants. In other words, far from demonstrating the egalitarian and multicultural credentials of the Western participant it signals instead her refusal to vacate the seat of power. As Narayan argues,

> such foreclosures can leave Third-World individuals unsure about whether their failures to make sense will be pointed out, or whether their failures to convince will be subject to interrogation. Being in such situations feels like participating in some sort of 'ritual of diversity,' where the 'Insider' has the instrumental role of 'speaking difference' but is not seen to have her own stakes in hearing a rich range of responses and criticisms that would enable her to refine, rearticulate, or defend her account … I find it unsettling to think that when I present my views in public or academic contexts, I need to specifically signal that critical responses to my views from mainstream members of the audience are permissible or welcome. I would argue that, in public discursive encounters, refraining from criticism as a form of 'deference' to 'Authentic Insiders' functions to defer a rich and genuine engagement with their views and work.[32]

However, the dangers of discussing the propriety of criticism *only* in the contexts of 'third world feminism' is that it reduces the need for Western feminists to attend to their own ideological assumptions. Consequently, Woodhull's valuable plea for combining a critical rejection of Arab racism in America with a critical stance towards patriarchy in Arab societies needs to be supplemented with the need for Western feminists to examine their own societies and assumptions with the same critical vigour.

In order to achieve this I would suggest that Western feminists combine their analysis of the fraternal basis of nation-states with a critical attention to those who claim that 'our' nationalism is inherently different to 'their' nationalism. This is not to 'deny' difference but rather to look at how it is that nation states with very different ideological and cultural foundations still manage to create and maintain patriarchal authority. Regarding nation-states as the embodiment of similar

principles and purposes is to go against the grain of most contemporary male-authored studies of nationalism.[33] Instead, after the collapse of the Soviet Union and the demolition of the Berlin Wall in 1989, minds have been focused upon the 'outbreak' or more often, the 'resurgence' of nationalism across the globe.[34] This sense that there is simultaneously something 'new' and 'old' about these contemporary wars has led to the frequent connection between war and 'ethnicity' culminating in the notion that there is a 'new barbarism' at large in the world today.[35] Arguably, labelling these wars 'ethnic' enables commentators to define and place these wars whilst at the same time allowing them a useful distance from any knowledge of the contexts for these wars. This, of course gives Western elites a convenient flexibility in terms of their intervention into contemporary wars Intervention is thus only appropriate when changes can be made but if 'ethnic' violence spirals too far out of control then the West is entitled to leave 'them' to their own devices. As David Keen points out, the argument that 'we' should simply withdraw from these conflicts is becoming commonplace.[36] In 1997, Douglas Hurd, the former British Foreign Secretary, expressed this idea more bluntly:

> It is perfectly defensible ... after examining the difficulties, to say that the international community can do nothing effective and must stay out of the way until those concerned have come to their senses.[37]

However, while 'ethnicity' may be a useful term with which to apply to wars that 'we' are not involved in its capacity to obscure, rather than clarify, the reasons for conflicts has not passed unnoticed. Thus, Richard Fardon notes that the immediate translation of the war in Rwanda as a violent struggle between two competing ethnic groups quickly transpired to have been 'a gross oversimplification of a complex set of circumstances'.[38]

However, for Michael Billig,[39] the crucial issue underlying contemporary discussions of nationalism lies in the assumptions on the part of Western commentators that 'our' nationalism is entirely different from 'their' nationalism; insofar as 'we' have completed the task of nation-building and in doing so are living out entirely different national experiences to those who are attempting to create their own nation-states. For Billig, the difference between 'our' nationalism and 'their' nationalism is better viewed as a matter of power and legitimacy rather than anything intrinsic to nationalism, or nations. Thus, it is not so much that Western commentators deny their own national contexts but that

they regard them as secure, benign products of an 'enlightened' struggle against the absolutist state and, as such providing a stark contrast to the volatile irrationality that accompanies contemporary nation-building.

Indeed, so innocuous are 'our' national contexts that 'we' are not obliged to define them as national unless 'we' are discussing 'other' people's nationalism. It is this, Billig contends, that leads academics, such as Stuart Hall, David Helm and Zygmunt Bauman, to perceive the nation-state as an institution that has been successfully challenged and has in the process lost much of its former power and influence. As Bauman's comment, '[e]xit the nation-state enter the tribe' makes clear, the alleged erosion of the nation-state has been accompanied by the corresponding rise to power of states that apparently lack any claim to the principles that led to the establishment of nation-states in North America and Western Europe. As Billig observes,

> the new so-called nations lack 'viability' they are too small to be sovereign and in any case sovereignty is disappearing. The rhetoric implies that France and the US having been established in the heyday of nationhood, were (and perhaps still are) 'real' nations. But Slovenia and Byelorus are *arrivistes*, seeking entrance after all the tickets to genuine nationhood have been sold.[40]

Neil Lazarus agrees, commenting:

> 'Our' nationalisms, classed as finished projects, are taken somehow to have had benign effects: modernising unifying, democratising. 'Their' still unfolding nationalisms, on the other hand, are categorised under the shop-worn rubrics of atavism, anarchy, irrationality and power-mongering. Thus, arguably, the contemporary term 'ethnic nationalism', which seems to me to have little analytical substance.[41]

However, Billig is less interested in contributing to the debate about 'other' people's nationalism than in analysing the ways in which 'we' fail to admit to or fail to notice the strength of our own national contexts. He argues that given that we all live in this world of nations, it is striking how little mention is made of the nationalism of the Western world:

> At the present juncture, special attention should be paid to the United States and its nationalism. This nationalism, above all, has appeared so forgettable, so 'natural' to social scientists, and is today so globally important.[42]

For Billig, the routine emphasis upon the strident nationalism of 'others' depends upon the erroneous assumption that established Western nation-states and North America have somehow reached a point where nationalism is no longer of primary importance for people. As Billig points out, there is 'no name for the banal reproduction of life in Western states' and such 'gaps' in political language are rarely innocent:

> By being semantically restricted to small sizes and exotic colours, 'nationalism' becomes identified as a problem: it occurs 'there' on the periphery, not 'here' at the centre. The separatists, the fascists and the guerrillas are the problem of nationalism. The ideological habits, by which 'our' nations are reproduced as nations are unnamed and, thereby, unnoticed. The national flag hanging outside a public building in the United States attracts no special attention. It belongs to no special sociological genus. Having no name it cannot be identified as a problem. Nor, by implication, is the daily reproduction of the United States a problem ... Daily the nation is indicated, or 'flagged', in the lives of its citizenry. Nationalism, far from being an intermittent mood in established nations, is the endemic condition.[43]

In established nations, he continues, it is not so much that nationalism signifies an 'imagined community'[44] but that we cannot imagine life without it. Billig cites Michael Ignatieff's widely publicised *Blood and Belonging*[45] as a leading contributor to the idea that the contemporary world 'order' is currently facing the challenge of irrational ethnic wars. The point, Billig emphasises, is not that we should to ignore the rising popularity of fascism,[46] but that we cannot afford to ignore our own powerful investments in nationalist ideologies. Thus he challenges Ignatieff's attempt to distinguish his own 'civic nationalism' from 'ethnic nationalism' as telling us little more than that we should regard Ignatieff's nationalism as benign and uncontroversial compared to the compelling subject of violent 'ethnic' nationalism. The result is that 'our' nationalism does not need to enter the discussion and by extension does not require the benefits of critical analysis.

Billig's proposal that Western commentators should take the 'banality' of Western nationalism seriously is certainly a useful corrective to those who insist upon their ability to 'diagnose' the contemporary world order from some objective and 'civilised' standpoint. However, Billig's exposure of the ethnocentrism of other prominent discussions of nationalism is curiously inattentive to the implications of his own proposed unitary 'we'.

Thus, his evocation of 'a' national homeland in which 'we' all participate overlooks the extent to which people within Western nations are divided in their relation to the dominant national culture.

Indeed, the only way that Billig's reading can work is if the assumed member of this national collectivity is white and male, which is presumably why he is at some pains to stress that women (even feminists) willingly participate in the maintenance of a national homeland. Thus he incorporates his brief attention to gender and nationalism with his own authorial 'confession'. Citing the sports pages of British national papers as evidence of the daily 'flagging' of nationalism, Billig notes his own unthinking nationalism:

> I read the sporting pages, turning to them more quickly than is appropriate, given the news of suffering on the other pages. Regularly I answer the invitation to celebrate national sporting triumphs. If a citizen from the homeland runs quicker or jumps higher than foreigners I feel pleasure. Why, I do not know ... Daily I scan the papers for yet more scores, thoughtless of the future to which this routine activity might be pointing. I do not ask myself why I do it, I just do it, habitually.

The point is, Billig argues, that this 'personal' confession is in fact the confessions of the national community in general. 'We' are all more interested in the national news than the international news; and while sport is, of course, primarily played by, aimed at and consumed by men, 'Wimbledon Tennis' proves that women can be every bit as involved as their male counterparts.

Similarly, war, although it divides men and women in terms of who is risking death, does nevertheless rely on the equal support of men and women for their respective roles in war making. Billig cites the female 'just war' advocate, Jean Elshtain,[47] to document the willingness of women to serve their countries as patriotic mothers and carers and draws upon a single poll to argue that support for the Gulf War was roughly equivalent between men and women:

> Most strikingly, the authors report that 'feminists were as likely to support the war effort as non-feminists' ... The daily deixis of the homeland crosses the divides of gender. 'We' all are daily reminded that 'we' are 'here', living at home in 'our' precious homeland. ... Liberals, socialists and feminists, whatever ideals for the future are

entertained, cannot pretend to present absent-mindedness which forgets which is 'their' nation.[48]

Billig's determination to present a homogenised account of the Western nationalism leads him to overlook entirely the wealth of material documenting women's reservations and objections to nationalism and to ignore the fact that the failure of many black British fans (and indeed, white British fans) to support 'their' country continues to preoccupy the dominant culture. The growing insistence that 'England' be a rallying point for 'the' nation is reflected in the increasing involvement of schools with English football. Meanwhile, the objections of many white British people to the adoption of a British nationality by 'foreigners' continues to complicate the efforts of the dominant culture to both elevate Britishness to a general inclusiveness whilst preserving the hierarchies of race and class that themselves feed into 'British' identity.

Accounts such as Billig's demonstrate that the problem is not necessarily that women are ignored in male-authored accounts of nationalism, as that they are included in ways that suppress any dissension with patriarchal discourses.

Arguably, the most ambitious attempt to include women within a radical political narrative occurs in Marxist theory. Frederick Engels wrote his 1884 treatise, *The Origin of the Family, Private Property and the State*,[49] as a bequest for Marx, using Marx's critical notes and reproducing them as best as he could. Engels' text has been cited as a compelling and revolutionary account of women's oppression by Marxists, while Marxist-feminists have sought to elaborate further upon Engels' main argument. Thus, Sharon Smith[50] argues that Marx and Engels correctly located the origins of women's oppression in the rise of a divided class society. Consequently, she argues that feminists who attempt to locate the origins of women's oppression elsewhere are placing women outside of society and are compelled to find reasons for women's oppression in far more contested concepts such as nature and biology.

For Smith the power of the Marxist account of women's oppression is derived from its 'materialism'. Unlike other accounts that can only conjecture about the reasons for women's oppression, Marxist theory is produced from 'what we actually know about the evolution of human society'.[51] And it is this that enables Engels to both account for women's oppression and give us 'strategies' for ending that oppression. But evolutionary theory is more supple than Smith's reading implies. The move from discovering or observing the physical evidence of humanity's past to interpreting that past has always been a matter of conjecture and contestation. Marxist theory is not, in this sense, 'produced' by

'what we know' but an interpretation of historical, anthropological and geographical evidence.

Moreover, evolutionary theory has been a narrative written, for the most part, by history's victors who have been keen to account for contemporary inequalities and hierarchies by locating their 'sources' in earlier organisations and structures. Women, the colonised and non-Western societies in general have, not surprisingly, fared badly in narratives of evolution which is precisely why evolutionary discourses continue to provide elites with the ammunition to 'explain' the persistence of contemporary inequalities. It is in this sense that evolutionary theory always was a contemporary project.

Evolutionary theory, then, despite its overt connection to a distant past is surely better viewed as a way of giving contemporary humanity a coherent and more importantly, 'empirical' and 'scientific' past. Unfortunately, this overlooks the level of human invention that goes into 'science' reflected in the fact that scientific research in the same way as research in the 'humanities' continues to re-interpret and revisit its foundations. Thus, Engels may well have located earlier evidence of matriarchal societies that practiced sexual freedom but his account as to *how* and *why* these societies 'developed' into the modern monogamous patriarchal family relies upon precisely those contexts that readers such as Smith would prefer us to banish from the realm of Marxist theory. In other words, what Smith overlooks is that Marx and Engels too were reliant upon the intersection of dominant notions about nature, gender, sexuality, biology and culture and that without them a 'materialist' account of history would not even be possible.

For Marx and Engels, the context for their investigation into women's oppression lay in the need to find in human evolution evidence for the 'progression' of women from earlier times to 'real' sexual freedom in a future classless society. The evidence that human society was once matriarchal and practiced sexual freedom was, from the outset, an evolutionary 'fact' that had to be tied in with the *future* liberation of women. Matriarchy and sexual freedom, in other words, had to be in some way anathematic to women. Engels proposed that the roots of women's dissatisfaction with their earlier power lay in the 'shame' and 'humiliation' that they experienced in 'free' love. Thus, Engels' description of the processes of economic development and their impact on the development of the family emphasises women's burdens under traditional arrangements:

> The more the traditional relations lost the naïve character of primitive forest life, owing to the development of economic conditions ... the

more oppressive and humiliating must the women have felt them to be, and the greater their longing for the right of chastity, of temporary or permanent marriage with one man only as a way of release.[52]

Engels' assumption that women 'longed' to be 'released' into the chaste comfort of monogamous marriage is the context and explanation for why women instigated their own forthcoming oppression. Women in this reading are the 'virtuous', 'chaste' sex that were mobilised by favourable economic developments and their own growing sense of 'shame' to overthrow the old sexual 'dis'order. Thus, Engels introduces the modern patriarchal family as, above all, a product of female desire:

> This advance could not ... have originated with the men if only because it never occurred to them, even to this day, to renounce the pleasures of actual group marriage. Only when the women had brought about the transition to pairing marriage were the men able to introduce strict monogamy – though indeed only for women.[53]

Thus, economic progress and women's acquirement of their 'longed' for chastity together bring about the 'world historical defeat of the female sex'[54] and provide the grounds for the emerging antagonism between the sexes. Engels' uncompromising descriptions of women's servitude and oppression within the monogamous patriarchal family are analogous to Marx and Engels' sympathy for the fate of the proletariat under capitalism and the colonised under colonialism. In all cases exploitation and oppression are the harrowing but necessary contexts for the eventual liberation of humanity from conditions of exploitation.

Significantly, however, Engels in his discussion of women's oppression and its impact upon society goes further and asserts that in fact men are *more* degraded by women's oppressed condition than women. For while women are removed from 'public' life and transformed into wageless domestic servants, men, although nominally 'free', undergo a far deeper impoverishment. Engels explains:

> The more the hetaerism of the past is changed in our time by capitalist commodity production and brought into conformity with it, the more, that is to say, it is transformed into undisguised prostitution, the more demoralizing are its effects. And it demoralizes men far more than women. Among women, prostitution degrades only the unfortunate ones who become its victims, and even those by no

means to the extent commonly believed. But it degrades the whole character of the male world.[55]

In other words, women's oppression as the first instance of class oppression becomes an oppression that can be theorised without women necessarily laying claim to that oppression. For, while Marx and Engels viewed class as a category that could and should be abolished in the coming revolution, gender, by contrast, remained resolutely in place attached to traditional assumptions about female nature and sexuality. And while it was possible to propose that class differences should be abolished and replaced by a community of classless equals, the prospect of imagining a society predicated on an overhaul of traditional assumptions about gender and sexuality proved to be far less palatable. Instead, Engels retained a firm allegiance to notions of women's natural chastity and her desire for monogamy. Individual sex love, as opposed to the anarchy of polygamy, and, worse still, polyandry, emerges as a historical presence that has been developing quietly in the background since the Middle Ages when it was restricted to the adulterous exploits of the ruling class.

Subsequent male Marxists have indeed been remarkably faithful to Engels' treatise. The valorisation of heterosexual relations and the automatic assumption that because gender differences are 'natural' they are therefore immune to processes of historical change is succinctly captured in Perry Anderson's assertion:

> If the structures of sexual domination stretch back longer, and go deeper, culturally than those of class exploitation, they also typically generate less collective resistance, politically. The division between the sexes is a fact of nature: it cannot be abolished, as can the division between the classes, a fact of history.[56]

Anderson, in much the same way as Sharon Smith, takes it as read that history and the movement of class through history are irrefutable facts rather than a hypothesis that can be subjected to much the same critical enquiry as concepts such as 'nature'. More importantly, however, such readings overlook the fact that arguments based upon 'history' and 'class' cannot necessarily be opposed to those that wish to ground their theories upon nature or biology. In other words, ideas concerning history and class are as marked by their complex relations with ideas about biology and nature as ideas about race, gender and sexuality are interwoven with ideas about history and class.[57] Indeed, as anthropological

studies have demonstrated, ideas about gender and sexuality are culturally specific[58] rendering the notion of the existence of some kind of
universal agreement as to what constitutes masculinity and femininity
and appropriate sexual relations 'between' the genders difficult to
substantiate.[59]

For Smith, Engels' somewhat unthinking 'Victorian' morality and the
fact that gay oppression is 'entirely absent' in *The Origin of the Family* are
both inevitable consequences of Engels' own historical contexts. Thus if
his ideas about class and history proved him to be 'ahead' of his time
his ideas about gender and sexuality were simply ideas that were more
obviously linked to prevailing nineteenth-century thought. For Smith,
the important point is that these shortcomings do not detract from
the overall veracity of Engels' text and have been remedied by later
Marxist scholarship. Accordingly, contemporary Marxist theory has
now remedied this 'absence' and 'pinpointed' gay oppression within the
class system.

Unfortunately, what Smith overlooks is that Marxist theory has
made a particular connection between homosexuality and ruling-class
depravity that makes the issue less one of updating what was previously
absent, as Smith asserts has taken place, than of accounting for the
presence of heterosexism in texts such as *The Origin of the Family.*

Subsequent Marxist theorists and practitioners have combined their
radical reading of class with an accompanying puritanical moralism
towards gender and sexuality to such an extent that embracing 'class'
politics has often seemed to necessitate a dismissal of gender and sexual
oppression. As James N. Green and Florence E. Babb point out, the
international communist movement that emerged in the late 1920s
explicitly associated homosexuality with upper-class men and in doing
so was able to define it as merely a sign of 'bourgeois decadence'.[60] This
reading of 'the' homosexual as a weak and depraved subject served as
a stark contrast to the moral energy that was required of the new
revolutionary subject. Neil Harding points out that Gramsci regarded
the transformation of the 'simple man-in-the-mass' as primarily a
matter of renouncing his coarse and vulgar sexual instinct. For Gramsci,
both industrialisation and philosophy involved a concerted struggle
against an earlier and more primitive animal instinct. Thus, Gramsci
argued that

> the truth is that the new type of man demanded by the rationaliza-
> tion of production and work cannot be developed until the sexual
> instinct has been suitably regulated and it too has been rationalized.[61]

Gramsci's strictures were clearly in evidence in the early years of the Cuban Revolution where the Cuban government sought to overcome the association of Havana with the eroticism that many Americans, who visited it in order to escape the sexual restrictions and customs of their own nation, ascribed to it.[62] Arguably, the imperialism of American sexual tourists only served to validate a sexual puritanism that was already there in the heart of Marxist theory. Rafael Ocasio cites Fidel Castro's interview in 1965 as providing the explanatory contexts for Cuba's early criminalisation of homosexuality:

> Nothing prevents a homosexual from professing revolutionary ideology and, consequently, exhibiting a correct political position. In that case he should not be considered politically negative. And yet we would never come to believe that a homosexual could embody the conditions and requirements of conduct that would enable us to consider him a true Revolutionary, a true Communist militant. A deviation of that nature clashes with the concept we have of what a militant communist should be.[63]

And it is this evocation of a brotherhood with an accompanying suspicion of female sexuality and prohibition upon sexual desire between men that connects the Marxist project to that of the nationalist one. For as Peterson points out:

> Typically represented as a passionate brotherhood, the nation finds itself compelled to distinguish its 'proper' homosociality from more explicitly sexualized male-male relations, a compulsion that requires the identification, isolation, and containment of male homosexuality.[64]

For many Western commentators the Marxist and anti-colonial project should properly be viewed as, at best, a well-intentioned attempt to end oppression and inequality through a commitment to universal goals of equality and justice, and at worst, as a tragic repression of individual freedom and consciousness.

The increasing focus upon postmodernism in Western academic debate in the 1990s was secured by the collapse of communism and the accompanying loss of faith in universal and utopian illusions about a common humanity. Commentators, such as Zygmunt Bauman,[65] insisted that 'our' postmodern age afforded us the unique opportunity to live in a world no longer tied down to illusory and repressive certainties. Male commentators, in particular, focused upon the excitement of

losing 'our' former political certainty and enthusiastically welcomed in a new era of political uncertainty, humility and improvisation. Robert Young captured the mood of the time with his 1990 declaration:

> Postmodernism can best be defined as European Culture's awareness that it is no longer the unquestioned and dominant centre of the world.[66]

Meanwhile Keith Jenkins[67] and Hans Bertens[68] confirmed that postmodernism offered humanity a chance to begin again without the illusory comforts of ideological certainty that had unravelled most dramatically in the failure of the Marxist project in the Soviet Union and Eastern Europe. The humility of postmodernism was a much repeated claim throughout male scholarship – no longer were 'we' the centre, no longer were 'we' presuming to know anything; instead 'we' were embarking for the first time without preconceptions ready to 'accept' the world for what it really is. Therefore, because 'we' had discarded our illusions of centrality and supremacy, it followed that what 'we' would produce would be for the first time in history a genuinely democratic and radical interpretation of the world. Humanity as a project could, in this sense be reclaimed precisely because it had been stripped of the artifices of modernist certainty. As Jenkins argued:

> We Postmodernists are people who recognise that we are finite creatures in an unintelligible, existential condition with nothing to fall back on 'beyond the reach of time and chance.' With no skyhooks, no transcendental foundations and no point we are, to recall Rorty's remark, 'just one more species doing its best', a best that, bereft of history and ethics, we might still *choose* to articulate in emancipatory ways.[69]

The parallel reclamation of humanity and 're-enchantment' of the world could not, of course, proceed without some clarification and definition of both humanity and the world. While commentators, such as Jenkins, revelled in the freedom that postmodern ambiguity and uncertainty offered them, other commentators, notably Bauman, were more interested in spelling out the solemn implications of this postmodern world. Thus, throughout his texts Bauman reiterates that there is no guarantee that 'we' will make the right ethical choices, since all that postmodernism has done is to make each of us individually responsible for our actions. Bauman's postmodern individual is the hero of his

texts; battling against the confusing array of choices and dilemmas that a globalised world brings:

> At the end of the ambitious project of universal moral certainty ... the bewildered and disoriented self finds itself alone in the face of moral dilemmas without good (let alone obvious) choices, unresolved conflicts and the excruciating difficulty of being moral.[70]

And if Bauman has profound sympathy for the plight of 'his' postmodern individual learning how to negotiate a world that suddenly does not require (or care) whether he is moral or not, then he has no such tolerance towards those who shirk this business of being human and attempt to comfort themselves in the oppressive embrace of 'the herd':

> In the question of happiness, numbers carry no authority. Relying on majority opinion won't help you in your search. The odds are that listening to the majority's view will divert you from the goal. The herd is the last place where the pattern of happy life could be found.[71]

While male advocates of postmodernism celebrated the loss of modernist certainty and concentrated upon the implications of this new 'freedom' feminist commentators focused upon its implications for gender.

The possibility of rethinking what being female means enabled feminist commentators to challenge the supposedly 'natural' characteristics of gender. The radical potential for feminist commentators such as Judith Butler[72] lay in the ability of postmodernism to call gender, arguably, the most seemingly obvious and natural identity, into question. She pointed out that we cannot effect radical political change without extending that transformation to ourselves and particularly to our most deeply held assumptions and beliefs:

> I would suggest that a fundamental mistake is made when we think we must sort out philosophically or epistemologically our 'grounds' before we can take stock of the world politically or engage in its affairs actively with the aim of transformation ... To be so grounded is nearly to be buried: it is to refuse alterity, to reject contestation, to decline the risk of self-transformation perpetually posed by democratic life.[73]

However, the problem that confronted all advocates of postmodernism was that their assumption that the loss of modernist certainty in

itself amounted to a loss of power was contradicted by two interrelated problems. First, postmodern theory effortlessly replaced modernist theory as elite theory within Western critical debate, and, secondly, postmodern theorists tended to assume that they could talk about the non-West only this time it did so *without* authority and in the process often advanced sweeping and inaccurate generalisations about 'the third world'.[74] The postmodern world (or 'challenge') that Bauman, in particular, described as confronting us all, was one that was too quick to dismiss those who were unable to 'play' the 'game'. And it is this sense that postmodernism was too quick to celebrate the 'end' of certainties and rigid classifications, given that most of the world is still living out the consequences of class, race and gender oppression, that dogged postmodern debate from its inception. Edward Said's reference to the 'astonishing sense of weightlessness with regard to the gravity of history' was a much-repeated charge in the field of postcolonial studies in particular.[75]

Certainly, the most striking limitation of the postmodern individual of Bauman, Rorty, Bertens and Jenkins' imagination lies in the fact that 'his' valuable fallibility never lies in economic or material deprivation but is a psychic alienation. The universalisation of such a hero in a world of ever greater inequality and impoverishment is a strikingly parochial subject given that 'he' is supposedly representative of 'the' world today. The postmodern hero has little to offer those without the freedom to engage in or consume the 'choices' of contemporary capitalism.

Unsurprisingly, it was not in the West that people have decided to make different choices but in Latin America, where the intensification of the effects of global capital brought an end to the conservative leaderships of Brazil, Venezuela and Bolivia. Moreover, the transformations in Latin America were predicated on precisely those values of class, oppression and equality that Western postmodernism had declared to be dead and buried. And it is within Latin America that a genuinely radical experiment is taking place as the Mexican Zapatistas (EZLN)[76] bring their rethinking of orthodox Marxism and political theory and activism to the forefront of contemporary political debate. The Zapatistas have proved to be a complicated and contested political entity for Mexican and Western commentators. The determination of the Zapatistas to resist the closure of traditional politics and to work with an inclusive definition of membership (all those who are against neoliberal globalisation and for humanity) has persuaded some that they are a 'postmodern' entity since they are not interested in state power and are skilful users of the globalised media.[77] For others, the fact that they engage in armed struggle and make clear use of a narrative of class oppression means that they must be a traditional Marxist

guerrilla force.[78] The involvement of indigenous people in the Zapatistas leads others to emphasise the indigenous contexts of the Zapatistas reflected in their contemporary support base.[79]

For me, what is valuable about the Zapatistas is their willingness to critically rethink traditional concepts and assumptions (notably those concerning gender and nationality). The evolution of their origins from a small vanguard, preparing to lead the peasants into political enlightenment, into a political force that is marked by its high numbers of indigenous people and women is a powerful demonstration of how radical the outcome can be when political assumptions are challenged and overturned. As the Zapatistas spokesperson, Subcomandante Marcos[80] relates, his arrival with five other comrades in the Lacandon Jungle, in 1983, quickly transformed a teaching exercise into a learning one. Thus, he describes the EZLN's origins as

> a group of 'illuminati' who came from the city in order to 'liberate' the exploited and who looked, when confronted with the reality of the indigenous communities, more like burnt out light bulbs than 'illuminati'. How long did it take us to realize that we had to learn to listen, and afterwards, to speak? ... what had been a classic revolutionary guerrilla war in 1984 (armed uprising of the masses, the taking of power, the establishment of socialism from above, many statues and names of heroes and martyrs everywhere, purges, etcetera, in sum, a perfect world) by 1986 was already an armed group, overwhelmingly indigenous, listening attentively and barely babbling its first words with a new teacher: the Indian peoples.[81]

The Zapatistas emphasis upon consultation and listening, captured in their description of a revolution that 'walks asking',[82] and their commitment to opening up a space in civil society in order for people to express and organise themselves against neoliberalism has brought sharp criticism from the traditional left. Their refusal to incorporate themselves into the traditional left, combined with their pursuit of a new way of theorising politics and political activism has often proved to be an inconveniently critical presence for those who wish to celebrate the left-wing electoral victories in Latin America.[83]

The debate about the Zapatistas tends to focus upon how they fit (or more often do not fit) into the existing political landscape rather than addressing the more significant question of how far the existing left is able to incorporate a movement that is committed to rethinking and overcoming established hierarchies. The high numbers of women and peasants[84] in the Zapatistas ensured that this was a rebellion that

was set to challenge prevailing assumptions about their place in radical struggle from the start. Central to their attempts to re-capture public space and political debate is the Zapatistas insistence upon the need for more affluent supporters to respect the dignity of the indigenous poor.

As John Holloway points out, the Zapatistas emphasis upon the dignity of those most exploited by the capitalist free market is apt to strike Western commentators as a concept that lacks theoretical power, whereas in fact it offers us all a way to work with the dual nature of oppression and resistance:

> The consistent pursuit of dignity based on the denial of dignity is itself revolutionary. But it implies a different concept of revolution from the 'storming of the Winter Palace' concept that we have grown up with. There is no building of the revolutionary party, no strategy for world revolution, no transitional programme. Revolution is simply the constant, uncompromising struggle for that which cannot be achieved under capitalism: dignity, control over our own lives.[85]

The readiness of the Zapatistas to challenge not just the oppressive political realities of neoliberalism but also the constraints of orthodox radical politics has ensured their vulnerability. The militarisation of Chiapas and the low-intensity war against the Zapatistas has been accompanied by the exclusion of the Zapatistas from prestigious international events such as the 'World Social Forum'. The attempts to marginalise and discredit the Zapatistas should concern all of us who wish to undo the damage of the hierarchical assumptions embedded within radical theory and activism. Moreover, their commitment to breaking down the barriers that isolate people on the basis of nationality, gender and sexuality seems to me to offer a compelling revision to orthodox radical theory. For as Marcos explained just months after the capture of San Cristobel in 1994:

> something was broken in this year, not just the false image of modernity, which neoliberalism was selling to us, not just the falsity of governmental projects … but also the rigid schemas of a left dedicated to living from and of the past. In the midst of navigating from pain to hope, the political struggle finds itself bereft of the worn-out clothes bequeathed to it by pain; it is hope which obliges it to seek new forms of struggle, new ways of being political, of doing politics. A new politics, a new political ethic is not just a wish, it is the only way to advance, to jump to the other side.[86]

Notes

1 Introduction: The Role of the Intellectual

1. Stefan Collini, *Absent Minds: Intellectuals in Britain* (Oxford: Oxford University Press, 2006).
2. See ibid., for details about the same charge of the absence or decline of intellectuals being voiced across Europe.
3. Stefan Collini, '"Every Fruit-juice Drinker, Nudist, Sandal-wearer. ..."': Intellectuals as Other People', in Helen Small (Ed.) *The Public Intellectual* (Oxford: Blackwell Publishing, 2002), p. 206.
4. See Michael Walzer, *The Company of Critics: Social Criticism and Political Commitment in the Twentieth Century* (London: Peter Halban, 1989).
5. See Richard Rorty, *Contingency, Irony and Solidarity* (Cambridge: Cambridge University Press, 1989).
6. See Zygmunt Bauman, *Legislators and Interpreters: On Modernity, Post-Modernity and Intellectuals* (Oxford: Polity Press, 1987).
7. See Edward Said, *Representations of the Intellectual: The 1993 Reith Lectures* (London: Vintage, 1994).
8. See Julien Benda, *La Trahison des clercs* (Paris: Grasset, 1927).
9. Michael Walzer, *Interpretation and Social Criticism* (Cambridge: Harvard University Press, 1987). pp. 36–40.
10. Bauman, op. cit., p. 192.
11. Jeremy Jennings and Anthony Kemp-Welch (Eds) *Intellectuals in Politics: From the Dreyfus Affair to Salman Rushdie* (London: Routledge, 1997).
12. Richard Rorty, cited in Jennings and Kemp-Welch, *Intellectuals in Politics*, p. 298.
13. Both the Brazilian Landless People's Movement (MST) and the Mexican Zapatistas have been engaged in a critical reassessment of the relation of social protest and intellectuals to the state apparatus. The work of educationalist Paulo Freire has been influential throughout Latin and Central America and he was appointed to oversee the radical literacy programme/experiment that began in Nicaragua in 1980. Detailed in David Archer and Patrick Costello, *Literacy and Power: The Latin-American Battleground* (London: Earthscan Publications, 1990), pp. 23–32.
14. The criticisms that followed the publication of *Representations of the Intellectual* did not dissuade Said and in 2002 he published his essay, 'The Public Role of Writers and Intellectuals' in *The Public Intellectual,* in which he expanded upon his original argument.
15. Stefan Collini details the level of attention that followed Said's Reith Lectures in *Absent* Minds, pp. 422–3.
16. Bauman, op. cit., p. 192.
17. Charles F. Gattone, *The Social Scientist As Public Intellectual: Critical Reflections in a Changing World* (New York: Rowman & Littlefield Publishers, 2006).
18. Ibid., p. 145.

19. Ibid., p. 146.
20. Colin Gordon (Ed.) *Power/Knowledge: Selected Interviews and Other Writings 1972–1977 by Michel Foucault* (Hemel Hempstead: Harvester Wheatsheaf, 1980).
21. Ibid., p. 126.
22. Pierre Bourdieu, *Acts of Resistance: Against the New Myths of Our Time* (Cambridge: Polity Press, 1998).
23. Ibid., p. 7.
24. Ibid., pp. 56–7.
25. Ibid., pp. 73–4.
26. Archer and Costello, op. cit.
27. Paulo Freire was the Brazilian educationalist whose work transformed the teaching of literacy across Latin America. He was directly involved in the 1980 National Literacy Crusade advanced by the Sandinistas.
28. Freire, cited in Archer and Costello, op. cit., p. 24.
29. Foucault helped to find the Prison Information Group (GIP) which manipulated the celebrity of its members to create a space in which the voices of prisoners could be heard. Detailed in Mark Poster, *Foucault, Marxism & History: Mode of Production versus Mode of Information* (Cambridge: Polity Press in association with Basil Blackwell, Oxford, 1984), p. 155.
30. The 'Parliament of Writers' that Bourdieu and other intellectuals established in 1993 eventually folded but reflected Bourdieu's commitment to work collectively as a 'critical countervailing power' rather than as an 'incarnation of the universal conscience'. Detailed in *Intellectuals In Politics*, p. 79.
31. Collini draws particular attention to the sustained attack upon intellectuals undertaken by George Orwell and notes that Orwell is, 'guilty of that most unlovely and least defensible of inner-contradictions, the anti-intellectualism of the intellectual'. Stefan Collini in Small, op. cit., p. 204.
32. Ibid.
33. A striking example of this is Steve Fuller's recent polemic *The Intellectual* (Cambridge: Icon Books, 2006).
34. Ibid., pp. 113–6.
35. Collini in Small, op. cit., p. 214.
36. Collini, *Absent Minds*, p. 505.
37. Ibid., p. 494.
38. Ibid.
39. Ibid., p. 495.
40. Pierre Bourdieu's response to the anti-intellectualism that has accompanied the rhetoric and policies of the North American and British administrations was to emphasise the need for 'critical intellectuals' to preserve their autonomy. *Acts of Resistance,* in this sense was an attempt to galvanise critical intellectuals into political action.
41. For example, after the attack upon the World Trade Centre (September 2001), critical voices were marginalised by the dominant culture which stressed the 'ivory tower' idealism of intellectuals which though tolerated in times of peace was entirely inappropriate in times of national and international crisis.
42. This is particularly marked in modern art which is frequently criticised for being something that 'anyone' could have done thus confirming that the proper function of 'high' art is to be extraordinary. Modern art is a particularly

aggravating case for conservative critics as it has the status of 'high art'. This was particularly evident when the work of Tracy Emin and other artists such as Damien Hirst, Chris Ofili and Jake and Dinos Chapman was destroyed by a fire that broke out in an East London warehouse on 26 May 2004. The fire inspired a stream of commentaries in the tabloid and broadsheet press suggesting that such art was neither a loss nor a problem since it could easily be remade. The common ground that conservative elites invoke with 'the people' is thus sought on the basis that Emin and artists like her have renegaded on their proper duty as artists and intellectuals and are therefore being paid extravagant sums of money that ordinary people themselves cannot hope to earn. Of course, what remains firmly in place here is the idea that 'proper' art (that is to say art that ordinary people cannot or do not produce) deserves to be highly paid.

2 Matthew Arnold, Culture and the Intellectual

1. See, for example, Stefan Collini's introduction to Matthew Arnold [1869] *Culture and Anarchy: An essay in political and social criticism* (Cambridge: Cambridge University Press, 1993). Collini introduces Arnold's text as 'one of the most celebrated works of social criticism ever written' and notes that he did more than any other single figure to endow the role of the critic with the cultural centrality it has come to enjoy in the English-speaking world. Furthermore, Collini argues, 'the text has left a lasting impression upon subsequent debate about the relation between politics and culture.' (p. ix).
2. Chris Baldick notes that Arnold looked to the study of English literature as an agent of harmony, and this social project moulded the forms of literary education as they were applied to the teachings of workers, school children, women and Indians. Chris Baldick, *The Social Mission of English Criticism 1848–1932* (Oxford: OUP, 1987) p. 84.
3. Deborah Cameron, *Verbal Hygiene* (London: Routledge, 1993) p. 12.
4. See, for example, Deborah Cameron's discussion of the Thatcher government's failed attempts to enlist the support of linguists when it embarked on its radical programme of educational 'reform', detailed in *Verbal Hygiene*. Philip Pullman's caustic assessment of the National Curriculum is as polemical as any of Arnold's writings on education: *The Guardian* 22 January 2005.
5. See in particular Chris Baldick's account of Walter Raleigh who after his initial enthusiasm found the task of teaching literature to be depressingly mechanical: Baldick, *Social Mission of English Criticism*, pp. 76–80.
6. See, for example, John Taylor Gatto, *Dumbing Us Down: The Hidden Curriculum of Compulsory Schooling* (Canada: New Society Publishers, 1991). Also see, Ivan Illich, *Deschooling Society* (London: Marion Boyars, Publishers, 1971).
7. Stefan Collini, Introduction to M. Arnold, *Culture and Anarchy:* p. ix.
8. Matthew Arnold [1869] *Culture and Anarchy and other writings*.
9. Terry Eagleton, *The Function of Criticism: From the Spectator to post-structuralism* (London: Verso, 1984), details these as an increase in bookseller power, expansion of wealth, population and education, technological developments in printing and publishing and the growth of a middle-class eager for literature.

10. Eagleton discusses Samuel Johnson's periodicals in *The Function of Criticism*, pp. 31–5.
11. Ibid., p. 9.
12. E.P. Thompson, *The Making of the English Working Class*, cited in Terry Eagleton, *The Function of* Criticism, p. 36.
13. Ibid., p. 36.
14. Matthew Arnold, 'The Popular Education of France' in *Democratic Education*, cited in Terry Eagleton, *Criticism & Ideology* (London: ILB, 1976) pp. 105–6.
15. Arnold, *Culture & Anarchy* cited in Raymond Williams (1961) *Culture and Society 1780–1950* (London: Penguin, 1961) p. 132.
16. Baldick, *Social Mission of English Criticism*, p. 29.
17. Baldick, op. cit., pp. 60–7.
18. Lord Playfair who formed the London Society for the Extension of University Teaching and F.D. Maurice, Professor of English Literature and History at King's College London, in the 1840s, and founder of the model of the Working Men's College are detailed in Baldick, op. cit., pp. 64–5.
19. Ibid., p. 66.
20. Robinson, 'English Classical Literature' cited in Baldick, Ibid., p. 66.
21. M. Arnold, cited in Baldick, Ibid., p. 32.
22. Baldick, op. cit., p. 43.
23. Ibid., p. 25.
24. Matthew Arnold, *Culture & Anarchy* cited in Raymond Williams, *Culture and Society*, p. 124.
25. Robert J.C. Young, *Torn Halves: Political conflict in literary and cultural theory* (Manchester: Manchester University Press, 1996) p. 204.
26. K. Anthony Appiah and Henry Louis Gates Jr, *The Dictionary of Global Culture* (Harmondsworth: Penguin, 1998).
27. Ibid., p. 32.
28. Ibid., p. 33.
29. Ibid., p. 33.
30. Raymond Williams, op. cit., p. 128.
31. Ibid., p. 304.
32. Ibid., p. 127.
33. Ibid., p. 132.
34. Ibid., p. 133.
35. Ibid.
36. Matthew Arnold, *The Bishop and the Philosopher* (1863), cited in Eagleton, *Criticism and Ideology*, p. 109.
37. Patricia J. Williams, in T. Morrison (ed.) *Race-Ing Justice, En-Gendering Power. Essays on Anita Hill, Clarence Thomas and the Construction of Social Reality* (New York: Pantheon, 1995) p. 167.
38. K. Appiah and A. Gutmann, *Color Conscious: The political morality of race* (Princeton, New Jersey: Princeton University Press, 1996), was the winner of the American Political Science Association's 1997 Ralph J. Bunche Award.
39. Ibid., p. 179.
40. Ibid., p. 91.
41. Ibid., p. 47.
42. Ibid., p. 32–8.

43. Marek Kohn, *The Race Gallery: The return of racial science* (London: Vintage, 1996).
44. For example the survey of American psychologists which found that over half of them believed that differences in IQ scores observed between different races were partly genetic in origin. Detailed in Kohn, op. cit., p. 110.
45. Ibid., p. 26.
46. Verena Stolcke, 'Gender, race and class in the formation of colonial society'. In M. Hendricks & P. Parker (Eds), *Women, 'Race,' & Writing in the Early Modern Period* (London: Routledge, 1994) p. 285.
47. Toni Morrison, *Playing In The Dark: Whiteness and the literary imagination* (London: Picador, 1993), p. 38.
48. Ibid., pp. 63–4.
49. Robyn Wiegman, *American Anatomies: Theorizing race and gender* (London: Duke University Press, 1995) p. 35.
50. Appiah, op. cit., p. 85.
51. Toni Morrison cited by Joy James in Naomi Zack, *Women of Color and Philosophy* (Oxford: Blackwell, 2000), p. 34.
52. Uma Narayan, *Dislocating Cultures: Identities, traditions, and Third-World feminism* (London: Routledge, 1997). Narayan notes the Indian rhetoric of women as goddesses that took place alongside the oppressive treatment of poor and low-caste women (p. 15).
53. Appiah, op. cit., p. 98.
54. Ibid., p. 165.
55. Ibid., p. 100.
56. Pierre Bourdieu, *Pascalian Meditations* (Cambridge: Polity Press, 2000) trans. by R. Nice.
57. Ibid., p. 80.
58. Appiah, op. cit., pp. 100–1.
59. Detailed in Neera Chandhoke, *State And Civil Society: Explorations in political theory* (London: Sage Publications, 1995) p. 105.
60. Ibid.
61. Ibid.
62. Appiah, op. cit., p. 172.

3   The Habermasian Public Sphere

1. A. Callinicos, *Against Postmodernism: A Marxist critique* (Cambridge: Polity 1989) p. 95.
2. Ibid.
3. See Noam Chomsky, *Deterring Democracy* (London: Vintage, 1992), for extensive details of American foreign policy.
4. Pauline Johnson, 'Distorted communications: Feminism's dispute with Habermas', *Philosophy & Social Criticism*, 27, no. 1 (January 2001) 41.
5. Jürgen Habermas, cited in Callinicos, *Against Postmodernism*, p. 97.
6. Ibid., p. 115.
7. Ibid.
8. Ibid.

9. Ibid.

10. Habermas, *Between Facts and Norms: Contributions to a discourse theory of law and democracy* (Cambridge, MA: MIT Press, 1996) p. 449.

11. Habermas, cited in Callinicos, *Against Postmodernism* p. 102.

12. Habermas, cited in Johnson, 'Distorted communications feminism's dispute with Habermas', p. 43.

13. Neera Chandhoke, *State and Civil Society: Explorations in political theory* (London: Sage Publications, 1995) p. 205.

14. Stale R.S. Finke (2000) 'Habermas and Kant: Judgement and communicative experience', *Philosophy and Social Criticism,* vol. 26, no. 6 (2000).

15. Maeve Cooke, *Language and Reason: A study in Habermas's pragmatics* (Cambridge, MA and London: MIT Press, 1994) p. 169.

16. Trinh T. Minh-Ha, *When The Moon Waxes Red: Representation, gender and cultural politics* (New York: Routledge, 1991) p. 228.

17. Antje Gimmler, 'Deliberative democracy, the public sphere and the internet', *Philosophy & Social criticism,* vol. 27 no. 4 (July 2001).

18. Ibid., p. 24.

19. See Jan Blommaert and Jef Verschueren, *Debating Diversity: Analysing the discourse of tolerance* (London: Routledge, 1998) for details of asylum laws in Western Europe. Also see Frances Webber, 'Europe J'accuse', extract from the prosecution's counsel's indictment of the EU for violation of human rights laid before the Basso Tribunal on the Right of Asylum in Europe, Berlin, December 1994, in *Race and Class* Issue 36, vol. 3 (1995), pp. 86–8.

20. Blommaert & Verschueren, *Debating Diversity*, p. 15.

21. Gayatri Chakravorty Spivak, *The Post-Colonial Critic: Interviews, strategies, dialogues,* ed. Sarah Harasym (London: Routledge, 1990), p. 72.

22. Gimmler op. cit., p. 24.

23. Rey Chow, *Ethics After Idealism: Theory, culture, ethnicity, reading* (Bloomington: Indiana University Press, 1998), pp. 12–13.

24. Lucius T. Outlaw, *On Race and Philosophy* (London: Routledge, 1996) p. 35.

25. Ibid., p. 151.

26. Ibid., p. 153.

27. W.E.B. Du Bois, *Russia and America,* cited in Kate Baldwin, *Beyond The Color Line And The Iron Curtain: Reading encounters between black and red, 1922–1963* (Durham: Duke University Press, 2002), pp. 167–8.

28. Ibid.

29. Kate A. Baldwin discusses this in detail in, *Beyond The Color Line,* pp. 149–61.

30. Ibid., p. 153.

31. Outlaw, *On Race and Philosophy*, p. 177.

32. Du Bois, *Russia and America*, p. 163.

33. The mildly inconvenient record of the changing status of those such as Saddam Hussein, Osama bin Laden and Mohammar Qadaffi from friend to foe and back again is testimony to the overriding importance of economic advantage to those currently protecting 'our way of life'.

34. Alexander Kluge and Oskar Negt, *Public Sphere and Experience: Toward an analysis of the bourgeois and proletarian public Sphere* (Minneapolis: University of Minnesota Press, 1993).

4   The Counter-Public Sphere

1. Jürgen Habermas, The Structural Transformation of the Public Sphere: An inquiry into a category of bourgeois society (Cambridge: Polity Press, 1989).
2. Oskar Negt and Alexander Kluge, op cit.
3. Cited in Habermas, op cit. pp. 109–10.
4. Ibid.
5. Cited in Susanne Kappeler, *The Will To Violence: The politics of personal behaviour* (Cambridge: Polity Press, 1995) p. 210.
6. Ibid., p. 210.
7. Couze Venn, *Occidentalism: Modernity and subjectivity* (London: Sage Publications, 2000) pp. 144–5.
8. Ibid, pp. 174–5.
9. Kappeler, op. cit., p. 212.
10. Habermas cited by Negt & Kluge, op. cit., p. 10.
11. Juliana Schiesari in Hendricks & Parker op. cit., p. 57.
12. Kathryn Church, *Forbidden Narratives: Critical autobiography as a social science* (London: Gordon & Breach Science Publishers Ltd., 1995) pp. 73–90.
13. Ibid., p. 90.
14. Valerie Walkerdine (1986), cited in Church op. cit., p. 135.
15. Kluge & Negt, *Public Sphere and Experience*, pp. 45–6.
16. Ferruccio Rossi-Landi, 'Kapital und Privateigentum der Sprache,' in *Asthetic und Kommunikation* 7(1972): 44, cited in Kluge & Negt, op. cit., pp. 3–4.
17. Ibid., p. 4.
18. Miriam Hansen points out that it is worth remembering that in Marxist philosophy the proletariat, though predicated on the working class as the historical subject of alienated labour and living, is not an empirical category. It is a category of negation in both a critical and utopian sense, referring both to the fragmentation of human labour and existence and its dialectical opposite, the practical negation of existing conditions in their totality. In Foreword to *Public Sphere and Experience*, p. xxxi.
19. The Zapatistas challenged the Mexican government, in 1994, over its capitulation to crippling 'free' trade conditions of the World Bank and IMF. They have articulated their struggle in terms of global capital and hence in terms of a global opposition.
20. Kluge & Negt, op. cit., p. 32.
21. Adorno left his native Germany in 1934 to escape the growing persecution of Jews and did not return for 15 years, two years before he returned to Germany with his colleague Max Horkheimer, they co-authored the widely influential *Dialectic of Enlightenment* (New York: Continuum, 2001 [1972]), a polemical attack upon the philosophical and scientific embrace of rationality. They depicted society as labouring under the tyrannical oppression of a capitalist economy that had colonised all forms of life. Most crucially, culture had been stripped of all its previous attachments to freedom, creativity and imagination and had become merely another arm of the capitalist market. Adorno described the logic of capitalist production as one that had subjugated all of society with 'the rhythm of an iron system'. In this nightmare of capitalist regulation, Adorno depicted the masses as incapable of escaping from the nullifying logic of capitalist production.

5 Thinking Subjects

1. Adorno expressed his bewilderment at the submission of the oppressed throughout history: 'Immovably, they on the very ideology that enslaves them. The misplaced love of the common people for the wrong which is done to them is a greater force than the cunning of the authorities', Adorno and Horkheimer, *Dialectic of Enlightenment*, p. 134.
2. Adorno, op. cit., pp. 120, 138.
3. Antonio Gramsci, *Selections from the Prison Notebooks* (London: Lawrence and Wishart, 1971) p. 333.
4. Kluge & Negt, *Public Sphere and Experience*, p. 25.
5. Ibid., p. 43.
6. Ibid., p. 29.
7. Ibid., p. 40.
8. Ibid.
9. Ibid., p. 41.
10. Ibid., pp. 23–4.
11. Gramsci, op. cit., p. 417.
12. Kluge & Negt, op. cit., pp. 86–7.
13. See Pierre Bourdieu, *Pascalian Meditations* (Cambridge: Polity Press, 2000).
14. Bourdieu, *Sociology in Question* (London: Sage, 1993) p. 1.
15. Bourdieu, *Pascalian Meditations*, pp. 67–8.
16. See for example, David Barton and Mary Hamilton, *Local Literacies: Reading and writing in one community* (London: Routledge, 1998).
17. Steadman, *Landscape for a Good Woman*, p. 12.
18. Kluge & Negt, op. cit., p. 23.
19. Steadman, op. cit., p. 11.
20. Bourdieu, *Pascalian Meditations*, p. 20.
21. Bourdieu, *Sociology in Question*, p. 17.

6 The Savage and the Proletariat

1. Karl Marx [1844] *Economic and Philosophical Manuscripts* in Bottomore and Rubel, *Karl Marx: Selected Writings in Sociology and Social Philosophy* (Harmondsworth: Pelican Books, 1971) pp. 249–50.
2. Karl Marx (1845–6) *German Ideology* in Bottomore & Rubel, op. cit., p. 232.
3. Karl Marx (1847), ibid., pp. 244–5.
4. Marx and Engels, *The German Ideology* (ed) C.J. Arthur. (London: Lawrence & Wishart, 1982) pp. 58–9.
5. Bottomore and Rubel, op. cit., pp. 23–4.
6. Georg Wilhelm Friedrich Hegel, *Lectures On The Philosophy of World History Introduction* (Cambridge: Cambridge University Press, 1975 [1822]) pp. 23–4. and pp. 30–1.
7. Karl Marx (1845), *The Holy Family*, cited in Bottomore op. cit., p. 73.
8. Ibid., p. 73.
9. Marx, *Capital* cited in Bottomore, op. cit., pp. 103–4.
10. Marx, *The Holy Family*, ibid., p. 78.

11. Michel-Rolph Trouillot, *Silencing The Past: Power and the production of history* (Boston: Beacon Press, 1995), p. 49.
12. Karl Marx, *Introduction To A Critique of Political Economy* in *The German Ideology* (1982) pp. 125–6.
13. Ibid., pp. 150–1.
14. Marx, *Capital*, cited in Bottomore, op. cit., p. 119.
15. Ibid., p. 119–20.
16. Bottomore, op. cit., pp. 35–6.
17. Karl Marx (1859), *Preface to A Contribution to the Critique of Political Economy* cited in Bottomore, op. cit., pp. 68–9.
18. Gayatri Chakravorty Spivak, *A Critique of Postcolonial Reason: Toward a history of the vanishing present* (Cambridge, MA: Harvard University Press, 1999) p. 83.
19. Victor Serge notes, that the first year of the Russian revolution was characterised by improvisations since the Bolsheviks had yet to possess a clear programme for the control of industry. Serge concludes that , '[A]n excess of improvisation rather than ideological rigidity was the real weakness of Russian Communism in the critical Year One.' Victor Serge *Year One Of The Russian Revolution* (London: Pluto Press, 1992 [1930]), pp. 15–6.
20. Spivak, op. cit., p. 83.
21. Mayfair Yang, 'Tradition, travelling anthropology and the discourse of modernity in China', in *The Future of Anthropological Knowledge,*(1996) [Ed.] Henrietta Moore (London: Routledge, 1996).
22. Ibid., p. 96.
23. Mayfair Yang notes in particular the work of Guo Moruo and Hu Sheng. Ibid., p. 96.
24. Mayfair Yang observes that 'Where landlords did not exist they had to be invented, in order to carry out the state policy of class struggle ... in the mountains of Yunnan during the Cultural revolution ... [a] work team from higher levels of government was sent down to divide [the] people up into the standard class categories of "landlord", "rich peasant", "poor peasant", etc. that applied all over China ... When the work team departed, A. Cheng writes ...' they left behind a very confused bunch of "landlords and poor peasants"', Friedman et al. (1991) cited by Mayfair Yang, op. cit., p. 102.
25. Spivak, op. cit., p. 80.
26. Ibid., pp. 289–90.
27. Gramsci, op. cit., p. 20.
28. Ibid., p. 21.
29. For a detailed overview of scientific racism see Stephen Jay Gould, *The Mismeasure Of Man* (Harmondsworth: Penguin, 1981) pp. 62–104.
30. Indeed, the output of black American writers in the early C20 is striking for its engagement with the issue of American culture and the relation of black Americans to that white America. See for example Zora Neale Hurston, Jessie Fauset, Nella Larsen, Charles W. Chesnutt, James Weldon Johnson and Ralph Ellison who all pondered with varying degrees of criticism, the implications of white America for black people.
31. Cedric J. Robinson, *Black Marxism: The Making Of The Black Radical Tradition* (Chapel Hill, NC: University of North Carolina Press, 2000). p. 81.
32. Gramsci, op. cit., p. 21.

33. Ronaldo Munck 'Postmodernism, Politics, and Paradigms in Latin America' in *Latin American Perspectives* issue 113, vol. 27, no. 4. July 2000 13–14.
34. Isak Niehaus argues that witchcraft beliefs are not unique to Africa. He notes their presence in pre-revolutionary Russia, contemporary France and India and in the tales of satanic child abuse in the United States and the United Kingdom. and in France and India. Cited in Henrietta Moore and Todd Sanders [Eds.] *Magical Interpretations, Material Realities: Modernity, Witchcraft and the Occult in Postcolonial Africa* (London: Routledge, 2001). p. 199.
35. Ibid., p. 2.
36. Ibid., p. 19.
37. Ibid., Introduction.
38. M. Taussig, *Shamanism, Colonialism and the Wild Man: A study in terror and healing* (Chicago: The University of Chicago Press, 1987). pp. 463–4.
39. Moore & Sanders, op. cit., p. 13.
40. Structural Adjustment Policies are economic policies which countries must follow in order to qualify for new World Bank and IMF loans and help them make debt repayments on older loans to commercial banks, governments and the World Bank. Although they are designed for individual countries structural 'reforms' have common guiding principles – export-led growth, privatisation, 'liberalisation' and the efficiency of the 'free market'. 'Latin American Perspectives' and 'Race & Class' provide detailed information on the terms and reactions to structural adjustment policies in the third world. See especially 'The New Conquistadors', *Race & Class* (London: Institute of Race Relations, vol. 34, no. 1, 1992) and *Latin American Perspectives* (Chapel Hill; University of North Carolina Press, issues 114, vol. 27, no. 5 September 2000, Issue 120, vol. 28, no. 5, September 2001 and Issue 115, vol. 27, no. 6, November 2000).
41. Todd Sanders, 'Save our Skins: Structural adjustment and the occult in Tanzania' in Moore and Sanders, op. cit., p. 161.
42. Ibid., p. 178.
43. Moore & Sanders, op. cit., pp. 12–3.
44. Ibid., p. 13.

7   Proletariats and Urban Intellectuals

1. Karl Marx [1844], *Hegel's Philosophy of Right*, in Bottomore and Rubel, *Karl Marx*, pp. 187–191.
2. Ibid., p. 189.
3. Ibid., p. 188.
4. Karl Marx [1845], *The Holy Family*, in Bottomore and Rubel, p. 190.
5. Ibid., pp. 237–8.
6. I discuss Oskar Negt and Alexander Kluge's reading of capitalist society in detail in chapters five, six and seven.
7. Adorno & Horkheimer, *Dialectic of Enlightenment*, p. 161.
8. Karl Marx [1844] *Hegel's Philosophy of Right*, in Bottomore and Rubel, op. cit., pp. 190–1.
9. Ibid., p. 191.
10. This was the argument that Marx advanced in *The Holy Family*, where he argued that '[A]lready with Hegel the *absolute spirit* of history has its material

in the *masses*, but finds only adequate expression in *philosophy*.' But the philosopher appears merely as the instrument by which the absolute spirit, which makes history, arrives at self-consciousness after the historical movement has been completed. The philosopher's share in history is thus limited to this subsequent consciousness. The philosopher arrives *post festum*.' Ibid., p. 73.

11. Karl Marx [1845–6] *The German Ideology*, op. cit., pp. 255–6.
12. Karl Marx (1847), *The Poverty of Philosophy*, Bottomore and Rubel, op. cit., pp. 80–1.
13. Negt and Kluge extended Adorno's observation that intellectual production does not serve the needs of capital and the bourgeoisie by claiming that 'scientific and theoretical activity is the form of human labor that is still most fully based upon the pleasure principle', op. cit., p. 25.
14. Ibid., pp. 8–9.
15. Ibid., p. 12.
16. Gramsci is particularly influential in debates about adult education. See for example, Peter J. Mayo, *Gramsci, Freire and Adult Education: Possibilities for transformative action* (London: Zed Books, 1999).
17. Gramsci, op. cit., p. 347.
18. Ibid., p. 356.
19. Negt and Kluge, op. cit., p. 297 n.3.
20. See Pierre Bourdieu, *Pascalian Meditations* (Cambridge: Polity Press, 2000), p. 23.
21. Gramsci, op. cit., p. 333.
22. Ibid.
23. Ibid., p. 334.
24. Ibid., pp. 334–5.
25. Ibid., p. 340.
26. Ibid., pp. 340–1.
27. I discuss Appiah and Gutmann in detail in chapter three.
28. Ibid., p. 325.
29. Ibid., p. 429.
30. The Italian Communist Party (PCI), led initially by Amadeo Bordiga and later by Gramsci, was formed in 1921 during the first period of fascist terror and took its place alongside an assortment of other leftist parties. Exacerbating the existing differences within the Italian left between the radicals and the reformists were the strained relations with the international communist organisation, the influential Comintern, who in 1921 were promoting the policy of the 'United Front'. The Soviet response to the succession of workers' defeats that occurred in Germany and Italy was to argue for the need for the international left to band together in order to defeat the threat from capital and the right. However, the leading Italian communists were reluctant to working with reformists on the Italian left who they blamed bitterly for sabotaging the succession of workers' revolts. Moreover, Bordiga's equally implacable suspicion of movements, such as the Turin factory councils, increased tensions both within the Comintern and the PCI. See Gramsci, op. cit., pp. xvii–xviii.
31. Victor Serge, *Year One Of The Russian Revolution* (London: Bookmarks and Pluto Press, 1992), p. 59.
32. Ibid., pp. 57–8.
33. Ibid., p. 58.

34. See Victor Serge, *Memoirs Of A Revolutionary* (Iowa City: Iowa University Press, 2002).
35. Stalin used terror and repression throughout his regime. Violent repression reached its height in the political purges of the 1930s. Stalin consolidated his dictatorship by liquidating all opposition within the party. The purge began with the murder, in 1934, of S.M. Kirov, Stalin's lieutenant, which led to prosecutions for an alleged plot led by Trotsky and aided by Nazi Germany which was seeking to overthrow Stalin's government. In the purge trials, many old Bolsheviks, including Kamenev, Zinoviev, Aleksey, Rykov and Bukharin, were accused, pleaded guilty and were executed. The purge extended to the head of the secret police, G.G. Yagoda and to some of the most senior army officers. As the purges drew to a close, in 1939, the efforts of the secret police were focused on eliminating those elements of the population that might be disloyal in case of war. The Soviet system of forced labour camps was hugely expanded during this period.
36. Victor Serge (1922) cited in David Cotterill [Ed.] (1994) *The Serge-Trotsky Papers: Correspondence and other writings between Victor Serge and Leon Trotsky* (London: Pluto Press, 1994) p. 16.
37. Twenty years after the revolution and eleven years after his expulsion from the party were not enough to persuade Serge that his support for the revolution had been in vain. See Victor Serge, *Memoirs Of A Revolutionary*, p. 384.
38. Karl Marx (1875), 'Critique of the Gotha Programme', in Bottomore and Rubel, op. cit., p. 261.
39. For Lenin Marxist theory was unique insofar as it was inextricable from reality. Marxism, as a theory of practice, was thus incapable of simply being an abstract formula but had to constantly adapt to changing historical circumstances: 'To different moments of economic evolution, there correspond different forms of struggle'. Lenin (1906) 'On Guerrilla Warfare' in Victor Serge, *Year One of the Russian Revolution*, pp. 44–5.
40. As Serge documents, there is no evidence that Bolshevik industrial policy in the pre-revolutionary period possessed any disposition towards centralisation and state planning. In fact, the Bolsheviks had no desire to govern alone and far from being rigidly doctrinaire in the early years of the revolution were constantly improvising their methods and policies. Lenin's Land Decree, which abolished landownership immediately and without compensation was passed in order to give peasants the freedom to organise their own lives. Lenin's response to his critics was emphatic: 'As a democratic government, we cannot simply ignore the wishes of the popular masses, even if we are in disagreement with them ... Will the peasantry act in the spirit of our programme or that of the SRs? It is of little importance, the main thing is for them to have the firm assurance that there will be no more landlords and that they can set about organising their own lives', *Lenin Collected Works* in Victor Serge, *Year One of the Russian Revolution* p. 82.
41. Ibid., pp. 196–7.
42. Ibid., p. 239.
43. Victor Serge, *Memoirs,* p. 375–6.
44. Marx and Engels, *The Communist Manifesto,* in C. Robinson op. cit., p. 330 n.18.
45. Detailed in Bottomore and Rubel, op. cit., p. 42.
46. The questions are reprinted in Bottomore and Rubel, op. cit., pp. 211–18.

47. The *Revue Socialiste*, three months after its publication of the questionnaire, noted that it had received very few replies and urged its readers to respond. Again the response was negligible and no further mention of the questionnaire was made.
48. Gramsci, op. cit., p. 335.

8 Speaking for the People

1. Johannes Fabian, *Time And The Other: How Anthropology makes its object* (New York: Columbia University Press, 1983).
2. Ibid., pp. 30–1.
3. Ibid., p. 67.
4. Ibid.
5. Ibid., p. 105.
6. Ibid., p. 158.
7. Ibid.
8. Ibid., p. 165.
9. Ibid., p. 155.
10. Robinson, *Black Marxism* op. cit., p. 66.
11. Robinson cites Oliver Cox who argued that the affiliations of the European white working classes was as much marked by nationalist allegiances as it was to a radical class consciousness. (Oliver Cox, 'Capitalism as a System', 1964.) Ibid., p. 372, n. 32.
12. As Aimé Césaire's resignation from the American Communist party demonstrates. Robinson, op. cit., p. 184.
13. Robinson, op. cit., p. 202.
14. Ibid.
15. Ibid., p. 288.
16. For example, the Haitian revolution continues to be marginalised in critical discussions. Michel-Rolph Trouillot details the extent to which the Haitian revolution, as opposed to the French and American revolutions of the same period, continues to be viewed as a historical impossibility. See Trouillot, op. cit.
17. Ibid., p. 317.
18. Robinson, op. cit., p. 317.
19. Ibid.
20. Ibid., pp. 299–300.
21. See Ntongela Masilela, 'Pan-Africanism or Classical African Marxism?' in Sidney Lemelle and Robin D.G. Kelley (eds), *Imagining Home: Class, culture and nationalism in the African diaspora* (London: Verso, 1994) p. 327.
22. Ibid., p. 317.
23. Ziauddin Sardar, *Postmodernism And The Other: The new imperialism of western culture* (London: Pluto Press, 1997).
24. Amílcar Cabral, *Revolution in Guinea: An African People's Struggle*, cited in Benita Parry, 'Liberation Movements' in *Interventions: International Journal of Postcolonial Studies*. 1-1 1998–9, p. 47.
25. Sardar, op. cit., p. 281.
26. Edward Said, *Orientalism* (London: Routledge and Kegan Paul, 1978).

27. Ibid., p. 42.
28. Ibid., p. 291.
29. Rey Chow, *Writing Diaspora: Tactics of intervention in contemporary cultural studies* (Bloomington: Indiana University Press, 1993).
30. Ibid., p. 30.
31. Ibid., p. 17.
32. Parry, op. cit., 1–1 1998–9.
33. Parry, op. cit., pp. 46–7 cites in particular the Portuguese colonies in Africa and the French territory of Upper Volta/Burkina Faso.
34. Benita Parry, 'Problems in Current Theories of Colonial Discourse', cited in Bill Ashcroft, Gareth Griffiths and Helen Tiffin (eds) *The Postcolonial Studies Reader* (London: Routledge, 1995) p. 43.
35. Ibid.
36. As Peter Quartermaine demonstrates, failing to attend to the historical contexts of representations of 'native' cultures can affirm the perceptions of colonialists rather than the indigenous peoples that progressive commentators align themselves with. Thus, John Pilger's employment of Lindt's nineteenth-century photographs as evidence of Aboriginal life, overlooks the fact that such photographs were, in their time, important trophies for nineteenth-century drawing rooms, serving the interests of empire rather than those of Aboriginal culture or existence. Peter Quartermaine, 'Johannes Lindt: Photographer of Australia and New Guinea', in Mark Gidley (ed.), *Representing Others: White views of indigenous peoples* (Exeter: University of Exeter Press, 1992).
37. Parry, 'Liberation Movements: Memories Of The Future' in *Interventions*, p. 46.
38. For example, Walter Rodney a Guyanese historian and theorist combined his intellectual output with efforts to contribute towards the 'self-emancipation' of the working people that he grew increasingly anxious about in the face of an increasingly corrupt and authoritarian post-independence government in Guyana. At the Sixth Pan-African Congress in Tanzania (1974) he drew attention to the 'silent classes' on whose behalf national claims were being made, demonstrating that for him at least, the question of the equitable relation between the masses and the anti-colonial intellectuals and leaders was one worth considering. See Walter Rodney, *How Europe Underdeveloped Africa* (London: Bogle-L'Ouverture Publications, 1978), detailed in, Horace Campbell, 'Pan-Africanism and African Liberation', in Lemelle and Kelley (eds), *Imagining Home* pp. 180–1.
39. Jean Rhys, *Wide Sargasso Sea* (London: Penguin, 1968).
40. Mayfair Yang points out that that the prohibition of Native American Indian customs by the Canadian government was accompanied by the collection of ceremonial heirlooms and masks in museums. Dominant discourses of modernity need a counter-discourse of ancient native wisdom which become figured as precious relics of an age that they themselves have superseded. In this sense, the celebration of past culture is an exhibition of precisely who holds current cultural-political power. See Mayfair Yang, 'Tradition, Travelling Theory, Anthropology and the Discourse of Modernity in China', in H. Moore, *The Future Of Anthropological Knowledge*, op. cit. Nicola Miller, in her discussion of Spanish America, notes that across the region the cultural rediscovery of oppressed groups by intellectuals followed on from, or

went in tandem with, the calculated destruction of their political power by modernizing states. Thus, the Aztec empire could be represented in murals and manifestos as the glorious ancestry of the modern Mexican nation, but its descendents were perceived as obstacles to economic advancement. In Chile, only a few Mapuche survived the 'pacification' programmes of the 1860s to 1890s to become living reminders of the proud Araucanian warrior of the country's semi-invented past. Nicola Miller, *In The Shadow Of The State: Intellectuals and the quest for national identity in twentieth-century Spanish America* (London: Verso, 1999) p. 172.

41. María Elena García, 'The Politics of Community Education, Indigenous Rights and Ethnic Mobilization in Peru', in *Latin American Perspectives: Indigenous Transformational Movements in Contemporary Latin America*, Issue 128, vol. 30, Number 1. January 2003. 70–95.

42. Cited in María Elena García, Ibid., p. 80.

43. Ibid., p. 85.

44. Patrick Wilson, 'Ethnographic Museums and Cultural Commodification: Indigenous organizations, NGOs, and Culture as a resource in Amazonian Ecuador', ibid.

45. Jésus González, ibid., p. 162.

46. Ibid., p. 170.

47. Ibid., p. 175.

48. Cited in Rey Chow, *Writing Diaspora*, op. cit., p. 28.

49. Ibid.

50. Alcida Ramos, 'From Eden to limbo: the construction of indigenism in Brazil', in George C. Bond and Angela Gilliam (Eds.), *Social Construction of the Past: Representation as Power* (London: Routledge, 1994) p. 79.

51. Ibid., pp. 79–80.

52. For example, Duncan Campbell's article, reporting on the Goshute Indians' agreement to their land in Skull Valley, Utah being used by utility companies looking to store 40,000 tonnes of highly radioactive nuclear waste in advance of the construction of the permanent site at Yucca Mountain in Nevada, carried the headline, 'Alarm as tribe offers land for nuclear dump'. 'The Guardian' May 30th 2002.

53. See David B. Coplan, 'Fictions that save: Migrants' Performance and Basotho National Culture', in George E. Marcus (Ed), *Rereading Cultural Anthropology* (Durham and London: Duke University Press, 1995) pp. 267–292.

54. Parry 'Liberation Movements', op. cit., p. 47.

55. Ibid.

56. Amílcar Cabral (1969) *Revolution in Guinea: An African People's Struggle*, cited in Parry 'Liberation Movements', p. 47.

57. Andrew Spiegel cites Webster's study of the Thonga state under Mabadu (now Mozambique), which revealed the conflict between men's identifications as Zulu and women's identification as Thonga. Although women presented themselves as Zulu in public they preferred to identify themselves as Thonga in the domestic sphere where men retained their identity. This gender division reflected the fact that Zulu traditions were more patriarchal than the Thonga tradition which gave wives more independence. The fact that Zulu traditions and identity are more powerful in the public arena attests to the pre-colonial existence of competing traditions and to the post-colonial

entrenchment of patriarch privilege through recourse to notions of a colonised people's traditional Zulu heritage. In, 'Struggling with tradition in South Africa: the multivocality of images of the past', in Bond & Gilliam, op. cit., pp. 194–6.

58. Z. Sardar, op. cit., p. 282.
59. Parry, op. cit., p. 46.
60. Parry points out, that the aims of the Mozambique Liberation Front were to overthrow the structures and principles of colonial society. In 1976, Samora Moisés Machel argued that, "To 'Africanise' colonialist and capitalist power would be to negate the meaning of our struggle … our objective is to liberate ourselves, to build a new society". Ibid., p. 46.
61. Amílcar Cabral (1969) cited in, Parry, ibid., p.46.
62. Thomas Sankara (1988), ibid., pp. 46–7.
63. Amílcar Cabral, cited in Carlos Pinto Santos, 'Amílcar Cabral: 'Freedom Fighter, 1924–1973', http://www.vidaslusofonas.pt/amilcar_cabral_2.htm.
64. Parry, op. cit., p. 47.
65. Barbara Harlow documents the litany of committed intellectuals who have been the victims of political assassination: Naji al-Ali (Palestinian, died 1987); Malcolm X (African American, died 1965); Amil Cabral (Guinea Bissau, died 1973); Steve Biko (South African, died 1977); Walter Rodney (Guyana, died 1980); Roque Dalton (Salvadoran, died 1975), Ghassan Kanafani (Palestinian, died 1972) and Ruth First (South African, died 1982). Cited in 'Writers and Assassinations', ibid., pp. 172–3.
66. Cabral was assassinated by members of his own organisation working in collaboration with the Portuguese military regime. The Portuguese were able to exploit the differences in the PAIGC between the 'Cape Verdeans' who comprised the higher levels of the party and the Guineans who dominated the lower echelons of the organisation. Portugal's colonial divide and rule policy thus produced useful tensions within the anti-colonial movement itself. Moreover, Cabral's commitment to the fight against imperialism and his internationalism threatened both the old colonial power and those within the PAIGC who aspired to a more traditional notion of the transfer of power rather than any radical transformation of the colonial state. Cabral's murder, like Patrice Lumumba's before him, was an act that dealt a crushing blow to Africa. As Harlow points out, 'Critical to Cabral's philosophy was the international vision of emancipation that he represented within Africa in the combined resistance movements of Cape Verde and Guinea-Bissau as well as globally in his emphasis on the necessarily collective struggles of Africans and the Portuguese working class against imperialist exploitation.' Barbara Harlow, Writers and Assassinations', in, *Imagining Home*, op. cit., p. 177. Horace Campbell notes that Walter Rodney's efforts to rethink African liberation led to his assassination by a government that claimed to be at the forefront of the struggle of African liberation. Horace Campbell, 'Pan-Africanism and African Liberation', ibid., p. 300.
67. Parry, op. cit., pp. 47–8.
68. Steve Pile, 'The Troubled Spaces of Frantz Fanon' in Mike Crang and Nigel Thrift (eds.), *Thinking Space* (London: Routledge, 2000).
69. Ibid., p. 271.
70. Frantz Fanon (1961), ibid., p. 272.

71. Ibid., pp. 274–6.
72. Ntongela Masilela, 'Pan-Africanism or Classical Marxism' in Lemelle and Kelley, op. cit., p. 318.
73. See for example, Basil Davidson, *Africa In History* (London: Phoenix Press, 2001). Davidson signals his agreement with Cabral that imperialism, brutal though it was, did introduce development and industry to Africa: 'The colonial experience was undoubtedly heavy in its consequences. Most of these consequences were bad for Africans. But the total experience was dialectical by nature. The ills of Africa today derive partly from the colonial heritage, but also partly from Africa's still existing need for profound structural transformation ... Though wastefully and planlessly, with reluctance or contempt, the colonial rulers nonetheless opened a few new doors to the outside world', pp. 316–8.
74. Amílcar Cabral (1966) 'The weapon of theory' cited in Masilela, 'Pan-Africanism or Classical Marxism' in Lemelle and Kelley, op. cit., p. 320.
75. Frantz Fanon (1964) 'Toward the African Revolution', ibid., p. 316.
76. See Basil Davidson, op. cit.
77. Amílcar Cabral (1965: series of 9 lectures), cited in, Lemelle and Kelley, op. cit., p. 329.
78. Ibid., p. 319.
79. Ibid.
80. R. Chow (1998) *Ethics After idealism*, op. cit., p. 71.

9 Outsiders: Women and Radical Theory

1. Cynthia Enloe (1989) cited in Rick Wilford and Robert L. Miller (eds), *Women, Ethnicity and Nationalism: The politics of transition* (London: Routledge, 1998), p. 2.
2. Mary K. Meyer, 'Ulster's red hand: gender identity and sectarian conflict', in Sita Ranchod-Nilsson and Mary Ann Tétreault (eds), *Women, States And Nationalism: At home in the nation?* (London: Routledge, 2000).
3. V. Spike Peterson, 'Sexing political identities/nationalism as heterosexism', ibid., p. 69.
4. See Stephen Reicher and Nick Hopkins, *Self And Nation: Categorization, Contestation and Mobilization* (London: Sage, 2001) pp. 93–4.
5. Ibid., p. 95.
6. Edmund Burke (1775), ibid., p. 95.
7. Cited in Nicola Miller, *In the Shadow of the State: Intellectuals and the quest for national identity in twentieth-century Spanish America* (London: Verso, 1999) p. 60.
8. Luce Irigaray (1977) cited by S. D Kristmundsdottir, '"Father did not answer that question": Power, gender and globalisation in Europe', in Angela Cheater (ed.), *The Anthropology of Power: Empowerment and disempowerment in changing structures* (London: Routledge, 1999). p. 51.
9. Sigmund Freud, *Totem and Taboo: Some points of agreement between the mental lives of savages and neurotics* (London: Routledge, 2001 [1913]).
10. Chow, *Ethics after Idealism*, op. cit., p. 61.
11. Frantz Fanon, *Black Skin, White Masks* (London: Pluto Press, 1986 [1967]) p. 222.

12. Jacqui Alexander (1997) cited in V. Spike Peterson, 'Sexing political identities/ nationalism as heterosexism' in Ranchod-Nilsson, op. cit., p. 63.
13. Frantz Fanon, *Black Skin White Masks*, cited in Rey Chow, *Ethics After Idealism* p. 59.
14. See T. Morrison, *Race-Ing Justice, En-Gendering Power*, op. cit.
15. Spike Peterson, 'Sexing political identities/nationalism as heterosexism' in Ranchod-Nilsson, op. cit., p. 63.
16. This is a vast subject that gathered pace during the 1980s when working class women, lesbian women, black women and women of color began to challenge the assumptions of prominent white feminists who, they argued, were too quick to speak in the name of all women.
17. Zillah Eisenstein, *Hatreds: Racialized and sexualized conflicts in the 21st century* (London: Routledge, 1996) p. 53.
18. Sardar, op. cit.
19. Detailed in Sardar, *Orientalism* (Buckingham: Open University Press, 1999) pp. 64–5. I discuss this more fully in chapter eight.
20. Spike Peterson, 'Sexing political identities/nationalism as heterosexism' in Ranchod-Nilsson, op. cit., p. 67.
21. Cherrie Moraga (1994) in U. Narayan, op. cit., p. 30.
22. Ibid., p. 22.
23. Spike Peterson, 'Sexing political identities/nationalism as heterosexism' in Ranchod-Nilsson, op. cit., p. 70.
24. Winifred Woodhull, 'Unveiling Algeria' in Reina Lewis and Sara Mills (eds), *Feminist Postcolonial Theory: A reader* (Edinburgh: Edinburgh University Press, 2003).
25. Ibid., p. 574.
26. Ibid., p. 576.
27. See Wilford and Miller, op. cit.; Ranchod-Nilsson, op. cit.; and Chilla Bulbeck *Re-Orienting Western Feminisms: Women's diversity in a post-colonial world* (Cambridge: Cambridge University Press, 1998).
28. Marie-Aimee Helie-Lucas, cited in Narayan op. cit., p. 31.
29. Barbara Harlow (1987) 'Resistance Literature' New York: Methuen, in Winifred Woodhull, 'Unveiling Algeria', Lewis & Mills, op. cit., p. 580.
30. Ibid.
31. Marilyn Friedman (1995) 'Multi-cultural Education and Feminist Ethics' cited in Narayan, *Dislocating Cultures*, pp. 148.
32. Ibid., pp. 149–50.
33. See for example, Michael Ignatieff, *Blood and Belonging: Journeys into the new nationalism* (London: Chatto & Windus, 1993). Billig notes that the book was accompanied by a BBC television series with rights sold worldwide, Michael Billig, *Banal Nationalism* (London: Sage Publications, 1995), p. 46.
34. See Tim Allen and Jean Seaton (eds), *The Media of Conflict: War reporting and representations of ethnic violence* (London: Zed Books, 1999) and David Wood in Keith Ansell-Pearson, Benita Parry and Judith Squires (eds), *Cultural Readings of Imperialism: Edward Said and the gravity of history* (London: Lawrence & Wishart, 1997) p. 194.
35. See David Keen, in Allen & Seaton, op. cit., p. 81.
36. Ibid., p. 82.
37. Douglas Hurd, ibid., p. 82.

38. Richard Fardon, ibid., p. 65.
39. Michael Billig, op. cit.
40. Ibid., p. 140.
41. Neil Lazarus in Ansell-Pearson, op. cit., pp. 28–9.
42. Ibid., p. 9.
43. Ibid., p. 6.
44. Billig is referring to Benedict Anderson's widely quoted reading of the significance of print-capitalism as providing a new point of origin for society and ushering in a 'new' community. Benedict Anderson, *Imagined Communities: Reflections on the origin and spread of nationalism* (London: Verso, 1983).
45. Michael Ignatieff, op. cit.
46. Ibid., p. 46.
47. See Jean Bethke Elshtain, *Just War against Terror: The burden of American power in a violent world* (New York: Basic Books, 2004).
48. Billig, op. cit., p 126.
49. Frederick Engels [1884], *The Origin of the Family, Private Property and the State* (London: New Era Books, 1978).
50. Sharon Smith, *Engels and the origins of women's oppression'*, International Socialist Review, Issue 2, Fall 1997, online edition.
51. Ibid.
52. Engels, op. cit., p. 60.
53. Ibid.
54. Ibid., p. 65.
55. Ibid., p. 86.
56. Perry Anderson cited in Young, *Torn Halves,* op. cit., p. 136.
57. See Donald S. Moore, Jake Kosek and Anand Pandian (eds), *Race, Nature and the Politics of Difference* (Durham NC; London: Duke University Press, 2003).
58. See Moore, *The Future of Anthropological Knowledge,* op. cit.
59. Lynn Stephen documents how while some pre-Hispanic societies were characterised by dichotomous gender systems for elites that focused upon male/female complementarity other indigenous communities had far more flexible gender systems offering the possibility of androgyny and a third gender. Detailed in (2002) 'Sexualities and Genders in Zapotec Oaxaca' in *Latin American Perspectives*, Issue 123, vol. 29, no. 2, March 2002, pp. 55–6.
60. James N. Green and Florence E. Babb in 'Gender, Sexuality and Same Sex Desire in Latin America' *Latin American Perspectives* Issue 123, vol. 29, no. 2, March 2002. The association of homosexuality with upper-class men and bourgeois decadence permeated the international communist movement. They note that the pro-Soviet Brazilian Communist party continued to maintain that position. Pro-Chinese and pro-Albanian Maoist groups had considerable influence in Colombia, Peru and Brazil and followed suit, p. 11.
61. Ibid.
62. See David William Foster, 'The Homoerotic Diaspora in Latin America' in *Latin American Perspectives* Issue 123, vol. 29, no. 2, March 2002.
63. Fidel Castro, cited in Rafael Ocasio, 'Gays and the Cuban Revolution' in *Latin American Perspectives* Issue 123, vol. 29, no. 2, March 2002. California: Sage, p. 82.
64. Spike Peterson, 'Sexing political identities/nationalism as heterosexism' in Ranchod-Nilsson, op cit., p. 66.

65. See Zygmunt Bauman, *Postmodern Ethics* (Oxford: Blackwell, 1993) and *Postmodernity and Its discontent* (Cambridge: Polity Press, 1997).
66. Robert Young, *White Mythologies: Writing history and the west* (London: Routledge, 1990) p. 19.
67. Keith Jenkins, *Why History: Ethics and postmodernity* (London: Routledge, 1999).
68. Hans Bertens, *The Idea of the Postmodern: A history* (London: Routledge, 1995).
69. Jenkins, op. cit., p. 204.
70. Bauman, *Postmodern Ethics*, op. cit., pp. 248–9.
71. Bauman, *Society Under Siege* (Cambridge: Polity Press, 2002), p. 127.
72. Judith Butler in N. Fraser, *Feminist Contentions* (London: Routledge, 1995).
73. Judith Butler in Fraser, op. cit., pp. 129–32.
74. See, for example, Robert Young's discussion of 'the third world' and 'the west' in *White Mythologies*. Young argued that African and Asian nations had a 'choice' of political systems when they became independent. The 'choice' was between a Western free-market demand economy, a Sino-Soviet centralised one or an indigenous mixed economy. Young argues that these 'choices' were abruptly curtailed after the collapse of the Soviet bloc. Young's neutral assertion omits any reference to the brutal processes of decolonisation that made the 'choice' to adopt a socialist programme one that risked the military aggression and political interference of Western governments and elites.
75. See Ansell-Pearson, op. cit.
76. Zapatista Army of National Liberation (Ejército Zapatista de Liberación Nacional).
77. See June Nash, *Mayan Visions: The quest for autonomy in an age of globalisation* (London: Routledge, 2001).
78. See Henry Veltmeyer, 'The Dynamics of Social Change and Mexico's EZLN' and Mark T. Berger, 'Romancing the Zapatistas: International intellectuals and the Chiapas rebellion' in *Latin American Perspectives,* Issue 114, vol. 27. no. 5, September 2000.
79. See Kevin Gosner and Arij Ouweneel (eds) *Indigenous Revolts in Chiapas and the Andean Highlands* (The Netherlands: CEDLA, 1998).
80. George A. Collier details how Rafael Santiago Guillién Vicente is 'Marcos' the name that Vicente adopted in order to speak for the Zapatistas. See G. Collier, *Basta: Land & The Zapatista Rebellion In Chiapas* (California: Food First Books, 1994) p. 167. The focus upon Marcos as the charismatic leader of the movement arises from Vicente's visibility and frequent communiqués posted in the Internet to international supporters. However, Marcos is primarily a reference to the 'other': 'Marcos is a human being in this world. Marcos is every untolerated, oppressed, exploited minority that is resisting and saying "Enough!"', cited in John Holloway and Eloína Peláez (eds), *Zapatista: Reinventing revolution In Mexico* (London: Pluto Press, 1998) p. 11. The Zapatistas and Marcos stress the importance of accountability, and consultation in their movement which is reflected in the priority given to negotiation and agreement.
81. Subcomandante Marcos, 'Chiapas, the thirteenth stele, Part Two, A Death', ZNet/Chiapas, www.Zmag.
82. See Subcomandante And The Zapatistas, *The Other Campaign* (San Francisco, CA: City Lights Books, 2006).

83. For example their rejection of Evo Morales's invitation to attend his 2006 presidential inauguration in Bolivia. The Zapatistas made it clear that their refusal to attend was due to their refusal to accept the legitimacy of existing political structures whoever happened to win.
84. Márgara Millán notes that many senior posts are held by women. Roughly 30 per cent of EZLN members are women. Women's voices were promptly heard after the uprising and The Woman's Law was included among the proclamations published on 1 January 1994. Other commentators put the involvement of women even higher. The most important military action undertaken by the Zapatistas – the occupation of the town hall in San Cristobál on 1 January 1994 was led by Ana María, John Holloway and Eloína Peláez (eds), op. cit., p. 64.
85. Ibid., pp. 159–60.
86. Ibid., p. 15.

Bibliography

T. Adorno and M. Horkheimer, *Dialectic of Enlightenment* (New York: Continuum, 2001 [1972]).

T. Allen and J. Seaton (Eds), *The Media of Conflict: War reporting and representations of ethnic violence* (London: Zed Books, 1999).

B. Anderson, *Imagined Communities: Reflections on the origin and spread of nationalism* (London: Verso, 1983).

K. Ansell-Pearson, B. Parry and J. Squires (Eds), *Cultural Readings of Imperialism: Edward Said and the gravity of history* (London: Lawrence & Wishart, 1997).

K. Appiah and H.L. Gates Jr, *The Dictionary of Global Culture* (Harmondsworth: Penguin, 1998).

K. Appiah and A. Gutmann, *Color Conscious: The political morality of race* (Princeton, NJ: Princeton University Press, 1996).

D. Archer and P. Costello, *Literacy and Power: The Latin-American battleground* (London: Earthscan Publications, 1990).

M. Arnold [1869] *Culture and Anarchy: An essay in political and social criticism* (Cambridge: Cambridge University Press, 1993).

B. Ashcroft, G. Griffiths and H. Tiffin (Eds), *The Postcolonial Studies Reader* (London: Routledge, 1995) p. 43.

C. Baldick, *The Social Mission of English Criticism 1848–1932* (Oxford: OUP 1987).

K. A. Baldwin, *Beyond The Color Line and the Iron Curtain: Reading encounters between black and red, 1922–1963* (Durham: Duke University Press, 2002).

D. Barton and M. Hamilton, *Local Literacies: Reading and writing in one community* (London: Routledge, 1998).

Z. Bauman, *Legislators and Interpreters: On modernity, post-modernity and intellectuals* (Oxford: Polity Press, 1987).

——, *Postmodern Ethics* (Oxford: Blackwell, 1993).

——, *Postmodernity And Its Discontents* (Cambridge: Polity Press, 1997).

——, *Society Under Siege* (Cambridge: Polity Press, 2002).

J. Benda, *La Trahison des clercs* (Paris: Grasset, 1927).

H. Bertens, *The Idea Of The Postmodern: A history* (London: Routledge, 1999).

M. Billig, *Banal Nationalism* (London: Sage Publications, 1995).

J. Blommaert and J. Verschueren, *Debating Diversity: Analysing the discourse of tolerance* (London: Routledge, 1998).

G. Bond and A. Gilliam (Eds), *Social Construction of the Past: Representation as Power* (London: Routledge, 1994).

T. Bottomore and M. Rubel, *Karl Marx: Selected Writings in Sociology and Social Philosophy* (Harmondsworth: Pelican Books, 1971).

P. Bourdieu, *Acts of Resistance: Against the new myths of our time* (Cambridge: Polity Press, 1998).

——, *Pascalian Meditations* (Cambridge: Polity Press, 2000) translated by R. Nice.

——, *Sociology in Question* (London: Sage, 1993).

C. Bulbeck, *Re-Orienting Western Feminisms: Women's diversity in a post-colonial world* (Cambridge: Cambridge University Press, 1998).

A. Callinicos, *Against postmodernism: A Marxist critique* (Cambridge: Polity Press, 1989).

D. Cameron *Verbal Hygiene* (London: Routledge, 1993).

N. Chandhoke, *State and Civil Society: Explorations in political theory* (London: Sage Publications, 1995).

A. Cheater (Ed.), *The Anthropology of Power: Empowerment and disempowerment in changing structures* (London: Routledge, 1999).

N. Chomsky, *Deterring Democracy* (London: Vintage, 1992).

R. Chow, *Ethics after Idealism: Theory, culture, ethnicity, reading* (Bloomington: Indiana University Press, 1998).

——, *Writing Diaspora: Tactics of intervention in contemporary cultural studies* (Bloomington: Indiana University Press, 1993).

K. Church, *Forbidden Narratives: Critical autobiography as a social science* (London: Gordon & Breach Science Publishers Ltd, 1995).

G. Collier, *Basta: Land & The Zapatista Rebellion In Chiapas* (California: Food First Books, 1994).

S. Collini, *Absent Minds: Intellectuals in Britain* (Oxford: Oxford University Press, 2006).

M. Cooke, *Language and Reason: A Study in Habermas's Pragmatics* (Cambridge MA: MIT Press, 1994).

D. Cotterill (Ed.), *The Serge-Trotsky Papers: Correspondence and other writings between Victor Serge and Leon Trotsky* (London: Pluto Press, 1994).

M. Crang and N. Thrift (Eds), *Thinking Space* (London: Routledge, 2000).

B. Davidson, *Africa In History* (London: Phoenix Press, 2001).

T. Eagleton, *The Function of Criticism: From the Spectator to post-structuralism* (London: Verso, 1984).

——, *Criticism and Ideology: A study in Marxist literary theory* (London: ILB, 1976).

Z. Eisenstein, *Hatreds: Racialized and sexualized conflicts in the 21st century* (London: Routledge, 1996).

J. Elshtain, *Just War against Terror: The burden of American power in a violent world* (New York: Basic Books, 2004).

J. Fabian, *Time And The Other: How anthropology makes its object* (New York: Columbia Press, 1983).

F. Fanon, *Black Skin, White Masks* (London: Pluto Press, 1986 [1967]) S.R.S. Finke 'Habermas and Kant: Judgment and communicative experience', *Philosophy and Social Criticism*, vol. 26, no. 6 (2000) 21–45.

N. Fraser, *Feminist Contentions* (London: Routledge, 1995).

S. Freud, *Totem and Taboo: Some points of agreement between the mental lives of savages and neurotics* (London: Routledge, 2001 [1913]).

S. Fuller, *The Intellectual* (Cambridge: Icon Books, 2006).

M. García, 'The Politics of Community Education, Indigenous Rights and Ethnic Mobilization in Peru', in *Latin American Perspectives: Indigenous transformational movements in contemporary Latin America*, Issue 128, vol. 30, no. 1 (January 2003) 70–95.

J.T. Gatto, *Dumbing Us Down: The hidden curriculum of compulsory schooling* (New Society Pub, 1991).

C. Gattone, *The Social Scientist as Public Intellectual: Critical reflections in a changing world* (New York: Rowman & Littlefield Publishers, 2006).

M. Gidley (Ed.), *Representing Others: White views of indigenous peoples* (Exeter: University of Exeter Press for AmCAS, 1992).

A. Gimmler, 'Deliberative democracy, the public sphere and the internet', *Philosophy & Social criticism* vol. 27, no. 4 (July 2001) 21–39.

C. Gordon (Ed.), *Power/Knowledge: Selected interviews and other writings 1972–1977 by Michel Foucault* (Hemel Hempstead: Harvester Wheatsheaf, 1980).

K. Gosner and A. Ouweneel (Eds), *Indigenous Revolts in Chiapas and the Andean Highlands* (The Netherlands: CEDLA, 1998).

S. Gould (1992) *The Mismeasure Of Man* (Harmondsworth: Penguin, 1981).

A. Gramsci (1996) *Selections from the Prison Notebooks* (London: Lawrence and Wishart, 1971).

J. Habermas, *Between Facts and Norms: Contributions to a discourse theory of law and democracy* (Cambridge, MA: MIT Press, 1996).

——, *The Structural Transformation of the Public Sphere: An inquiry into a category of bourgeois society* (Cambridge: Polity Press, 1989).

G. Hegel, *Lectures On The Philosophy of World History Introduction* (Cambridge: Cambridge University Press, 1975 [1822]).

M. Hendricks and P. Parker (Eds), *Women, 'Race,' & Writing in the Early Modern Period* (London: Routledge, 1994).

J. Holloway and E. Peláez (Eds), *Zapatista: Reinventing revolution in Mexico* (London: Pluto Press, 1998).

M. Ignatieff, *Blood and Belonging* (London: BBC Books, 1993).

I. Illich, *Deschooling Society* (London: Marion Boyars Publishers, 1971).

K. Jenkins, *Why History: Ethics and postmodernity* (London: Routledge, 1999).

J. Jennings and A. Kemp-Welch (Eds), *Intellectuals In Politics: From the Dreyfus affair to Salman Rushdie* (London: Routledge, 1997).

P. Johnson, 'Distorted communications: Feminism's dispute with Habermas' *Philosophy & Social Criticism*, 27. no. 1 (January 2001).

S. Kappeler, *The Will to Violence: The politics of personal behaviour* (Cambridge: Polity Press, 1995).

A. Kluge and O. Negt, *Public Sphere and Experience: Toward an analysis of the Bourgeois and Proletarian Public Sphere* (Minneapolis: University of Minnesota Press, 1993).

M. Kohn, *The Race Gallery: The return of racial science* (London: J. Cape, 1995).

Latin American Perspectives (Chapel Hill; University of North Carolina Press) Issue 114 vol. 27, no. 5 September 2000; Issue 120, vol. 28, no. 5, September 2001; Issue 115, vol. 27, no. 6, November 2000; Issue 123, vol. 29, no. 2, March 2002.

S. Lemelle and R. Kelley (Eds), *Imagining Home: Class, culture and nationalism in the African diaspora* (London: Verso, 1994).

R. Lewis and S. Mills (Eds), *Feminist Postcolonial Theory: A reader* (Edinburgh: Edinburgh University Press, 2003).

G. Marcus (Ed.), *Rereading Cultural Anthropology* (Durham and London: Duke University Press, 1995).

I. Marcos and the Zapatistas, *The Other Campaign* (San Francisco: City Lights Books, 2006).

K. Marx and F. Engels, *The German Ideology* (Ed.) C.J. Arthur (London: Lawrence & Wishart, 1982).

P. Mayo, *Gramsci, Freire and Adult Education: Possibilities for transformative action* (London: Zed Books, 1999).

N. Miller, *In the Shadow of the State: Intellectuals and the quest for national identity in twentieth-century Spanish America* (London: Verso, 1999).

T.T. Minh-Ha, *When The Moon Waxes Red: Representation, gender and cultural politics* (New York: Routledge, 1991).

D. Moore, J. Kosek and A. Pandian (Eds), *Race, Nature And the Politics of Difference* (Durham N.C; London: Duke University Press, 2003).

H. Moore (Ed.), *The Future of Anthropological Knowledge* (London: Routledge, 1996).

H. Moore and T. Sanders (Eds), *Magical Interpretations, Material Realities: Modernity, witchcraft and the occult in postcolonial Africa* (London: Routledge, 2001).

T. Morrison (Ed.), *Race-Ing Justice, En-Gendering Power. Essays on Anita Hill, Clarence Thomas and the Construction of Social Reality* (New York: Pantheon, 1992).

——, *Playing In The Dark: Whiteness and the literary imagination* (London: Picador, 1993).

R. Munck 'Postmodernism, Politics, and Paradigms in Latin America' in *Latin American Perspectives* Issue 113, vol. 27, no. 4 (July 2000).

U. Narayan, *Dislocating Cultures: Identities, traditions, and Third-World feminism* (London: Routledge, 1997).

J. Nash, *Mayan Visions: The quest for autonomy in an age of globalisation* (London: Routledge, 2001).

The New Conquistadors, *Race & Class*, vol. 34, no. 1 (London: Institute of Race Relations, 1992).

L.T. Outlaw, *On Race and Philosophy* (London: Routledge, 1996).

B. Parry, 'Liberation Movements' in *Interventions: International Journal of Postcolonial Studies,* 1–1 (1998/9) 47.

M. Poster, *Foucault, Marxism & History: Mode of production versus mode of information* (Cambridge: Polity Press in association with Basil Blackwell, Oxford, 1984).

S. Ranchod-Nilsson and M. Tétreault (Eds), *Women, States And Nationalism: At home in the nation?* (London: Routledge, 2000).

S. Reicher and N. Hopkins, *Self And Nation: Categorization, contestation and mobilization* (London: Sage, 2001).

J. Rhys, *Wide Sargasso Sea* (London: Penguin, 1968).

C. Robinson, *Black Marxism: The making Of the black radical tradition* (Chapel Hill, NC: University of North Carolina Press, 2000).

W. Rodney, *How Europe Underdeveloped Africa* (London: Bogle-L'Ouverture Publications, 1978).

R. Rorty, *Contingency, Irony and Solidarity* (Cambridge: Cambridge University Press, 1989).

E. Said, *Orientalism* (London: Routledge and Kegan Paul, 1978).

——, *Representations of the Intellectual: The 1993 Reith lectures* (London: Vintage, 1994).

Z. Sardar, *Orientalism* (Buckingham: Open University Press, 1999).

——, *Postmodernism And the Other: The new imperialism of Western culture* (London: Pluto Press, 1997).

V. Serge, *Memoirs Of A Revolutionary* (Iowa City: University of Iowa Press, 2002 [1951]).

——, *Year One Of The Russian Revolution* (London: Pluto Press, 1992 [1930]).

H. Small (Ed.) *The Public Intellectual* (Oxford: Blackwell Publishing, 2002).

G. Spivak, *A Critique of Postcolonial Reason: Toward a history of the vanishing present* (Cambridge, MA: Harvard University Press, 1999).

——, *The Post-colonial Critic: Interviews, strategies, Dialogues* ed. Sarah Harasym (London: Routledge, 1990).

C. Steadman, *Landscape for a Good Woman: A story of two lives* (London: Virago, 1986).

M. Taussig, *Shamanism, Colonialism and the Wild Man: A study in terror and healing* (Chicago: The University of Chicago Press, 1987).

M. Trouillot, *Silencing the Past: Power and the Production of History* (Boston: Beacon Press, 1995).

C. Venn, *Occidentalism: Modernity and subjectivity* (London: Sage Publications, 2000).

M. Walzer, *The Company of Critics: Social criticism and Political commitment in the twentieth century* (London: Peter Halban, 1989).

——, *Interpretation and Social Criticism* (Cambridge: Harvard University Press, 1987).

F. Webber, 'Europe J'accuse', *Race and Class,* Issue 36, vol. 3 (1995). 86–8.

R. Wiegman, *American Anatomies: Theorizing race and gender* (London: Duke University Press, 1995).

R. Wilford and R. Miller (Eds), *Women, Ethnicity and Nationalism: The politics of transition* (London: Routledge, 1989).

R. Williams, *Culture and Society 1780–1950* (London: Penguin, 1961).

R. Young, *Torn Halves: Political conflict in literary and cultural theory* (Manchester: Manchester University Press, 1996).

——, *White Mythologies: Writing history and the West* (London: Routledge, 1990).

N. Zack (Ed.), *Women of Color and Philosophy: A critical reader* (Oxford: Blackwell, 2000).

Index

Authors

AF352249